MW01628795

CELEBRATE

FOOD FAMILY SHABBOS

DISTRIBUTED BY

WHY WE COOK...

A home cooked meal says I want to take care of you.

A home cooked meal says I want to nourish you.

A home cooked meal says I care and I want you to be healthy.

A home cooked meal says I love you.

A home cooked meal is remembered forever.

CELEBRATE

FOOD FAMILY SHABBOS

ELIZABETH KURTZ

TO BENEFIT EMUNAH OF AMERICA

THANK YOU

Sometimes a small good deed leads to something more, something unexpected, and something truly extraordinary. This is how my relationship with EMUNAH began.

On a flight to Florida in February, 2013, I was seated next to a mother-daughter pair, clearly a wonderfully close duo, chatting and enjoying each other's company. I was taking advantage of the long flight to work, clicking away on my computer, reviewing new recipes for my website, editing food photos, and answering reader questions. The mom sporadically peeked over, checking out the photos and quietly commenting to her daughter about the yummy-looking food site.

Now to know Fran Hirmes is to know she's not shy, which is why she knows everyone—or certainly makes the effort to know everyone—and I was the next beneficiary of her engaging personality. As I was typing, Fran interjected, "My daughter Kimberly here knows that website and says it's great." And thus began a beautiful and rewarding friendship, one that ultimately yielded this wonderful EMUNAH partnership. To work with Fran and Kimberly is to understand that selfless commitment and positive energy are the cornerstones of their essence.

In developing this book, we kept the overarching mission of EMUNAH as our guide. I thank everyone for their connection to this mission and the good fortune to be a part of a dream and a chesed. I am particularly grateful and honored to have worked work with such amazing women at Emunah. Carol Sufian, Fran Hirmes, Bonnie Eizikovitz, Karen Spitalnick, Heddy Klein, Debby Siman Tov, Kimberly Rothstein, Randy Krevat, Michelle Schwartz and our invaluable recipe testing team. Their efforts, commitment, and energy brought a momentum and enthusiasm for the book that have girded me throughout this entire process. To be in their company was an incredible privilege and experience that I will forever cherish. To Bonnie and Kimberly, your devotion and commitment to this project coupled with your creativity and enthusiasm were truly invaluable.

I'm grateful to my friend Emuna Braverman who worked with me for many years on the website and the original version of this book concept. She is both a role model and mentor for me, and I cherish our friendship.

To the incredible sponsors, thank you for making the lives of so many people better through this project. Thank you for enabling me to inspire and enhance the Shabbos experience for so many readers.

The mechanics of creating a book are an overwhelming experience—unless you work with some of the best in the field like I did. My sincerest appreciation to Heather, Jon, Denise, Cindie, Paty, Tasha, Hudi, Renee, Eugene, Izzy, Suzanne, Martha, and Randall.

To my husband, and my biggest fan since the day we met. He has constantly encouraged me and was as eager and excited for this book as I was. On some days, when it seemed like the mountain might be a little bit too high, he just pushed harder and encouraged more. His perfect combination of love, creativity, and endless support is really my secret sauce. I'm so grateful that he is my lifetime love and partner.

Like my husband, my children are my best PR managers. I don't think there is a teacher, tutor, friend, acquaintance, or bus driver in their orbit who doesn't know that their mother runs a website, teaches cooking classes, and is a cookbook author. They are the best testers and helpers and always remind me of why, at the end of the day, this is a project worth doing. My beautiful and talented girls inspire me with their devotion to family, school, friends, and this enormous undertaking that has been a part of their daily meals for the past 10 years. In the process, Basia and Sarah have become accomplished salad chefs, and Ella has matured into my go-to prep cook with culinary skills well beyond her 13 years. CJ and Avi are great dessert bakers and cookie monsters. Their repertoire includes favorites like Hot Chocolate Pudding Chocolate Cake and Ballpark Cookies, neither of which is as delicious as they are. Thank you to my loves and my joys, my little helpers and biggest fans. I appreciate your feedback and your patience when I had to make something fifteen times before I thought it was just right. The good news is you came out perfect the first time!

TESTERS:

Elsa Adler
Chagit Alpert
Carole Alter
Chaviva Alter
Maureen Ash
Lauri Barbanel
Sabina Barbanel
Rita Bleicher
Deborah Brand
Shaina Braun
Estee Burg
Ashley Charnoff
Yael Eisenberg
Bonnie Eizikovitz
Marni Eizikovitz
Nina Eizikovitz
Faigy Elefant
Minda Fischer
Deena Fisher
Tova Fruchter
Robyn Gelberg
Robin Gelman
Yana Gilkin
Chaya Glikman
Aviva Golombeck
Shani Goodman
Goldie Gordon
Fran Hirmes
Riki Hirmes
Lori Huberfeld
Malkie Hyman
Shaynee Kessler
Esther Klein
Heddy Klein
Malkie Klein
Elissa Koffsky
Sarita Kohn
Louise Kramer
Mitch Krevat
Randy Krevat
Evie Leifer
Esty Malek
Fanny Malek
Hindi Mazel
Rabia Mitchell
Leiah Moskowitz
Monroe Musman
Naomi Nachman
Malkie Nathan
Rebecca Naumemberg
Gladys Neuman
Fayge Nissenbaum
Devora Resnick
Kimberly Rothstein
Adina Rubin
Jean Sadnoff
Nechama Schnall
Bonnie Schwartz
Beth Shubowitz
Betty Shusterman
Bailey Sigman
Judy Simpson
Sariva Sklar
Janet Spector
Carol Sufian
Rivka Wilamowsky
Toby Wolf
Arielle Wolfson
Sara Zalkin

EMUNAH OF AMERICA THANKS THE SPONSORS OF *CELEBRATE*

EXECUTIVE CHEF

Anonymous
Bonnie & Jack Eizikovitz
Michelle & Eli Salig
Rachel & Harry Skydell
Karen & Robert Spitalnick
Gisela Steigman
Rena & Elliott Steigman

PASTRY CHEF

Gila Alpert
Shelli & Harvey Dachs
In Memory of Yo & Bernie Lipschitz, A"H
Tracy & Sander Gerber
Yenny & Ralph Herzka
Elizabeth & Robert Kurtz
Basya & Jay Lobell
Arielle & Moshe Wolfson

SOUS CHEF

Michelle Chrein
Sharon & Sinclair Haberman
Heddy & Mendy Klein
Esther & Paul Lerer
Rivki & Lindsay Rosenwald
Judy & Yossie Simpson
Esther & Jerry Williams
In memory of Judith Williams, A"H

SAUCIER

Fran & Alan Hirmes

APPRENTICE

Anne & Sheldon Golombeck
Careena & Drew Parker

LINE CHEF

Ashley & Judah Charnoff
Hindi & Mark Mazel
Friends of Zila Besser A"H

TABLE OF CONTENTS

INTRODUCTION

It starts and ends with love.

My entire relationship with food, reading and writing recipes, cooking, and eating, is all about love. I didn't realize just how special it was at the time, but, my happiest times as a little girl were often spent with my mother in the kitchen. There were no expectations of excellence and achievement like there was for my school work, clubs, or gymnastics. There was just love. We would pick a favorite recipe or maybe try something new and then on went the apron and off we went into a magical place of creativity, happiness and love. As I think of it now it was the most wonderful time.

Then there was the bonus of sharing the love with family and friends.
I do many things for my family, but no carpool, camp application, or help with a complicated homework assignment brings anywhere near the smile that a delicious meal—especially on Shabbos or Yom Tov—brings. Absolutely nothing.

It's all about love.

It is often said that as much as the Jewish people keep the Sabbath, in truth is it is the Sabbath that keeps the Jews. I believe that with all of my heart, and at the very heart of our celebration of Shabbos is family gathered around the table enjoying a delicious Shabbos meal.

I started my blog, Gourmet Kosher Cooking, years ago in response to friends, relatives, and Shabbos guests often asking me for my recipes. Now, tens of millions of impressions and millions of recipe downloads later, my dream of publishing *Celebrate* is here!

The dream of sharing my love of cooking and delicious food with so many became something even deeper in my partnership with EMUNAH. If Shabbos keeps the Jews, then giving and caring for others in need keeps the soul. EMUNAH is all about caring for those who need extra care. My time at Bet Elazraki, one of their children's homes in Israel, was beyond inspiring—the eagerness of the children, their smiles, and their joy is a sign of the love and extra care they receive from EMUNAH. I prepared meals at EMUNAH's Golden Age Restaurant, where seniors can share a meal and a conversation with others. To watch the children and seniors at these EMUNAH facilities prepare and cook for Shabbos, to see them laugh and play and make delicious food tells me what I know to be true: It is, indeed, all about love.

ABOUT EMUNAH: Caring for a Nation since 1935.

EMUNAH, Shabbos, love, and delicious food —how perfect! Each enhances your life, emotionally, physically, and spiritually. To all of us at EMUNAH, it seems so fitting to collaborate with Elizabeth Kurtz on this incredible cookbook: For Elizabeth, renown for her wonderfully delicious food, all of her recipes start with love. It is the same, too, for us at EMUNAH. Our work and dedication to children and families in Israel who rely on us for help, this is all about love. The theme of *Celebrate* is Shabbos, a day that is all about love, a day that is entirely delicious.

The EMUNAH story began in 1935 when a few selfless and dedicated women banded together to bring assistance to the children and families of Israel's early pioneers who faced tremendous challenges. This fledgling movement (formerly called Hapoel Ha Mizrachi) has now burgeoned into the EMUNAH of today: the Israel prize-winning organization with 250 social service and educational programs throughout the Jewish State.

EMUNAH works to restore children and families in distress back to health, emotionally, physically, and spiritually. Children, from infants to teens, rescued from terrible and often perilous situations at home, come to us in our five children's homes, starving for love and attention. And love is what they get, often for the first time in their young lives. EMUNAH "feeds" them with all the care and support they need to grow and thrive into happy and productive adults.

In our 135 day care centers throughout the country, babies to children up to 5 years of age are nurtured and cared for while parents must work. Young women in need of an education are helped to become successful graduates with promising futures in our educational network of four high schools, mechina program, and college of art. Families in crisis, teens at risk, and victims of terror are counseled so they can heal and function in society. Seniors who are lonely and feel forgotten are physically and emotionally sustained. And all our services are provided within a Torah framework. This is EMUNAH. As an organization, we work to strengthen Israel, its people, and its Jewish future.

We know the amazing mouthwatering recipes in this cookbook will enhance your Shabbos—and the serendipitous partnership between Elizabeth Kurtz and EMUNAH elevates it with spirituality and with good deeds. Of all the wonderful ingredients you will find in this book, we're certain the one you will find the most delicious of all is—love.

As you sit at your Shabbos table gathered with family and friends, please take satisfaction in knowing that the purchase of this cookbook will touch the life of a child or adult who relies on EMUNAH for help.

CHALLAH

Challah is quicker to make in a machine, but all of these can be made by hand (I did it that way for years!). Alternatively, make in a large 6-quart stand mixer with a dough hook or a large-capacity bread mixer from Bosch or Magic Mill fitted with a dough hook. High-gluten flour (or high-gluten bread flour) is my recommendation for great challah making because it creates a chewy, soft, and elastic dough. Standard bread flour, though it has a lower protein content, will still yield a nice result, and you can even get by with all-purpose flour when bread flour is not available. Feel free to make these breads ahead—they all freeze beautifully. Wrap tightly in plastic wrap and then again in foil. Thaw in the refrigerator or on the counter, and refresh in a warming drawer, if desired.

Water Challah

Note

This recipe can be made by hand, in a large 6-quart stand mixer with a dough hook, or in a large-capacity bread mixer from Bosch or Magic Mill fitted with a dough hook.

Make Ahead

The breads in this book freeze beautifully. Wrap tightly in plastic wrap and then again in foil. Thaw in the refrigerator or on the counter.

If you want your challah without eggs, you can't get any better than this recipe, which works equally well as rolls or as a pull-apart challah. Simply roll the dough into balls about the size of golf balls. For rolls, place the balls in muffin tins. For a pull-apart challah, place the balls side by side, touching, in round challah pans. Follow the recipe topping and baking instructions. And if you want a terrific egg challah, add 5 eggs to this recipe. Thank you Ann-Michelle for helping me with this recipe and photo.

makes 6 large loaves

Dough:

1 teaspoon sugar

6 tablespoons or 8 (¼-ounce) packets active dry yeast

5 cups lukewarm water

14 to 15 cups high-gluten flour

2 tablespoons salt

1½ cups honey

1½ cups plus 2 teaspoons canola oil, divided

Topping:

1 tablespoon margarine, melted (optional)

Poppyseeds or sesame seeds, as needed

To make the dough: Dissolve sugar and yeast in warm water in a large bowl. (Note: For the yeast to proof, the water must truly be lukewarm. Dip your finger in the water. If it's too hot for your fingers, it's too hot for the yeast as well. If it's cool, it won't work either. Lukewarm is just right.) Wait 5 to 10 minutes to allow the yeast to proof. It will appear foamy.

In a separate large bowl, or mixer fitted with dough hook, mix flour and salt. Add proofed yeast, honey, and oil, mixing until fully incorporated. Knead dough until smooth and elastic, about 5 minutes by hand or mixer, adding additional flour if dough is too sticky.

Drizzle remaining 2 teaspoons oil in mixing bowl; roll dough in oil to coat. Cover with a towel and let rise until doubled, about 1 hour.

Grease six loaf or challah pans. Punch down dough. Divide into six pieces; divide each piece into at least three, and roll into long ropes about 12 inches long. Braid and place in prepared pans. Cover and let rise until doubled, about 1 hour.

Preheat oven to 350°F.

To prepare the topping: Gently brush tops of challahs with margarine with a pastry brush. Sprinkle poppyseeds or sesame seeds over loaves. Bake 30 to 40 minutes, or until loaves are golden brown and sound hollow when tapped. Cool for 10 minutes in the pan, and then remove the challahs to wire racks to cool.

Baking Challah with the Children at Bet Elazraki. *One of my most memorable moments in Israel was my visit to Bet Elazraki, EMUNAH's Children's Home in Netanya. The children and I made challah together there. Watching the joy on their beautiful faces as we baked warmed my own heart.*

Apple-Date Swirled Challah

The title says it all—delicious challah swirled with sweet apple and date compote—how perfect is that for Rosh Hashanah? The filling also makes a great holiday dip or spread so be sure to save any extra (or double the filling and serve it alongside for dipping). You can serve it alongside any challah recipe.

makes 5 loaves

Note

This recipe can be made by hand, in a large 6-quart stand mixer with a dough hook, or in a large-capacity bread mixer from Bosch or Magic Mill fitted with a dough hook.

Make Ahead

The breads in this book freeze beautifully. Wrap tightly in plastic wrap and then again in foil. Thaw in the refrigerator or on the counter, and refresh in a warming drawer, if desired.

Dough:

4 cups lukewarm water
3 tablespoons or 4 (¼-ounce) packets active dry yeast
1¼ cups plus 1 teaspoon sugar
14 cups high-gluten flour
1½ tablespoons salt
1½ teaspoons cinnamon
¼ teaspoon nutmeg
¼ cup honey
2 teaspoons vanilla extract
¾ cup plus 2 teaspoons canola oil, divided
4 eggs
2 egg yolks

Filling:

3 Granny Smith apples, peeled and diced
¾ cup pitted dates, chopped
½ teaspoon salt
1 cinnamon stick
¼ cup water
¼ cup red wine
1½ tablespoons balsamic vinegar
2 tablespoons packed light brown sugar

Topping:

1 egg
1 teaspoon water
1 teaspoon honey
¼ cup sugar
1¼ teaspoons ground cinnamon

To prepare the dough: Place the lukewarm water in a large bowl. (Note: For the yeast to proof, the water must truly be lukewarm. Dip your finger in the water. If it's too hot for your fingers, it's too hot for the yeast as well. If it's cool, it won't work either. Lukewarm is just right.) Add the yeast and 1 teaspoon of the sugar, and stir to dissolve. Wait 5 to 10 minutes to allow the yeast to proof. It will appear foamy.

In another large bowl (or in a large 6-quart stand mixer fitted with dough hook), mix the remaining 1¼ cups sugar, flour, salt, cinnamon, and nutmeg. Add the proofed yeast and mix. In a small bowl, mix the honey, vanilla, ¾ cup oil, eggs, and egg yolks. Add to the dough mixture. Knead the dough until smooth and elastic, about 5 minutes by hand or mixer, adding additional flour if the dough is too sticky.

Drizzle remaining 2 teaspoons oil in mixing bowl; roll dough in oil to coat. Cover with a towel, and let rise in a warm place until doubled, about 1 hour.

While the dough is rising, make the filling: Place the apples, dates, salt, cinnamon stick, water, red wine, balsamic vinegar, and brown sugar in a medium saucepan and bring to a boil. Reduce the heat to a simmer, and cook until mixture is reduced and most of the liquid is absorbed, 10 to 15 minutes. Discard the cinnamon stick. Remove from the heat and let cool for 5 minutes. With an immersion blender, purée until mostly smooth.

Grease five 9-inch round challah or pie pans.

Punch down the risen dough and divide into 5 pieces. With a rolling pin, roll each piece out into a large rectangle, about 6 inches wide and 14 inches long. Spread one fifth of the reserved apple filling (about ⅓ cup) to within ½-inch of the edges. Roll up each rectangle from the long side, jelly-roll style. Pinch the ends to seal.

Pull the ends of the dough around to form a concentric circle. (It will look like a big pinwheel.) Place in the prepared greased round pans. Cover and let rise in a warm place until doubled again in size, about 45 minutes.

Alternatively, cut the rolled log into 1-inch slices crosswise like cinnamon rolls. Place the cut rolls into a greased round pans, cut-side down so that you can see the swirl of the filling. The slices from one log will fit snugly into a 9-inch round pan or pie pan. Cover and let rise in a warm place until doubled again in size, about 45 minutes.

Preheat the oven to 350°F.

To prepare the topping: In a small dish, whisk the egg, water, and honey. In another small dish, mix the sugar and cinnamon. Gently brush each challah with the egg wash and sprinkle with the cinnamon sugar.

Bake until the loaves are golden and sound hollow when tapped, about 25 or 30 minutes. Cool for 10 minutes in the pan, and then remove the challahs to wire racks to cool.

Whole Wheat Challah

Note

This recipe can be made by hand, in a large 6-quart stand mixer with a dough hook, or in a large-capacity bread mixer from Bosch or Magic Mill fitted with a dough hook.

Make Ahead

The breads in this book freeze beautifully. Wrap tightly in plastic wrap and then again in foil. Thaw in the refrigerator or on the counter.

This challah is so good that no one will mind that it's made with some whole grain flour. I like to use white whole wheat flour from King Arthur. They use a wheat berry, which is much lighter than the darker variety, but any type of wheat flour works well in this recipe.

makes 6 loaves

Dough:

4 cups warm water

4 rounded teaspoons or 2 (¼-ounce) packets active dry yeast

1 cup plus 1 teaspoon sugar

2 eggs

½ cup honey

¼ cup plus 2 teaspoons canola oil, divided

1½ tablespoons salt

5 cups whole wheat flour

7 cups high-gluten flour, plus more if needed

Egg Wash:

1 egg yolk

1 teaspoon water

Sesame seeds, poppyseeds, or a mixture (optional)

To make the dough: Place the lukewarm water in a large bowl. (Note: For the yeast to proof, the water must truly be lukewarm. Dip your finger in the water. If it's too hot for your fingers, it's too hot for the yeast as well. If it's cool, it won't work either. Lukewarm is just right.) Add the yeast and 1 teaspoon of the sugar, and stir to dissolve. Wait 5 to 10 minutes to allow the yeast to proof. It will appear foamy.

In another large bowl (or in a large 6-quart stand mixer fitted with dough hook), mix the remaining cup sugar, eggs, honey, and ¼ cup of the oil. Add proofed yeast, and stir to combine. Add salt and flour, 4 cups at a time, mixing until fully incorporated. Knead dough until smooth and elastic, about 5 minutes by hand or mixer, adding additional flour if dough is too sticky.

Drizzle remaining 2 teaspoons oil in the mixing bowl; roll dough in oil to coat. Cover with a towel and let rise in a warm place until doubled, about 1 hour.

Grease six loaf or challah pans. Punch down the risen dough. Divide into six pieces, and divide each piece into three more pieces. Roll into long ropes about 12 inches long, and braid the loaves. Place one braided loaf in each prepared pan. Cover and let rise in a warm place until doubled, about 1 hour.

Preheat oven to 350°F.

To prepare the egg wash: In a small bowl, whisk together egg yolk and water, and gently brush over the challahs with a pastry brush. Sprinkle loaves with topping, if using.

Place risen loaves in oven; bake until loaves are golden brown and sound hollow when tapped, about 35 to 40 minutes. Cool for 10 minutes in the pan, and then remove the challahs to wire racks to cool.

Onion-Poppyseed Challah

Note

This recipe can be made by hand, in a large 6-quart stand mixer with a dough hook, or in a large-capacity bread mixer from Bosch or Magic Mill fitted with a dough hook.

Make Ahead

The breads in this book freeze beautifully. Wrap tightly in plastic wrap and then again in foil. Thaw in the refrigerator or on the counter.

Remember Ratner's restaurant on the Lower East Side? It was an iconic Jewish restaurant with blintzes, kugels, latkes, and the works. People came from far and wide to try their onion-poppyseed rolls. This challah is a re-creation of those soft onion rolls that smelled so good. If I do say so, this version gives Ratner's a run for their money. The presentation is beautiful and there is never a bite left. I make it every year on Succot, but it should not be limited to that! Many thanks to Judy Zeidler for sharing this treasure with us.

makes 2 large or 4 medium loaves

Dough:

2½ cups lukewarm water

4½ teaspoons or 2 (¼-ounce) packets active dry yeast

½ cup plus 1 teaspoon sugar

2 eggs

1 cup (2 sticks) margarine, melted

2 tablespoons salt

10 cups high-gluten flour

2 teaspoons canola oil

Filling:

4 cups finely chopped yellow onion

¾ cup poppyseeds

10 tablespoons (1¼ sticks) margarine, melted

1 teaspoon salt

Egg wash:

1 egg yolk

1 tablespoon water

To prepare the dough: Place the lukewarm water in a large bowl. (Note: For the yeast to proof, the water must truly be lukewarm. Dip your finger in the water. If it's too hot for your fingers, it's too hot for the yeast as well. If it's cool, it won't work either. Lukewarm is just right.) Add the yeast and 1 teaspoon of the sugar, and stir to dissolve. Wait 5 to 10 minutes to allow the yeast to proof. It will appear foamy.

In another large bowl (or in a large 6-quart stand mixer fitted with dough hook), mix eggs, margarine, and salt. Add proofed yeast and remaining ½ cup sugar, and mix to combine. Add flour, 4 cups at a time, mixing after each addition until fully incorporated. Knead dough until smooth and elastic, about 5 minutes by hand or mixer, adding additional flour if dough is too sticky.

Drizzle oil in the mixing bowl; roll dough in oil to coat. Cover with a towel and let rise in a warm place until doubled, about 1 hour. While the dough is rising, prepare the filling

To prepare the filling: Mix together onion, poppyseeds, margarine, and salt in a medium bowl. Reserve 1 cup of mixture in a small bowl for topping.

Grease two baking sheets. Punch down the risen dough; divide into four pieces. Roll each piece out into a large rectangle, about 12 x 16 inches. Spread ¾ cup of the reserved filling to within ½-inch of the edges. (Remember to reserve 1 cup for topping.) Roll up each rectangle from the long side, jellyroll-style. Pinch ends to seal.

Take two of the loaves and twist together. Repeat with the remaining two loaves. Place on prepared baking sheets. Cover and let rise until doubled, about 45 minutes.

Preheat oven to 350°F.

Prepare the egg wash: Lightly beat together egg yolk and water in a small bowl; brush over the loaves. Sprinkle with the reserved filling. Bake until loaves are golden and sound hollow when tapped, about 40 minutes. Cool for 10 minutes in the pan, and then remove the challahs to wire racks to cool.

Pumpkin Challah

I usually make this festive challah for Succot but there's really no reason not to make it all year round. It is not a cake and just has overtones of fall and pumpkin flavors. The pumpkin adds terrific richness and texture and the color is beautiful for the fall.

makes 4 loaves

Dough:

1 teaspoon sugar

1½ tablespoons or 2 (¼-ounce) packets active dry yeast

1⅓ cups warm water

4 cups canned pumpkin

3 teaspoons cinnamon

1 teaspoon nutmeg

¼ cup maple syrup

2 teaspoons vanilla extract

¾ cup packed light brown sugar

2½ tablespoons salt

⅓ cup plus 2 teaspoons canola oil, divided

1 egg

12 to 13 cups high-gluten flour

Topping:

1 egg yolk

1 tablespoon water

Pumpkin seeds (optional)

To make the dough, dissolve 1 teaspoon sugar and yeast in warm water in a large bowl. (Note: For the yeast to proof, the water must truly be lukewarm. Dip your finger in the water. If it's too hot for your fingers, it's too hot for the yeast as well. If it's cool, it won't work either. Lukewarm is just right.) Wait 5 to 10 minutes to allow the yeast to proof. It will appear foamy.

In a separate large bowl, or mixer fitted with dough hook, mix pumpkin, cinnamon, nutmeg, maple syrup, vanilla, brown sugar, salt, ⅓ cup oil, and egg. Add proofed yeast and flour, 4 cups at a time, mixing until fully incorporated. Knead dough until smooth and elastic, about 5 minutes by hand or mixer, adding additional flour if dough is too sticky.

Drizzle remaining 2 teaspoons oil in mixing bowl; roll dough in oil to coat. Cover with a towel and let rise until doubled, about 1 hour.

Grease four loaf or challah pans. Punch down dough. Divide into four pieces, and then divide each piece into at least three more pieces, and roll into 12-inch long ropes. Braid and place in prepared pans. Cover and let rise until doubled, about 1 hour.

Preheat oven to 350°F.

To prepare the topping: Lightly beat together egg yolk and water in a small bowl; brush over the loaves. Sprinkle pumpkin seeds over loaves. Bake 30 to 40 minutes, or until loaves are golden brown and sound hollow when tapped. Cool for 10 minutes in the pan, and then remove the challahs to wire racks to cool.

Note

This recipe can be made by hand, in a large 6-quart stand mixer with a dough hook, or in a large-capacity bread mixer from Bosch or Magic Mill fitted with a dough hook.

Make Ahead

The breads in this book freeze beautifully. Wrap tightly in plastic wrap and then again in foil. Thaw in the refrigerator or on the counter.

Sweet Challah with Streusel Topping

Note

This recipe can be made by hand, in a large 6-quart stand mixer with a dough hook, or in a large-capacity bread mixer from Bosch or Magic Mill fitted with a dough hook.

Make Ahead

The breads in this book freeze beautifully. Wrap tightly in plastic wrap and then again in foil. Thaw in the refrigerator or on the counter.

This is one of my favorite challah recipes and I make it almost every week—to rave reviews! It also looks great made in muffin tins when you need individual challettes. My kids love the sweet crumble topping, but feel free to omit it if you prefer a sweet challah that is not too babka-like.

makes 6 loaves

Dough:

2 cups plus 1 teaspoon sugar

4 rounded teaspoons or 3 (¼-ounce) packets active dry yeast

4 cups warm water

6 eggs

1½ cups plus 2 teaspoons canola oil, divided

2 tablespoons salt

14 to 15 cups high-gluten flour

Topping:

1 cup sugar

1 cup all-purpose flour

½ cup (1 stick) margarine, cut into pieces, or canola oil

½ teaspoon vanilla extract

½ teaspoon cinnamon (optional)

To prepare the dough: Place the lukewarm water in a large bowl. (Note: For the yeast to proof, the water must truly be lukewarm. Dip your finger in the water. If it's too hot for your fingers, it's too hot for the yeast as well. If it's cool, it won't work either. Lukewarm is just right.) Add the yeast and 1 teaspoon of the sugar, and stir to dissolve. Wait 5 to 10 minutes to allow the yeast to proof. It will appear foamy.

In a separate large bowl (or a large 6-quart mixer fitted with dough hook), mix remaining 2 cups sugar, eggs, 1½ cups of the oil, and salt. Add proofed yeast and mix. Add flour, 4 cups at a time, mixing after each addition until fully incorporated. Knead dough until smooth and elastic, about 5 minutes by hand or mixer, adding additional flour if dough is too sticky.

Drizzle remaining 2 teaspoons oil in mixing bowl; roll dough in oil to coat. Cover with a towel and let rise until doubled, about 1 hour. While the dough is rising, prepare the topping.

To prepare the topping: Combine sugar, flour, margarine, vanilla, and cinnamon, if using, in a small bowl; mix with a fork until coarse crumbs form.

Grease six loaf or challah pans. Punch down the risen dough. Divide into six pieces; divide each piece into at least three, and roll into long ropes about 12 inches long. Braid and place in prepared pans. Cover and let rise in a warm place until doubled, about 1 hour.

Preheat oven to 350°F. Sprinkle reserved topping over loaves. Bake until loaves are golden brown and sound hollow when tapped, about 35 minutes. Cool for 10 minutes in the pan, and then remove the challahs to wire racks to cool.

Vanilla Challah

Vanilla extract gives wonderful sweetness to this challah. It's a surprise ingredient that takes challah to a whole new level. I add vanilla extract to many of the other challah recipes too.

makes 6 loaves

Dough:

1¾ cups plus 1 teaspoon sugar

¼ cup or 5 (¼-ounce) packets active dry yeast

4 cups warm water

1½ cups plus 2 teaspoons canola oil, divided

3 eggs

1½ tablespoons salt

2 teaspoons vanilla extract

12 cups high-gluten flour

Egg Wash:

1 egg yolk

½ teaspoon honey

¼ teaspoon vanilla extract

1 teaspoon water

To prepare the dough: Dissolve 1 teaspoon sugar and yeast in warm water in a large bowl. (Note: For the yeast to proof, the water must truly be lukewarm. Dip your finger in the water. If it's too hot for your fingers, it's too hot for the yeast as well. If it's cool, it won't work either. Lukewarm is just right.) Wait 5 to 10 minutes to allow the yeast to proof. It will appear foamy.

In a separate large bowl, or mixer fitted with dough hook, mix remaining 1¾ cups sugar, 1½ cups oil, eggs, salt, and vanilla. Add proofed yeast and flour, 4 cups at a time, mixing until fully incorporated. Knead dough until smooth and elastic, about 5 minutes by hand or mixer, adding additional flour if dough is too sticky.

Drizzle remaining 2 teaspoons oil in mixing bowl; roll dough in oil to coat. Cover with a towel and let rise until doubled, about 1 hour.

Grease six loaf or challah pans. Punch down dough. Divide into six pieces; divide each piece into at least three, and roll into long ropes about 12 inches long. Braid and place in prepared pans. Cover and let rise until doubled, about 1 hour.

Preheat oven to 350°F.

To prepare the egg wash: In a small dish, whisk together egg yolk, honey, vanilla, and water. With a pastry brush, gently brush loaves with mixture.

Bake about 35 minutes, or until loaves are golden brown and sound hollow when tapped. Cool for 10 minutes in the pan, and then remove the challahs to wire racks to cool.

Note

This recipe can be made by hand, in a large 6-quart stand mixer with a dough hook, or in a large-capacity bread mixer from Bosch or Magic Mill fitted with a dough hook.

Make Ahead

The breads in this book freeze beautifully. Wrap tightly in plastic wrap and then again in foil. Thaw in the refrigerator or on the counter.

Cinnamon Swirl Filling for Rosh Hashanah

This filling can be added to any challah recipe of your choice.

makes 2 challahs

Cinnamon Filling:
5 tablespoons margarine
¼ cup packed light brown sugar
1½ teaspoons light corn syrup
1 tablespoon cinnamon
2 tablespoons all-purpose flour
Pinch of salt
½ teaspoon vanilla extract

For the cinnamon filling: In a mixer, beat margarine, brown sugar, corn syrup, cinnamon, flour, salt, and vanilla, until smooth, about 2 minutes. Set aside.

Grease 2 baking sheets. Separate enough dough to make 2 challahs (about 2 (5-inch) balls of dough) and then separate into 4 total pieces. Roll each piece out into a large rectangle. Spread with 2 to 3 tablespoons of the filling to within ½-inch of the edges. Roll up each rectangle lengthwise, jellyroll-style. Pinch ends to seal.

Take two of the loaves and twist together. Repeat with the remaining two loaves. Place on prepared baking sheets. Cover and let rise until doubled, about 45 minutes. Sprinkle with additional cinnamon sugar. Bake as directed in the challah recipe of your choice.

When the Madricha, the children's supervisor at Bet Elazraki Children's Home, took the kids' freshly baked challah loaves out of the oven, I had never felt more proud of sharing my culinary skills. Seeing how excited the children were when they saw the beautiful finished loaves was gratifying beyond words.

Spelt Challah

Note

This recipe can be made by hand, in a large 6-quart stand mixer with a dough hook, or in a large-capacity bread mixer from Bosch or Magic Mill fitted with a dough hook.

Make Ahead

The breads in this book freeze beautifully. Wrap tightly in plastic wrap and then again in foil. Thaw in the refrigerator or on the counter.

Spelt flour is lower in gluten than other whole grain flours and therefore can be managed by people that have mild sensitivities to wheat. When used in baking, its consistency is light and easier to digest with all the whole grain benefits and none of the heaviness that is sometimes associated with whole grain wheat flours. My friend Arielle makes this every week and no one ever knows that it's made with spelt flour. Thanks for sharing the recipe with me!

makes 6 loaves

Dough:

1 cup plus 1 tablespoon sugar

¼ cup or 5 (¼-ounce) packets active dry yeast

4¼ cups warm water

4 eggs

1 cup plus 2 teaspoons canola oil , divided

3 tablespoons salt

1 (5-pound) bag spelt flour (we like the organic whole white spelt flour)

Egg Wash:

1 egg yolk

1 tablespoon water

To prepare the dough: Dissolve 1 tablespoon sugar and yeast in water in a large bowl. (Note: For the yeast to proof, the water must truly be lukewarm. Dip your finger in the water. If it's too hot for your fingers, it's too hot for the yeast as well. If it's cool, it won't work either. Lukewarm is just right.) Wait 5 to 10 minutes to allow the yeast to proof. It will appear foamy.

In a separate large bowl, or mixer fitted with dough hook, mix remaining cup of sugar, eggs, 1 cup oil, and salt. Mix in proofed yeast and spelt flour, 4 cups at a time, mixing until fully incorporated. Knead dough until smooth and elastic, about 5 minutes by hand or mixer. This dough will be sticky.

Drizzle remaining 2 teaspoons oil in mixing bowl; roll dough in oil to coat. Cover with a towel and let rise until doubled, about 1 hour.

Grease six loaf or challah pans. Punch down dough. Divide into six pieces; divide each piece into at least three, and roll into long ropes about 12 inches long. Braid and place in prepared pans. Cover and let rise until doubled, about 1 hour.

Preheat oven to 350°F.

To prepare the egg wash: Whisk egg yolk and water in a small dish. Gently brush on top of challah.

Bake about 30 minutes, or until loaves are golden brown and sound hollow when tapped. Cool for 10 minutes in the pan, and then remove the challahs to wire racks to cool.

Gluten-Free Challah

So many people have gluten sensitivity today that I receive tons of emails asking for gluten free conversions. My friend Esther gave me this great recipe and people love it. It's wonderful to have this satiating and tasty challah as an option. The dough is sticky and hard to braid. I recommend using a silicone challah mold to get a great look without the need to braid the challah. It also works well as a pull-apart challah.

makes 1 to 2 loaves

Dough:

⅓ cup plus 1 teaspoon sugar

1½ tablespoons or 2 (¼-ounce) packets active dry yeast

1½ cups warm water

2 cups oat flour

1 cup gluten-free flour (I like and only use Authentic Foods Multi Blend Flour)

2 teaspoons salt

1 tablespoon xanthan gum

¼ cup plus 2 teaspoons canola oil, divided

1 egg

¼ teaspoon distilled white vinegar

Egg Wash:

1 egg yolk

1 tablespoon water

To prepare the dough: Dissolve 1 teaspoon sugar and yeast in water in a large bowl. (Note: For the yeast to proof, the water must truly be lukewarm. Dip your finger in the water. If it's too hot for your fingers, it's too hot for the yeast as well. If it's cool, it won't work either. Lukewarm is just right.) Wait 5 to 10 minutes to allow the yeast to proof. It will appear foamy.

In a separate large bowl, or mixer fitted with dough hook, mix remaining ⅓ cup sugar, oat flour, gluten-free flour, salt, xanthan gum, ¼ cup oil, egg, and vinegar. Mix in proofed yeast and knead dough until smooth and elastic, about 5 minutes by hand or mixer. This dough is often sticky, especially on a humid day and may need a little more flour; add a few tablespoons if necessary.

Drizzle remaining 2 teaspoons oil in mixing bowl; roll dough in oil to coat. Cover with a towel and let rise until doubled, about 1 hour.

Punch down dough. Place dough in a silicone challah mold or roll into balls and place side by side in a round pan or a challah pan. The dough is sticky but can be braided if you prefer. Grease a bread or challah pan. Braid dough and place in prepared pans. Cover and let rise until doubled, about 1 hour.

Preheat oven to 350°F.

To prepare the egg wash: Whisk egg yolk and water in a small dish. Gently brush on top of challah.

Bake 35 minutes, or until loaves are golden brown and sound hollow when tapped. Cool for 10 minutes in the pan, and then remove the challahs to wire racks to cool.

Note

This recipe can be made by hand, in a large 6-quart stand mixer with a dough hook, or in a large-capacity bread mixer from Bosch or Magic Mill fitted with a dough hook.

Make Ahead

The breads in this book freeze beautifully. Wrap tightly in plastic wrap and then again in foil. Thaw in the refrigerator or on the counter.

קידוש

KIDDUSH

Kiddush is all about a warm welcome . . . a welcome to Shabbos, a welcome to guests, a welcome to the upcoming meal. I like to elevate it with delicious dips and bite-size treats, heart-warming cholents, and my favorite comfort food, overnight kugel. That's my kind of Shabbos welcome!

Fresh Tuna, Chickpea, and Rosemary Salad

The creaminess of the chickpeas, the briny bite of olive, and the scent of rosemary throughout the dish make this Mediterranean twist on traditional tuna salad a winner. This is the rare salad that tastes even more delicious the next day, when the vinaigrette has had time to flavor all the ingredients. I like to serve this salad in mini clay pots from the gardening store—washed thoroughly, of course! Build a nest of clean, chopped lettuce in the bottom of the pot (to block the water hole) and top with the tuna salad. For an elegant presentation, serve the tuna medium rare, in slices atop the salad.

makes 8 to 10 servings

1 teaspoon canola oil
2 pounds fresh Ahi tuna steaks
2 tablespoons Dijon mustard
2 tablespoons red wine vinegar
2 teaspoons fresh lemon juice
½ teaspoon ground cumin
½ teaspoon kosher salt
½ teaspoon ground black pepper
⅔ cup extra-virgin olive oil
1 (15-ounce) can chickpeas, rinsed and drained
1 cup kalamata olives
2 teaspoons fresh rosemary leaves or ¾ teaspoon dried
¾ cup grape tomatoes, sliced in half
¼ cup sliced scallions

Set a large, heavy skillet over medium heat and add the canola oil. Add tuna steaks to skillet, working in batches if needed to keep from crowding. Cook until lightly browned on each side, about 3 minutes each side for rare or 5 minutes for well done. (Alternatively, you can bake the tuna in a 350°F oven. Brush tuna with a little canola oil and bake for 12 minutes.)

Remove the tuna from the pan to a cutting board. When cool enough to handle, cut into 1-inch pieces.

Combine Dijon, vinegar, lemon juice, cumin, salt, and pepper in a large bowl. Whisk in olive oil in a steady stream until emulsified. Add cooked tuna, chickpeas, olives, rosemary, tomatoes, and scallions. Toss gently to coat. Refrigerate until ready to serve and serve at room temperature.

Passover

Substitute olive oil for the canola. Use Passover mustard instead of Dijon mustard. Substitute jícama, apple, or quinoa for chickpeas.

Make Ahead

Can be prepared a day or two ahead of time. Store, covered, in the refrigerator.

Skewered Gefilte Fish with Zesty Ratatouille

Gefilte fish is such an important part of traditional Shabbos food. I like to serve it with this ratatouille sauce because it mixes familiar with some unfamiliar, yet fantastic, flavors. The sauce can be made days ahead of time and frozen for future use. I usually serve the fish cut in square pieces and then skewered, but it also works well sliced with the sauce served on the side. For a lovely salad course, serve in martini glasses.

makes 10 servings

Fish:

1 yellow onion, halved
2 carrots, peeled and diced
8 cups water
¼ cup sugar
1 teaspoon kosher salt
1 (22-ounce) frozen loaf gefilte fish or salmon loaf

Ratatouille:

3 tablespoons extra-virgin olive oil
1 large yellow onion, finely chopped
1 zucchini, finely chopped
1 red bell pepper, seeded and finely chopped
2 cloves garlic, chopped
1 (15-ounce) can tomato sauce
½ teaspoon ground cumin
¾ teaspoon turmeric
½ teaspoon curry powder
1 teaspoon kosher salt
¼ teaspoon ground black pepper
12 (5-inch) wooden skewers
Fresh herbs, for garnish

To prepare the fish: Combine onion, carrots, water, sugar, and salt in a large stockpot; bring to a boil over high heat. Gently lower paper-wrapped fish loaf into boiling water. Cover and reduce heat; simmer until firm, about 1 to 1½ hours. Drain and cool. Store in refrigerator until ready to serve.

Alternatively, preheat oven to 350°F. Remove fish from its paper wrapper and place fish in a loaf pan. Pour 1 tablespoon water around sides of fish so that it runs down the sides of the pan. Sprinkle 1 tablespoon sugar on the fish. Bake until the fish is soft but cooked through, 45 to 60 minutes. The fish should look slightly dry.

To prepare the ratatouille: Heat oil in a large skillet over medium-high heat. Add onion, zucchini, bell pepper, and garlic; cook until softened, about 8 minutes, stirring occasionally. Add tomato sauce, cumin, turmeric, curry, salt, and pepper. Cook on low until sauce thickens slightly, about 4 minutes. Cool slightly; cover and chill until ready to serve.

To assemble: Bring ratatouille to room temperature. Spoon 2 tablespoons of ratatouille onto each serving plate. Slice gefilte fish into 1-inch slices, then into 1-inch squares. Thread gefilte fish pieces onto a skewer and place atop sauce. Sprinkle with fresh herbs and serve.

Passover

Omit the curry and turmeric and make as instructed above.

Make Ahead

Both the fish and ratatouille can be prepared 2 days ahead of time and stored, covered, in the refrigerator. Bring to room temperature before serving.

Salmon Ceviche

This chic version of salmon tartare has super colors and crunch running throughout the dish. It's gorgeous, so you'll want to show it off in a martini or sherbet glass or a small demitasse glass cup. It would also look lovely shaped with a food mold, such as a can with the top and bottom removed. No make-aheads here—the ingredients should be perfectly fresh and the dish should be served immediately.

serves 8

Dressing:

¼ teaspoon cumin

Zest and juice of 1 lime (about 2 teaspoons juice)

1½ teaspoons finely grated fresh ginger

2 tablespoons cilantro

½ teaspoon kosher salt

¼ teaspoon ground black pepper

2 tablespoons extra-virgin olive oil

Ceviche:

1 pink grapefruit, skin and pith removed, cut into ¼-inch pieces

1 cup peeled, diced English cucumber

½ apple, peeled and diced into ¼-inch pieces

2 tablespoons finely diced red onion

½ pound sushi-grade fresh salmon (or imitation crab meat), cut into ¼-inch dice

1 avocado, diced

¼ cup pomegranate seeds (p. 104)

To make the dressing: In a small bowl, mix cumin, lime zest and juice, ginger, cilantro, salt, and pepper. Slowly add oil to mixture, whisking to emulsify.

To make the ceviche: Gently mix grapefruit, cucumber, apple, onion, and salmon in a medium bowl. Give the dressing another stir and add to the salmon mixture, tossing gently to coat. Fold in avocado and pomegranate seeds. Refrigerate and serve within 2 hours. Serve in individual dishes or a serving dish with pita chips (p. 337) for scooping ceviche.

Passover

Perfect as-is!

Tips

If you cannot find pomegranate seeds in your local market, substitute them with diced fresh mango or finely diced cooked baby beets.

To use a can as a food mold for restaurant-quality presentation, remove the top and bottom of the can. Wash and dry it thoroughly. Place can in the middle of the plate. Spoon salad into the can, pressing gently, and refrigerate. When ready to serve, gently slide the can up and off of the salad.

Preparing Raw Fish

Buy the sushi-grade fish from a sushi vendor or a fish market that sells SUSHI-grade fish. I store it wrapped tightly in plastic wrap in the freezer until ready to use. When you are ready to cut it, defrost it slightly in the refrigerator. Remove it from the refrigerator when it is still slightly frozen and slice on a cutting board with a sharp knife. If the fish is still somewhat frozen it will cut into neat ¼-inch cubes and defrost quickly during prep.

Soy Ginger "Crab" Salad

Make Ahead

Can be prepared a day ahead of time. Store, covered, in the refrigerator. Serve chilled or at room temperature.

The lime juice and ginger pair beautifully with the "crab" in this salad. The result is an easy, fresh dish that would work as an appetizer, Kiddush dip, salad course, or light lunch.

serves 8

½ cup fresh lime juice
¼ cup rice vinegar
2 tablespoons canola oil
1 tablespoon soy sauce
½ teaspoon minced fresh ginger
2 cloves garlic, minced
2 pounds imitation crab, cut into ½-inch pieces
¼ cup minced fresh cilantro or parsley
1 tablespoon toasted sesame seeds

In a large bowl, whisk together the lime juice, rice vinegar, oil, soy sauce, ginger, and garlic until smooth. Add the imitation crab and toss gently to coat. Add the cilantro and sesame seeds and toss gently. Chill 1 to 3 hours before serving.

Egg Salad with a Twist

Passover

Substitute safflower or cottonseed oil for the canola. Omit the curry.

Make Ahead

Can be made up to 2 days in advance. Cover and refrigerate until ready to use.

Lighten Up

Use all the egg whites, but only half the yolks or none of the yolks.

This egg salad is creamy, rich, and delicious. The curry adds an unexpected flavor from typical egg salad recipes, and the scallions, celery and apple give it a nice crunch.

serves 8

2½ tablespoons canola oil
1 yellow onion, chopped
10 hard-boiled eggs (p. 49)
¼ cup sliced scallions
2 tablespoons chopped celery
3 tablespoons chopped apple
¼ cup mayonnaise
1 clove garlic, minced
1 tablespoon ketchup
1 teaspoon curry
1 teaspoon kosher salt

Heat a sauté pan over medium heat. Add oil. When oil is hot, cook onion until browned, about 12 to 15 minutes. Cool.

Peel hard-boiled eggs. In a medium bowl, mash 6 egg whites with 4 whole eggs. (Alternatively, for a richer dish, use all whole eggs.) Add cooked onion, scallions, celery, apple, mayonnaise, garlic, ketchup, curry, and salt. Gently mix until well combined. Store, covered, in the refrigerator until ready to use.

Chicken Livers with Brandy, Mushrooms, and Cherries

My friend Bonnie, an enthusiastic supporter of EMUNAH and seasoned tester and advisor for this book, tasted this dish at the Olive Restaurant in Jerusalem on an EMUNAH cooking trip in Israel. The entire group raved, and the restaurant was kind enough to share their recipe. It has found a permanent home in Bonnie's repertoire and mine as well. Bonnie prefers wine, and you may too. For my family table, I prefer the depth and sweetness of brandy. Try them both—you won't go wrong either way.

serves 8

¼ cup extra-virgin olive oil
2 large yellow onions, diced
1 pound large button mushrooms, chopped into ½-inch pieces
2 pounds chicken livers, kashered
½ cup brandy, dry red wine, or chicken broth
1 tablespoon kosher salt
¼ cup minced dried onions
1 cup dried cherries

Heat oil in a large skillet over medium heat. Add onions and cook until softened, about 10 minutes. Add mushrooms and continue to cook, stirring occasionally, until mushrooms are soft and onions are brown, about 5 to 7 minutes. Add chicken livers and cook, stirring occasionally, until livers are heated through, about 4 minutes. Pour brandy into pan and cook until the liquid has reduced by half, about 5 minutes. Add salt, dried onions, and dried cherries and cook until heated through. Serve warm or at room temperature, with pita chips (p. 337) or crackers for dipping.

Passover

Use wine instead of brandy.

Make Ahead

Can be prepared a day ahead of time. Store, covered, in the refrigerator. Rewarm in a 300°F oven for best results, or serve at room temperature.

Sun-Dried Tomato Dip

I love this rich and savory dip. The tomatoes sweeten as they cook and the wine adds depth of flavor. It's great spread on challah, as a dip for crackers or veggies, even as a topping for grilled chicken or salmon.

makes 1½ cups

- 1 (8-ounce) jar sun-dried tomatoes packed in oil, drained and chopped, 1 tablespoon oil reserved
- ½ yellow onion, thinly sliced
- 1 clove garlic, minced
- 1 cup water
- ½ cup pareve chicken broth
- ¼ cup red wine vinegar
- ¼ cup dry red wine
- 2 tablespoons sugar
- ½ teaspoon dried thyme
- ½ teaspoon kosher salt
- ½ teaspoon ground black pepper

Heat reserved sun-dried tomato oil in a large skillet over medium. Add tomatoes, onion, and garlic; cook 5 to 7 minutes, stirring frequently until onion is soft and beginning to brown at the edges.

Add water, broth, vinegar, wine, sugar, thyme, salt, and pepper to skillet; bring to a boil over high heat. Reduce to a simmer, cover, and cook 30 minutes. Uncover and continue simmering another 5 to 10 minutes, or until most of the liquid has evaporated and mixture is the consistency of jam.

With an immersion blender or food processor, purée until blended but still a little chunky.

Serve warm or at room temperature with pita chips (p. 337) or vegetable crudités. Store refrigerated in a clean glass jar (the one from the sun-dried tomatoes works great!) if not using immediately. It will keep 2 weeks.

Passover

Perfect as-is!

Make Ahead

Can be prepared 2 days ahead of time. Store, covered, in the refrigerator. Bring to room temperature before serving or freeze for up to three months.

Roasted Garlic Hummus

Make Ahead

Can be prepared 2 days ahead of time. Store, covered, in the refrigerator, or freeze for up to 2 months and thaw in the refrigerator. Serve at room temperature.

Prep Ahead

Be sure to allow enough time to roast the garlic—about 45 minutes. It removes all its sharpness and yields a sweet, subtle garlic flavor.

Sweet roasted garlic enhances almost anything, and certainly gives ordinary hummus a big lift. I use this basic recipe and add whatever stir-ins I have handy to change it up each week. It freezes well too.

serves 10

Hummus:

2 (15-ounce) cans chickpeas, rinsed and drained

6 cloves roasted garlic, or more to taste (p. 334) or 2 cloves minced garlic

¼ cup tahini paste

¼ cup fresh lemon juice

¼ cup plus 2 teaspoons extra-virgin olive oil, divided

1 teaspoon kosher salt

½ teaspoon paprika

1 tablespoon chopped fresh parsley

2 teaspoons extra-virgin olive oil (optional)

Stir-Ins:

¼ cup sliced green onion

¼ teaspoon cumin

½ cup chopped black olives

¼ cup chopped jalapeño peppers

¼ cup chopped roasted red peppers

1 tablespoon fresh dill

¼ cup pine nuts, toasted (p. 335)

1 tablespoon Sriracha sauce

To make the hummus: Combine chickpeas, garlic, tahini, lemon juice, ¼ cup oil, salt, and paprika in a blender or food processor. Squeeze out the cloves from the roasted garlic into the blender and add any remaining roasting oil. Blend for 1 minute or until very smooth.

If desired, stir in one or more of the extra toppings. To serve, swirl onto a plate, sprinkle with parsley, and drizzle with remaining 2 teaspoons oil, if desired. Serve with pita chips (p. 337), challah, or vegetable crudité.

Chunky Roasted Eggplant and Red Pepper Dip

This versatile dish does triple duty as a dip served with crostini, a side dish to grilled meats, or a filling for omelets and sandwiches. Make it pareve so that you have lots of options. With all due respect to the inimitable grilled cheese, I'm not sure there's a better sandwich than this slathered on Italian country bread, topped with cheese, and grilled in a Panini press. It's certainly one of my favorites. No panini press? Use your waffle iron—it works just as well!

makes 2½ cups

- 1 medium eggplant, cut into 1-inch cubes
- 2 red bell peppers, seeded and cut into 1-inch cubes
- 1 red onion, coarsely chopped
- 1 cup grape tomatoes
- ¼ cup extra-virgin olive oil
- 1½ teaspoons kosher salt
- ½ teaspoon ground black pepper
- 3 cloves garlic, minced
- 2 tablespoons balsamic vinegar
- 1 tablespoon red wine vinegar
- 1 tablespoon tomato paste
- ¼ cup fresh basil, thinly sliced in a chiffonade

Preheat oven to 400°F.

Combine eggplant, bell peppers, onion, tomatoes, oil, salt, pepper, and garlic in a large bowl. Spread mixture evenly on a rimmed baking sheet. Roast until vegetables are lightly browned and soft, about 35 to 45 minutes, turning once during cooking.

Transfer cooked vegetables to a large bowl. Add vinegars and tomato paste; toss and mash a little, leaving large chunks and just slightly blending the ingredients. Stir in basil. Serve warm or at room temperature.

Passover

Perfect as-is!

Make Ahead

Can be prepared 2 days ahead of time. In fact, it's better that way! Store, covered, in the refrigerator. Bring to room temperature before serving.

Tip

For a chiffonade, place a few clean, dry basil leaves on top of one another. Roll the bundle up from the short side to the other short side. With a sharp knife, slice the rolled leaves into thin strips to make ribbons—a chiffonade—of basil.

Olive Dip
Roasted Garlic Hummus
Chunky Roasted Eggplant and Red Pepper Dip
Triple Onion and Spinach Dip
New Eggplant Babbaganoush

Triple Onion and Spinach Dip

The base for this delicious dip is roasted onions and garlic. The onion trio gets sweet and caramelized from the addition of honey and then blended together with hearty spinach, woodsy dill, and creamy mayonnaise.

makes 2 cups

- 2 shallots, thinly sliced
- 1 small red onion, thinly sliced
- 1 leek, thinly sliced
- 3 cloves garlic
- 3 tablespoons extra-virgin olive oil
- 1 teaspoon honey
- ½ teaspoon kosher salt
- ¾ cup frozen spinach, thawed and squeezed dry
- ½ cup mayonnaise
- ⅓ cup Tofutti sour cream
- 1 tablespoon distilled white vinegar
- 2 teaspoons fresh lemon juice
- 1 tablespoon fresh dill or 1 teaspoon dried
- ½ teaspoon kosher salt
- ¼ teaspoon ground black pepper

Preheat oven to 425°F. On a large rimmed baking sheet, toss shallots, red onion, leek, and garlic with olive oil, honey, and salt. Spread in a single layer and roast in oven until slightly charred, about 20 minutes. Remove from oven and then coarsely chop when cool enough to handle.

With an immersion blender or a food processor purée spinach, mayonnaise, sour cream, vinegar, lemon juice, dill, salt, and pepper. Add roasted onion–garlic mixture and blend until smooth or slightly chunky.

Serve with vegetable crudités, pita chips (p. 337), crackers, or challah.

Passover

Omit Tofutti sour cream. Use an additional ¼ cup mayonnaise.

Make Ahead

This can be made 2 days ahead of time. Store, covered, in the refrigerator. Serve chilled or at room temperature.

Olive Dip

My entire family loves olive dip. It's creamier than a chunky tapenade, and they lather it on challah, schmear it on crackers or pretzels, and even like it topping a hot baked potato.

makes 2 cups

- 1 cup pitted green olives
- 1 cup fresh flat-leaf parsley
- 5 scallions, cut in chunks
- 1½ tablespoons capers, drained
- 1 clove garlic
- 2 teaspoons Dijon mustard
- 2 tablespoons extra-virgin olive oil
- 3 tablespoons mayonnaise

Combine all the ingredients in a food processor. Pulse until smooth and well blended.

Passover

Substitute Passover mustard for Dijon mustard.

Make Ahead

This dip stays good for about 2 weeks in the refrigerator and 3 months in freezer. I usually portion into ¾-cup servings, keeping some for immediate consumption and the rest in the freezer for my children's next round of olive dip cravings.

Roasted Red Pepper and Jalapeño Dip

This zesty dip is full of flavor and spices. It can be made days ahead of time and stored in the refrigerator. But fair warning: it tends to get spicier as time passes! Be careful when handling jalapeños as well. When slicing or deveining hot peppers, the fiery capsaicin will inevitably get onto your fingers. Touch your eyes or any other sensitive spot, and the result is no fun indeed. The best solution is to wear gloves when handling peppers. If you don't have those, use a napkin or towel to keep from touching the peppers directly. To cut peppers, slice them in half, and then scrape out the white membrane and seeds with a pairing knife or spoon. Do not use your fingers, or you will transfer the irritating components to your eyes or nose. Discard the seeds, and slice or chop the pepper according to the recipe directions. Always wash your hands, cutting board, and knife with soap and water before proceeding. Trust me on this.

makes 1½ cups

1 red bell pepper
1 jalapeño
2 cloves garlic
Pinch of kosher salt
2 tablespoons chopped mint leaves
2 tablespoons chopped fresh parsley
1 tablespoon extra-virgin olive oil
2 tablespoons non-dairy creamer or soy milk
2 tablespoons Tofutti sour cream
1 tablespoon sugar

Preheat oven to 425°F. Place the red bell pepper and jalapeño on a baking sheet and roast in oven until lightly charred and blackened, 25 to 35 minutes. Remove from oven and immediately place in a resealable plastic bag and close bag. Let peppers steam until cool enough to handle. Using your fingers, peel the charred skin off peppers. (It's okay if a bit of charring remains—it's good for flavor.)

Alternatively, you can roast the peppers individually in the flame of a gas stove. Using tongs, place the pepper directly on the grate above a burner turned to high. Turn occasionally until the pepper is well charred on all sides. Place in resealable plastic bag, steam, and peel as directed above.

Remove the stem and any seeds from the peppers and discard. Purée the roasted peppers with the remaining ingredients in a food processor, blender, or with an immersion blender until smooth.

Passover

Use non-dairy creamer in place of soy milk. Use mayonnaise in place of Tofutti sour cream.

Make Ahead

Can be made a few days ahead of time and stored, covered, in the refrigerator. Bring to room temperature before serving.

Tip

You can make this dip with store-bought roasted peppers, but it'll be all the better if you do it yourself. Give it a try—it's not hard!

New Eggplant Babbaganoush

I know you already make another babbaganoush recipe or even buy it premade and you are about to gloss over this one. Stop: try this recipe. It's a bit different. The garlic slowly softens and roasts into the eggplant skin, infusing it with garlic essence. It gets great flavor from balsamic vinegar, and terrific crunch from tomatoes and pine nuts. It's also enhanced with sweet raisins. Serve this at room temperature so that all the flavors are the correct consistency and well balanced.

serves 8

2 eggplants
4 cloves garlic, thinly sliced
¾ teaspoon kosher salt
½ teaspoon ground black pepper
1 teaspoon balsamic vinegar
1 tomato, seeded and chopped
4 tablespoons extra-virgin olive oil
⅓ cup golden raisins
⅓ cup pine nuts, toasted (p. 335)
3 tablespoons chopped fresh parsley

Preheat oven to 350°F.

Cut eggplants in half. Make slits in the eggplant skin all over and insert garlic into the slits. Place, cut-side down, in an ovensafe baking dish. Bake for about 1 hour, until eggplants are soft. Cool.

Scoop flesh from the eggplant skins. With an immersion blender or a food processor, purée eggplant. Add salt, pepper, balsamic vinegar, tomato, olive oil, and raisins. Refrigerate overnight. Before serving, mix in pine nuts and parsley. Serve at room temperature.

Passover

Perfect as-is!

Make Ahead

Can be prepared 2 days ahead of time. Store, covered, in the refrigerator. Serve at room temperature.

Cholent

Passover

Omit beans and barley. Use kosher for Passover spices. Add additional potatoes or sweet potatoes, if desired. The kishka recipe is not kosher for Passover.

Prep Ahead

The beans need to soak at least 6 hours and preferably overnight.

Make Ahead

The very nature of cholent is a dish that is made ahead and so it can be kept warm in a crockpot, a warm oven, or a warming drawer for several hours.

Cholent is a very personal dish and the flavor is very specific to each person. It evokes feelings of history, legacy, and family and thus taste and texture need to be altered based on your own preferences. You can use whatever dried beans you like or a combination of several. My family prefers kidney or white beans. Water can be adjusted, spices added or omitted, and cooking technique altered to create different results. I recommend experimenting. Remember, you'll need to add more liquid to the crockpot than called for in the recipe if you cook on high heat more than 8 hours. The warm setting will absorb less water over long periods of heating.

serves 10

1½ cups dried beans
2 tablespoons extra-virgin olive oil
1 yellow onion, chopped
3 cloves garlic, minced
2 to 3 pounds boneless flanken meat or beef stew meat
1 teaspoon paprika
1 teaspoon onion powder
½ teaspoon garlic powder
¼ cup barley
1 teaspoon kosher salt
½ teaspoon ground black pepper
½ cup red wine (optional)
Chicken broth or water to cover
4 potatoes, peeled and cut into large chunks

In a large bowl, soak beans in enough water to cover for at least 6 hours or overnight, and then drain.

Place oil, onion, and garlic in bottom of crockpot and turn heat to high. Let onion mixture soften, about 30 minutes to 1 hour. Add flanken, drained beans, paprika, onion powder, garlic powder, barley, salt, and pepper. Add red wine and enough broth or water to cover the ingredients by about ½ inch. Scatter potatoes around, submerging in liquid. Cook on high for 6 to 8 hours, and then reduce setting to warm until ready to serve.

Barbecue Cholent

To the cholent recipe above, add

1 teaspoon chili powder
½ cup barbecue sauce
2 tablespoons tomato paste

Moroccan Cholent

To the cholent recipe above, add

¼ cup ketchup
½ teaspoon more salt
1 tablespoon dried orange or lemon peel
1 tablespoon Ras el Hanout Moroccan spice blend
1 teaspoon ground cumin
1 teaspoon ground ginger
½ teaspoon cinnamon
½ teaspoon ground coriander
½ teaspoon cayenne pepper
½ teaspoon ground allspice
¼ teaspoon ground cloves

Marrow Cholent

1 cup mixed dried beans
2 tablespoons canola oil
1 large yellow onion, chopped
3 cloves garlic, minced
3 marrow bones
1 cup barley
1 (8-ounce) can tomato sauce
1½ pounds flanken
3 potatoes, cut into large chunks
1 teaspoon kosher salt
½ teaspoon ground black pepper
1 teaspoon garlic powder
1 teaspoon onion powder
1 teaspoon paprika
1 tablespoon honey
½ cup red wine
1 cup chicken broth or water

In a large bowl, soak beans in enough water to cover for at least 6 hours or overnight, and then drain beans.

Place oil, onion, and garlic in bottom of crockpot and turn heat to high. Let onion mixture soften, about 30 minutes to 1 hour. Place the marrow bones on top of the onion mixture. Add the beans, barley, tomato sauce, flanken, potatoes, salt, pepper, garlic powder, onion powder, paprika, and honey.

Add red wine and enough chicken broth or water to cover the ingredients by about ½ inch. Scatter potatoes around, submerging in liquid. Cook on high for 6 to 8 hours, and then reduce setting to warm until ready to serve.

Smoked Turkey-Garbanzo Bean Cholent

1 teaspoon canola oil
1 onion, cut into 1-inch chunks
3 potatoes, peeled and chopped into 2-inch chunks
2 cloves garlic, minced
½ cup barley
1 large smoked turkey leg and thigh
½ cup spicy prepared garbanzo beans (available in the refrigerator section of most markets or in a can)
2 tablespoons ketchup or barbecue sauce
1 teaspoon garlic powder
½ teaspoon cumin
½ teaspoon kosher salt
½ teaspoon ground black pepper

Approximately 2 hours before Shabbos begins, place oil, onion, potatoes, garlic, barley, and turkey in a large crockpot and turn heat to low. Cook for 1 hour. Add prepared garbanzo beans, ketchup (or barbecue sauce), garlic powder, cumin, salt, and pepper, and enough water to cover ingredients by about ½ inch. Stir and cook on low until ready to serve.

Kishka

⅔ cup all-purpose flour
⅓ cup old-fashioned oats
⅓ cup corn flake crumbs
1 yellow onion, grated (use juice and onion)
1 carrot, grated
½ teaspoon garlic powder
1 teaspoon paprika
1 teaspoon kosher salt
½ teaspoon ground black pepper
⅓ cup canola oil
⅓ cup water

In a large bowl, mix all ingredients together. With your hands, form batter into a log about 8 inches long and 4 inches wide. Wrap in parchment paper or foil and refrigerate for at least 1 hour. Leave wrapped—or unwrap—and place the kishka on top of or slightly submerged into the cholent while cholent is cooking.

Overnight Potato Kugel

Passover

Substitute safflower or cottonseed oil for the canola.

Prep Ahead

This dish needs to be started the day before so it can bake through the night.

This kugel is what Shabbos should smell and taste like. The aroma will have you ready for lunch before your Shabbos morning coffee. The overnight cooking technique makes the outside of the kugel crispy and browned while the inside stays super soft and almost pudding-like. I make it in a glass bowl with a lid, and then gently invert it before serving. It retains the molded dome shape until ready to serve. Slice it like a bombe, and use a spoon to scoop out the soft center.

serves 8

- Nonstick cooking spray, as needed
- ¾ cup canola oil, divided
- 6 large potatoes, grated by hand or in food processor
- 1 large yellow onion, grated
- 3 eggs, beaten
- 3 tablespoons maple syrup
- 1 tablespoon matzo meal
- 1½ teaspoons kosher salt
- ½ teaspoon ground black pepper

Preheat oven to 350°F. Lightly coat a round 2½-quart ovensafe glass Pyrex bowl with cooking spray; pour in ¼ cup of the oil. Place in oven and warm 15 minutes.

Meanwhile, combine potatoes, onion, eggs, maple syrup, matzo meal, salt, pepper, and the remaining ½ cup oil in a large bowl; mix well. Transfer mixture into oven-warmed dish (be careful as the oil can splatter!)

Bake 30 minutes. Reduce oven temperature to 225°F. Cover dish and cook through the night and until you serve it for Shabbos lunch, anywhere from 14 to 18 hours.

Healthy Spin Potato Kugel

Passover

Substitute safflower or cottonseed oil for the canola.

serves 8

- ¼ cup canola oil
- 2½ cups fresh cauliflower florets or 12 ounces frozen cauliflower, defrosted and squeezed dry
- 3 potatoes, peeled and quartered
- 1 yellow onion, peeled and quartered
- 2 eggs
- 2 egg whites
- 2 teaspoons maple syrup
- 1 tablespoon white whole wheat flour or matzo meal
- 1 teaspoon kosher salt
- ½ teaspoon ground black pepper

Preheat oven to 425°F. Pour canola oil into a 13 x 9 x 2-inch ovensafe baking dish and place in oven to warm for 15 minutes.

In a food processor, purée cauliflower until mashed and soft. Add potatoes, onion, eggs, egg whites, maple syrup, flour, salt and pepper and blend until smooth.

Pour mixture into oven-warmed dish. (Be careful as the oil can splatter!) Bake until top is browned and crispy, about 50 minutes or an hour.

Vegetarian Chopped Liver

I've tried this recipe in many variations, some made with just green beans and others with mixed vegetables. I like this one best because the mixture of vegetables gives it a true texture and taste similar to chopped liver. Make this a day ahead of time so that the flavors have time to blend.

makes 8 servings

- 3½ tablespoons canola oil, divided
- 2 large yellow onions, chopped
- 1 (15-ounce) can French-style green beans, drained
- 1 (15-ounce) can sweet peas, drained
- Whites from 4 hard-boiled eggs (see below)
- 1 cup walnuts, finely chopped
- ¾ teaspoon kosher salt
- ¼ teaspoon ground black pepper
- ½ to ¾ cup matzo meal

Heat skillet over medium-high heat and add 1 tablespoon oil. When oil is hot, add onions and cook until soft and golden brown, about 15 minutes.

Transfer onions to a food processor. Add green beans, peas, egg whites, remaining 2½ tablespoons canola oil, and walnuts, and pulse until the mixture is coarsely chopped but still chunky. Add salt and pepper, then matzo meal, starting with ½ cup, pulsing and adding more matzo as needed until blended and the consistency resembles chopped liver.

Refrigerate until ready to serve.

Make Ahead

Best made a day or two in advance. Store, covered, in the refrigerator. Bring to room temperature before serving.

Perfect Hard Boiled Eggs

Place 6 eggs—the older the better when it comes to peeling—in a medium heavy saucepan. Add water to cover by about 1½ inches and salt the water. Bring to a boil, and then immediately remove pot from the heat. Cover and let stand, undisturbed, for 10 minutes. While they're cooling, prepare a bowl of ice water. After 10 minutes, transfer eggs to the ice water to stop the cooking. Gently crack the eggs and peel under running water to release the membrane and get the shell off.

The Secret to Peeling an Egg

Crack a line around the middle of the egg with the edge of a spoon. Insert the tip of the spoon into the cracked shell, taking care to get under the membrane. Rotate the egg, keeping the spoon under the shell. The spoon breaks the suction so that the entire shell pops right off. It works best when the egg is warm.

מנות ראשונות

FIRSTS

For some, making similar recipes each week represents tradition, comfort, and familiarity. For others like me, trying new recipes adds much to my Shabbos table, and my favorite meals are a mix of classic Shabbos favorites with new and unexpected dishes. I truly believe the effort and energy one extends preparing these meals creates a connection and commitment to one's family and tradition that will be cherished forever. Not to mention it's the most delicious mitzvah!

Pan-Seared Duck Breast with Fig-Shallot Marmalade

Passover

Substitute safflower or cottonseed oil for the canola.

Make Ahead

This can be made 2 days ahead of time. Store, covered, in the refrigerator. Rewarm, covered, in a warming drawer or 300°F oven.

Duck is decadent and delicious, and this marmalade is its perfect accompaniment. The sweetness from the figs, the acid from the wine, and the piney scent of rosemary complement the rich and succulent meat. I love to serve this elegant dish in the winter on Yom Tov as an appetizer. It sets the mood for a most special of occasions.

serves 8 to 10

Fig-Shallot Marmalade:

2½ tablespoons extra-virgin olive oil
3 shallots, diced (about ⅓ cup)
2 cups dried figs, stemmed and quartered
1 cup Marsala wine
1½ tablespoons fresh rosemary or 1 teaspoon dried
1½ cups water

Duck:

6 boneless duck breast fillets, skin on
½ teaspoon kosher salt, plus more to taste
¼ teaspoon ground black pepper
2 tablespoons canola oil

Pan Sauce:

¼ cup balsamic vinegar
1 cup red wine
1 cup chicken or duck stock
⅓ cup packed dark brown sugar
2 tablespoons fresh rosemary or 2 teaspoons dried

For the marmalade: Heat olive oil in a small saucepan over medium heat. Add shallots; stir until soft, about 5 minutes. Add figs, Marsala, and rosemary. Increase heat and bring to a boil. Add 1½ cups water. Reduce heat to medium-low and simmer, stirring often, until figs are soft and easily mashed, about 20 minutes. If the marmalade seems too thick as it's cooking, add tablespoons of water until desired consistency. Mash figs and onions with a fork and blend into a jam-like consistency. Season with salt and pepper.

For the duck: Season duck breast with salt and pepper. Heat oil in a large sauté pan over medium-high heat. When the oil is just beginning to shimmer, brown duck breast, skin-side down, until the skin is crisp, golden brown, and releases easily from the pan. Flip duck breast, reduce heat, and cook other side until medium rare, about 10 minutes total cooking time. Remove duck breasts to a platter, reserving juices in pan. Work in batches, if necessary. Set aside cooked duck on plate and tent with foil to keep warm.

For the sauce: Set same pan over medium-high heat and add balsamic vinegar and red wine to deglaze. Use a wooden spoon to scrape up any browned bits from the bottom, and continue to cook over medium-high heat until reduced by half, about 7 minutes. Add stock and reduce by half again, about 5 minutes. Add brown sugar and rosemary; cook for 3 minutes.

Slice duck breast at an angle. Spoon about 1 tablespoon sauce on each appetizer plate. Top with 3 tablespoons of Fig-Shallot Marmalade. Place a few slices of duck on top of marmalade and spoon with more sauce.

Honey Garlic Meatballs

Make Ahead

Can be prepared 2 days ahead of time. Store, covered, in the refrigerator or freeze up to 3 months. Defrost in the refrigerator. Rewarm, covered, in a warming drawer or 300°F oven.

Lighten Up

Use 1 egg instead of 2. Omit soymilk and breadcrumbs. Instead of the ground beef, use 1 pound ground chicken combined with 1 pound lean ground turkey. Add ½ cup wheat germ, 1 teaspoon kosher salt, and ½ teaspoon ground black pepper. If the mixture is sticky, wet your hands with water before forming balls.

Made small, these simple but sweet and delicious meatballs make perfect appetizers. Larger, they work well as a main dish served over rice. Don't overwork the meat—it can make them tough.

8 servings

2 eggs
¾ cup soy milk
2 pounds ground beef
1 cup breadcrumbs
1 tablespoon onion powder
½ teaspoon kosher salt
¼ teaspoon ground black pepper
1 tablespoon canola oil
4 cloves garlic, minced
1¼ cups ketchup
½ cup honey
½ cup soy sauce
Cooked rice, for serving

Whisk together eggs and soy milk in a large bowl. Add beef, breadcrumbs, onion powder, salt, and pepper; mix with your hands until completely combined. Shape mixture into 1-inch balls and arrange evenly in two 13 x 9 x 2-inch pans. Bake 15 minutes. Drain off excess fat; set aside.

Heat oil in a large saucepan over medium heat. Add garlic and cook until softened and fragrant, 2 minutes, stirring frequently. Add ketchup, honey, and soy sauce, and stir to mix. Bring mixture to a boil over high heat; reduce to a simmer and cook 5 minutes. Add reserved meatballs and cook 5 more minutes. Serve with toothpicks on an appetizer buffet or over rice for a main dish.

Sweetbreads with Wild Mushrooms and Rich Broth

I only started making sweetbreads a few years ago. It is not a dish I grew up eating, but after trying chef and friend Jeff Nathan's version from the renowned Abigael's restaurant, I fell in love with their creamy texture. I used his recipe as a starting point for this dish. If you've not tried them before, you should. This recipe has a rich and flavorful sauce that makes everyone into a sweetbreads lover. Sweetbreads, by their nature, can be a bit salty. I soak them in cold water for about 30 minutes and rinse and drain them a few times before cooking.

serves 6

Mushrooms:

1 ounce dried porcini or other dried wild mushrooms
½ cup red wine
2 tablespoons balsamic vinegar
1 pound white mushrooms
½ pound fresh shiitake mushrooms
1 teaspoon fresh thyme leaves or ¼ teaspoon dried
½ teaspoon kosher salt
½ teaspoon ground black pepper
2 cups cold water

Sweetbreads:

1 pound sweetbreads
¼ cup all-purpose flour
¼ teaspoon ground cloves
¼ teaspoon ground black pepper
3 tablespoons canola oil
¼ pound shiitake mushrooms, stemmed and thinly sliced
1 teaspoon low-sodium soy sauce
1 tablespoon fresh thyme leaves or 1 teaspoon dried
¼ cup minced scallions
¼ cup finely chopped tomato

For the mushrooms: Combine all the ingredients in a large pot over medium-low heat and simmer for 30 minutes to 1 hour. Broth should be rich and dark. Strain and mince the mushrooms; return them to the broth, if desired.

While the mushrooms are simmering, prepare the sweetbreads: Bring a large pot of water to a boil over high heat, reduce to a simmer, and gently place sweetbreads in simmering water. Parboil for 20 or 30 minutes, or until membranes are easy to separate from the meat and sweetbreads are only slightly cooked. Remove partially cooked sweetbreads from water, reserving ½ cup cooking liquid. Gently peel membranes off meat and remove any other bone, tubes, or gristle.

Combine flour, cloves, and pepper in a medium bowl. Heat a large sauté pan over medium-high heat, and then add the oil. Dredge the sweetbreads in the mixture and gently set in pan. Cook until seared and lightly browned, about 4 to 6 minutes. Remove sweetbreads and deglaze pan with reserved cooking liquid, scraping the bottom of pan with a wooden spoon to remove any browned bits. Add mushrooms, soy sauce, thyme, scallions, and tomatoes to pan. Cook an additional 2 to 5 minutes, or until mixture is reduced slightly.

To serve, place sweetbreads in a dish or on a plate. Drizzle with wild mushroom broth.

Passover

Substitute potato starch for the flour. Use safflower or cottonseed oil for the canola. Substitute Passover soy sauce for regular soy sauce.

Make Ahead

The sweetbreads and broth can be prepared 2 days head of time or frozen for up to 2 months. Defrost in the refrigerator and rewarm, covered, in a 350°F oven or a warming drawer.

Salmon Croquettes with Dill Tartar Sauce

Kids and adults love these, so I couldn't resist including them in the book. They're equally good with the Spicy Mayonnaise (p. 331) if you don't have any dill handy.

makes 12 (3-inch) patties or 18 (2-inch) patties

Croquettes:

4 (14-ounce) cans salmon, drained, or 1 pound fresh salmon, ground
¼ cup minced yellow onion
4 cups cornflake crumbs, divided
4 eggs
⅔ cup mayonnaise or light mayonnaise
1 cup soy milk
1 tablespoon dried dill or ¼ cup fresh dill
1 teaspoon kosher salt
½ cup canola oil, divided

Tartar Sauce:

1 cup mayonnaise
1 tablespoon ketchup
3 tablespoons grated apple
2 pickles, chopped
⅓ cup chopped yellow onion
¼ cup fresh dill
1 tablespoon sugar

To prepare the croquettes: Line a large baking sheet with parchment paper. Mix salmon (canned or freshly ground), onion, 2 cups cornflake crumbs, eggs, mayonnaise, soy milk, dill, and salt in a large bowl. Form into 3-inch patties (or smaller for Kiddush size) and place on prepared baking sheet. Coat patties in remaining cornflake crumbs.

Heat ⅓ cup of the oil in a large skillet over medium-high heat. Add prepared patties in batches and fry until browned, 2 to 3 minutes per side. Drain on paper towel–lined plates. Add more oil between batches as needed.

For the tartar sauce: Place all ingredients in a food processor and process to desired consistency. Serve the tartar sauce with the salmon croquettes.

Passover

Substitute matzo meal for cornflake crumbs. Substitute non-dairy creamer for soy milk and use Passover safflower or cottonseed oil for canola.

Make Ahead

The sauce and croquettes can be made several days ahead of time and stored in the refrigerator until ready to use. The finished croquettes freeze well, too. Defrost in the refrigerator and rewarm in a warming drawer or a 350°F oven.

Sesame Chicken Hand Rolls

The chicken is best served warm in cold, crisp lettuce cups and eaten by hand. It's especially good with a dipping sauce like sweet chili sauce, hot and spicy duck sauce, Spicy Peanut Sauce (p. 330), or Peanut Dipping Sauce (p. 330). I like to have several on hand so that people can choose.

makes 8 servings

- 1½ pounds ground chicken
- 3 scallions, minced
- 4 tablespoons soy sauce, divided
- 1 teaspoon cornstarch
- 3 tablespoons sesame oil
- ¼ pound shiitake mushrooms, stemmed and chopped
- 3 teaspoons minced fresh ginger
- 3 cloves garlic, minced
- 1½ tablespoons packed light brown sugar
- 2 tablespoons water
- 20 large butter lettuce leaves
- ½ cup chopped roasted peanuts

Combine chicken, scallions, 3 tablespoons soy sauce, and cornstarch in a medium bowl. Marinate 10 minutes at room temperature.

Heat oil in a large nonstick skillet over medium-high. Add mushrooms and cook 1 minute, stirring occasionally. Add ginger and garlic; cook 30 seconds, stirring frequently. Add brown sugar, water, remaining tablespoon soy sauce, and reserved chicken mixture. Cook, stirring often, until golden brown and cooked through, 5 to 10 minutes.

Arrange lettuce leaves on a large platter. Spoon chicken mixture evenly among lettuce leaves. Garnish with peanuts. Serve immediately. To eat, roll leaves around filling and dip into chili sauces.

Make Ahead

The chicken can be made 2 days ahead of time and stored, covered, in the refrigerator or frozen. Defrost in the refrigerator. Rewarm, covered, in a 300°F oven for about 30 minutes.

Lighten Up

Use 3 tablespoons lite soy sauce in lieu of regular soy sauce. Reduce sesame oil to 2 tablespoons and brown sugar to 1 tablespoon. Omit peanuts.

Poached Salmon Two Ways

Passover

Use non-dairy creamer in place of soy milk in the dressing.

Make Ahead

The salmon and dressing can be made 2 days ahead of time, and the salsa can be made a day in advance. Store, covered, in the refrigerator until ready to serve.

Poaching creates a moist, flavorful fish that can be made a day ahead of time. This creamy green dressing tastes clean and bright with the citrus and fresh herbs, while the salsa pairs the meaty, briny olives with the freshness of oranges. Try them both and see which you prefer.

makes 10 servings

Salmon:

3 cups water
½ cup white wine
2 tablespoons fresh lemon juice
½ teaspoon kosher salt
10 (3-ounce) boneless, skinless salmon fillets

Green Goddess Dressing:

3 tablespoons white wine vinegar
1 teaspoon fresh lemon juice
1 tablespoon fresh lime juice
2 tablespoons sugar
1 ripe avocado
1 clove garlic, chopped
⅔ cup extra-virgin olive oil
¼ cup soy milk
3 tablespoons chopped fresh parsley
2 tablespoons chopped fresh tarragon
2 tablespoons chopped fresh cilantro
1 tablespoon chopped fresh basil
1 small shallot, finely chopped
Kosher salt and black pepper, to taste

Orange and Olive Salsa:

3 seedless oranges
3 tablespoons extra-virgin olive oil
3 tablespoons red wine vinegar
2 tablespoons balsamic vinegar
1 teaspoon paprika
1 teaspoon finely chopped garlic
½ teaspoon cayenne pepper
½ teaspoon kosher salt
¼ teaspoon ground black pepper
1 cup black and green olives
⅓ cup chopped fresh parsley

To prepare the salmon: Combine water, wine, lemon juice, and salt in a large skillet with 3-inch sides, and bring to a boil over high heat. Gently add salmon fillets and reduce to a bare simmer. Cook just until the fillets are opaque, about 5 minutes. Turn off heat and leave salmon in the cooking liquid until cool enough to handle, but still warm, about 5 minutes. Remove salmon from liquid with a slotted spatula, careful to keep pieces intact.

To prepare the Green Goddess Dressing: Combine vinegar, lemon juice, lime juice, sugar, avocado, and garlic in a food processor. With the machine running, gradually add oil and blend well. Transfer mixture to a large bowl and whisk in soy milk. Add parsley, tarragon, cilantro, basil, and shallot. Mix well and season with salt and pepper. Cover and chill at least 3 hours. Let stand at room temperature 20 minutes before serving. Whisk dressing to refresh and drizzle over the poached salmon.

To prepare the Orange and Olive Salsa: Slice the peel off the top and bottom of the oranges, and then slice the peel from top to bottom, removing any pith that remains. Cut next to each membrane to release each orange segment, placing a bowl below to catch any juice. Cut each segment into three pieces. Combine the oranges and their juice with the remaining ingredients and refrigerate at least 4 hours and up to overnight. Serve the salsa over the poached salmon.

Poached Salmon
with Orange and Olive salsa

Poached Salmon
with Green Goddess dressing

Pesto Flounder Pinwheels

These pinwheels have a beautiful presentation and a fresh and light taste. You can make them a day ahead of time and store them in the refrigerator until ready to serve.

Passover

Use matzo meal in place of breadcrumbs.

Make Ahead

Can be made one day ahead of time. Store, covered, in the refrigerator. Serve at room temperature or rewarm, covered, in a warming drawer or 300°F oven.

serves 8

- 1 pound flounder fillets, sliced into long, ¾-inch strips
- ¾ cup homemade pesto (p. 335) or store-bought
- ½ cup homemade breadcrumbs (p. 333) or store-bought
- Toothpicks, for securing
- 2 tablespoons white wine
- 2 tablespoons fresh lemon juice
- ½ teaspoon kosher salt
- ¼ teaspoon ground black pepper
- ¼ cup pistachios, toasted and coarsely chopped (p. 335)
- Serve with Sun-Dried Tomato Dip (p. 39), extra pesto (p. 335), or Honey Mustard Sauce (p. 328)

Place flounder strips on a clean, dry cutting board. Spread 1 teaspoon pesto atop the full length of each flounder strip. Sprinkle about 1 teaspoon breadcrumbs on top of pesto on each strip. Roll the flounder into a pinwheel, starting with the thickest part of the fish. Secure with a toothpick and place on a 13 x 9 x 2-inch baking dish.

Preheat oven to 400°F.

Drizzle pinwheels with white wine, lemon juice, salt, and pepper. Bake 10 to 14 minutes, until the flounder is just cooked through. Garnish with pistachios and serve warm or at room temperature with extra pesto (p. 335), Sun-Dried Tomato Dip (p. 39), or Honey Mustard Sauce (p. 328) on the side.

Tips for Fish Prep, Storage, and Cooking

Only buy fresh fish. How do you know if it's fresh? Smell it. Does it smell fishy or unpleasant? Then skip it. If it's a whole fish, look at the eyes? Are they bright and clear? That's good! Cloudy and dull? Skip those fish, too.

Buying pre-frozen fish is fine—it's often flash-frozen right on the boat, ensuring better quality than if they attempted to deliver it fresh. However, once thawed, it should not be refrozen. Grilled, baked, or roasted fish do not freeze well either.

Only freeze fresh fish or fish patty recipes, like the Salmon Croquettes on page 57. To freeze, wrap tightly in plastic wrap and then store in a resealable plastic bag. Defrost in the refrigerator, not at room temperature. If you need to prepare your fish ahead of time, you can do it the day before and store it, covered, in the refrigerator until ready to serve.

Gingersnap Sweet and Sour Stuffed Cabbage

My mother-in-law prefers to make reservations than dinner. But she has a few dishes that her family loves—with good reason. This stuffed cabbage is one of them. I've added gingersnaps to the sauce. Unexpected, yes, but I love the taste and texture it adds. Mom adds flanken to the sauce as well, and this is the ingredient that moves this dish from good to sensational. I am grateful to her not only for this delicious dish, but for the countless meals and memories we've shared together as family. You can serve this dish immediately, but it tastes even better on day two.

serves 20

Cabbage Rolls:

1 teaspoon canola oil
½ cup chopped yellow onion
2 pounds ground beef or steak
½ cup water
½ cup uncooked rice
2 tablespoons ketchup
½ to 1 teaspoon cumin (optional)
¼ teaspoon dried ginger (optional)
1 teaspoon kosher salt
½ teaspoon ground black pepper
1 large head cabbage
6 additional cabbage leaves

Sauce:

4 tablespoons extra-virgin olive oil
1 cup chopped yellow onion
3 pounds flanken, cut between the bones into individual pieces
1 (28-ounce) can crushed tomatoes
1 (8-ounce) can tomato paste
1½ to 2 cups water
⅓ cup packed brown sugar
3 tablespoons honey
¼ cup fresh lemon juice
8 gingersnap cookies, crumbled (or 5 graham crackers plus 1¼ teaspoons dried ginger)
2 teaspoons kosher salt

For the cabbage rolls: Heat a skillet over medium and add oil. When hot, add onion and sauté until golden. Remove from heat.

In a large bowl, combine ground beef with water, rice, ketchup, cumin (if using), ginger (if using), salt, and pepper. Add cooked onion and mix gently. Do not overmix, as it will toughen the meat.

With a sharp knife, remove the core from the cabbage and separate the leaves. Place the cabbage leaves in a large pot. Cover them with water and bring to a boil. Reduce heat and simmer for about 8 minutes, or until the leaves are soft and pliable. Drain and let cool.

Cut leaves in half, removing and discarding the hard core. Place 3 tablespoons meat mixture on each leaf. Fold edges toward center and roll up like an eggroll. Repeat until all leaves are filled.

Preheat oven to 350°F.

Passover

For cabbage rolls, use matzo meal in place of rice. For sauce omit gingersnaps.

Make Ahead

Best made a day or two ahead of time. Store, covered, in the refrigerator or freeze up to 3 months. Defrost in the refrigerator. Rewarm, covered, in a warming drawer or 350°F oven.

Tip

This recipe serves 20, which may be more than you're going to have at your dinnertable. You can halve the recipe or make the full amount and freeze what you don't need. Freeze in a 13 x 9-inch pan covered in foil. Defrost in the refrigerator. Rewarm, covered, in a warming drawer or 350°F oven.

Make the sauce: Heat a large, 12-quart pot over medium-high heat and add oil. (Alternatively, divide sauce recipe between 2 Dutch ovens.) When oil is hot, add onion and flanken and cook for 10 minutes, turning flanken over when slightly browned. Add tomatoes, tomato paste, water, brown sugar, honey, lemon juice, gingersnaps, and salt. Simmer for 10 minutes. Transfer half of sauce to a large roasting pan. Gently place cabbage bundles in sauce in roasting pan. Pour remaining sauce over cabbage bundles. Place additional cabbage leaves on top of cabbage and sauce. Cover roasting pan with heavy-duty foil and bake for 1½ to 2 hours, or until a knife or cake tester inserted through the cabbage and into the meat and comes out clean without any resistance.

To serve: Place one or two cabbage bundles on a plate. Add a piece of flanken, and spoon the sauce over rolls and meat. Serve with basmati rice or mashed potatoes so that guests can enjoy every drop of the delicious sauce.

Tip

Feeling like this is too time-consuming? Follow instructions for meat preparation and sauce preparation. But instead of making the cabbage rolls, form the meat mixture into meatballs and gently place in prepared sauce. Top with 1 or 2 (16-ounce) bags of shredded green cabbage. Bring to a boil, cover, and reduce heat. Cook for 1 hour at a gentle simmer. Gently stir before serving so that the cabbage is mixed with the sauce. Serve over rice.

Garden Fresh Gazpacho

Passover

For gazpacho, use Passover soy sauce in place of the Worcestershire sauce. The black bean cakes are NOT kosher for Passover.

Make Ahead

Both the gazpacho and black bean cakes are best prepared a day or two ahead of time. Store, covered, in the refrigerator. Serve gazpacho chilled. Rewarm black bean cakes in a warming drawer or 300°F oven.

This delightfully fresh gazpacho cools the palate on a hot day, and topping it with the Black Bean Cakes below makes it a full meal. The soup and the bean cakes work equally well on their own and can be made ahead. The gazpacho, in fact, tastes better on day two, and the bean cakes freeze well. For a restaurant-quality presentation, add the warm bean cakes to the chilled gazpacho and top with a smoked salmon garnish. Don't be intimidated by the long ingredient lists—both dishes come together quickly and the resulting flavor makes it all worth your time.

serves 8

1 clove garlic, chopped
2 teaspoons kosher salt
2 cups minced tomato
1¼ cup minced green or red bell pepper
1 cup minced yellow onion
1 cup diced celery
1 cup diced cucumber
1 tablespoon chopped fresh parsley
2 tablespoons chopped chives
1 teaspoon ground black pepper
1 teaspoon Worcestershire sauce, non-fish variety
½ teaspoon Tabasco sauce or other chili sauce
½ cup tarragon vinegar or distilled white vinegar
2 cups tomato juice
2 cups pareve chicken broth or vegetable broth
1 tablespoon honey
¼ cup chopped cilantro, plus more for garnish

Garnish: Tofutti sour cream, avocado, additional cilantro, tortilla chips, or smoked salmon

In a large bowl, stir together all of the ingredients. Cover and chill for at least 12 hours and up to 2 days. If desired, serve with the Black Bean Cakes and suggested garnishes.

Black Bean Cakes

You'll love having these delicious little bean cakes in your repertoire. You can serve them as an appetizer with guacamole and salsa, use them as garnish for a salad with mango and a tropical vinaigrette, or pair them with the guacamole for a lovely summer lunch.

serves 8

3 (15-ounce) cans black beans, drained, divided
2 large eggs
3 cups breadcrumbs, divided
1 cup red bell pepper, chopped
½ cup chopped scallions
½ cup chopped fresh cilantro
2 cloves garlic, minced
2 teaspoons chili powder
1 teaspoon ground cumin
1 teaspoon cayenne pepper
½ teaspoon onion powder
1 teaspoon kosher salt
½ teaspoon ground black pepper
2 to 3 tablespoons soy milk, non-dairy creamer, or water, if necessary
4 tablespoons canola oil, divided
8 thinly sliced pieces smoked salmon (optional)

In a food processor, purée 2 cups black beans and eggs in until smooth. Transfer to large bowl. Stir in remaining beans, 1¼ cup breadcrumbs, bell pepper, scallions, cilantro, garlic, chili powder, cumin, cayenne, onion powder, salt and pepper. Shape mixture into ten ½-inch-thick patties, using about ½ cup mixture for each. If mixture is too dry to hold together, add 1 to 3 tablespoons soy milk or non-dairy creamer to moisten slightly and help patties hold their shape.

Coat black bean cakes on both sides with remaining breadcrumbs. Heat 2 tablespoons oil in large skillet over medium heat. Add the patties, in batches adding more oil if necessary, and cook until golden brown, about 3 minutes each side. Serve immediately or keep warm in a 225°F oven.

Seared Cod with Corn Vinaigrette

Make Ahead

Can be made a day ahead of time. Store, covered, in the refrigerator. Serve at room temperature or rewarm, covered, in a warming drawer or 300°F oven.

This dish tastes of summertime, with a fresh corn vinaigrette and a rich basil pesto that elevates this simple fish. You can use whatever hearty white fish looks (and smells) freshest at your market, such as halibut, seabass, or mahi mahi.

serves 8

Vinaigrette:

¾ cup fresh corn kernels (cut from about 1 ear) or canned corn, drained
3 tablespoons extra-virgin olive oil
1 tablespoon red wine vinegar
1 teaspoon fresh lemon juice
2 teaspoons maple syrup
½ teaspoon kosher salt
¼ teaspoon ground black pepper
1 tablespoon chopped chives or scallions

Fish:

4 tablespoons extra-virgin olive oil
8 (4-ounce) cod fillets
1 teaspoon kosher salt
½ teaspoon ground black pepper
4 tablespoons margarine
Homemade pesto (p. 335) or store-bought, for garnish (optional)

For the vinaigrette: Place corn, olive oil, vinegar, lemon juice, maple syrup, salt, and pepper in a small bowl. With an immersion blender, purée until smooth or desired consistency, and then stir in chives.

For the fish: Heat the olive oil in a medium-size nonstick skillet set over medium-high heat. Season cod with salt and pepper. Once the oil is hot, sear cod for 3 to 4 minutes on the first side. Add margarine to pan and allow it to melt. Once margarine has melted, flip cod and finish cooking on other side, 3 to 4 minutes more, or until just cooked through.

Serve cod warm or at room temperature and drizzle with corn vinaigrette and a dollop of pesto, if desired.

Mini Moroccan Burgers in a Grilled Pita with Tzatziki Sauce

These burgers make a really adorable appetizer—they're grilled right in the pita so the bread gets toasty and full of flavor. I love them right off the grill, but they taste just as good made ahead of time and warmed in the oven. Store in the refrigerator until ready to use. If you have the time, start the tzatziki a few hours ahead for the flavors to meld together. My dad loves the addition of Zesty Ketchup to these, too (see page 329 for the recipe).

makes 16

Tzatziki Sauce:

1 cup Tofutti sour cream

1 cup finely diced or shredded cucumber

¼ cup fresh dill, finely chopped, or 2 tablespoons dried

1½ tablespoons fresh lemon juice

½ tablespoon white wine vinegar or distilled white vinegar

1 clove garlic, grated

½ teaspoon kosher salt

⅛ teaspoon ground black pepper

Burgers:

2½ pounds ground lamb or lean ground beef

1 medium-size yellow onion, very finely chopped

¾ cup chopped fresh flat-leaf parsley

1 tablespoon ground coriander

¾ teaspoon ground cumin

½ teaspoon ground cinnamon

2 teaspoons kosher salt

1½ teaspoon ground black pepper

¼ cup extra-virgin olive oil, plus more for greasing grill

16 mini-sized thick pita breads with pockets

For the tzatziki sauce: Combine all ingredients in a medium bowl and refrigerate several hours to let the flavors blend.

To make the burgers: Mix lamb, onion, parsley, coriander, cumin, cinnamon, salt, pepper, and ¼ cup oil in a large bowl with a fork. Cover and chill at least 1 hour.

Prepare grill or grill pan for medium heat and grease grates. Open each pita pocket by cutting along seam, halfway around perimeter. Spoon about ⅓ cup meat filling into each pitas, spreading to edges and packing filling tightly in pita.

Grill pitas over medium heat, until filling is cooked through and bread is crisp, about 4 minutes per side. Serve with tzatziki sauce.

Make Ahead

Filling can be made 8 hours ahead and pita breads can be stuffed 1 hour ahead. Keep chilled until ready to use. Rewarm cooked pitas in a warming drawer or a 300°F oven.

Horseradish Meringue-Topped Salmon

Passover

Substitute safflower or cottonseed oil for canola. Use ⅓ cup mayonnaise in place of Tofutti sour cream. Passover mustard for Dijon mustard.

This salmon is a show stopper when it comes out of the oven: Pillowy meringue atop moist baked salmon. It's best served warm. Make sure to use a skinless whole piece of salmon for easy slicing and serving.

makes 8 servings

- 1 (2½-pound) boneless, skinless salmon fillet
- 1 teaspoon canola oil
- 1 teaspoon kosher salt, divided
- ½ cup Tofutti sour cream
- ½ cup prepared white horseradish
- ½ cup chopped fresh dill
- 2 teaspoons Dijon mustard
- 6 egg whites
- 2 tablespoons sugar

Preheat oven to 425°F. Grease a large jellyroll pan.

Place salmon in prepared pan and brush with oil. Sprinkle with ½ teaspoon of the salt. Combine sour cream, horseradish, dill, Dijon, and remaining ½ teaspoon salt in a small bowl; whisk until smooth. Beat egg whites in a medium bowl until stiff peaks form. Gradually add sugar, beating until mixed. Fold in reserved sour cream mixture. Spread mixture evenly over salmon.

Bake 15 to 20 minutes, or until salmon flakes easily. Serve warm.

Sweet and Spicy Drumsticks

Whatever your preference—wings, drumsticks, drumettes, or chicken pieces on the bone—this recipe yields some divinely good eats. Sticky and lacquered and definitely divine. The end result is gorgeous, glossy pieces of chicken, coated in a delicious sauce of sweet jelly and spicy Sriracha, balanced with a splash of Japanese rice wine.

serves 8

1 cup all-purpose flour
1 tablespoon cornstarch
24 chicken drumsticks, or 2 chickens cut into eighths
½ cup Sriracha sauce, up to 1 cup for extra spicy
1 cup unseasoned rice vinegar
½ cup mirin (sweet rice wine)
½ cup strawberry jelly or cranberry sauce
1½ teaspoons kosher salt

Preheat oven to 450°F. Line a large, low-sided roasting pan with aluminum foil.

Whisk flour and cornstarch together in a medium bowl. Pat chicken pieces dry with paper towels and dredge in flour mixture, shaking off excess. Arrange on baking sheet and roast until skin is browned and crisp, about 40 minutes for drumsticks, 20 minutes for wings and drumettes, and 1 hour and 5 minutes for breasts and thighs. Remove from oven; they are not through cooking and may still be raw inside.

While chicken is roasting, make sauce. In a small saucepan, combine Sriracha, rice vinegar, mirin, jelly, and salt and bring to a boil over high heat. Reduce heat to medium and simmer, adjusting heat if necessary, until mixture is thick and reduced to about 1½ cups, about 10 minutes. The sauce should look glossy and reddish-orange.

Carefully pour the sauce over the drumsticks. Using a spoon (because the sauce is so hot), turn and coat the chicken well. Return to oven and cook until the skin is shiny and crisp and the sauce is beginning to brown, about 10 to 20 minutes more.

Make Ahead

This can be made two days ahead of time. Store, covered, in the refrigerator or freeze up to 3 months. Defrost in the refrigerator. Rewarm, covered, in a warming drawer or 300°F oven.

Tip

Spice averse? Cut back on the Sriracha.

Chicken, Pistachio, and Sun-Dried Tomato Terrine

This terrine is great twist on meatloaf. It's studded with pistachios, sun-dried tomatoes, and delicious dried herbs, and it's wrapped in pastrami for a smoky, flavorful finish. I serve it warm or at room temperature with Grainy Mustard Dipping Sauce (p. 328) or with Sri-Rancha Sauce (p. 331).

makes 10 servings

- 1 tablespoon extra-virgin olive oil
- 1 yellow onion, chopped
- 2 cloves garlic, minced
- 1 zucchini, grated
- 1 pound ground chicken or ground turkey
- 2 eggs
- 1 to 1½ cups breadcrumbs
- 2 tablespoons Dijon mustard
- 1 teaspoon herbes de Provence
- 1 teaspoon kosher salt
- ¼ teaspoon cayenne pepper
- ½ cup sun-dried tomatoes in oil, drained and chopped
- ½ cup coarsely chopped roasted and salted pistachios
- 12 slices pastrami, sliced thin
- Honey Dijon Mustard (p. 328), Grainy Mustard Dipping Sauce (p. 328), or Sri-Rancha (p. 331) for serving

Preheat oven to 350°F. Line an 8 x 4-inch loaf pan with a large piece of foil, pressing so that foil is tucked into the corners and overhangs the sides enough to cover top of terrine.

Heat oil in a large skillet over medium-high. Add onion and garlic; cook until softened, about 4 minutes. Add zucchini; cook an additional 2 minutes and then remove from the heat.

Combine chicken, eggs, breadcrumbs, Dijon, herbes de Provence, salt, and cayenne in a large mixing bowl. Add reserved onion mixture; stir to blend well. Fold in sun-dried tomatoes and pistachios.

Line the prepared loaf pan with the pastrami, slightly overlapping the slices to cover the bottom and sides of pan. Spoon the chicken mixture on top of the pastrami, spreading evenly to fill the loaf pan. Fold the overhanging pieces of pastrami over the chicken, and seal the top with the overhanging foil.

Make a water bath by filling a large roasting pan halfway with hot water. Gently place loaf pan in center of roasting pan with water. Bake 50 minutes. Let rest 10 minutes and then unmold unto a serving platter. Slice into individual pieces and serve with sauces.

Passover

Use matzo meal in place of breadcrumbs and Passover mustard for Dijon mustard.

Make Ahead

Can be made a day ahead of time. Store, covered, in the refrigerator or freeze up to 3 months. Defrost in the refrigerator. Rewarm, covered, in a warming drawer or 300°F oven.

Braised Short Ribs with Tomatoes and Mushrooms

Passover

Perfect as-is!

Make Ahead

Ribs can be made a day or two ahead of time. Store, covered, in the refrigerator or freeze up to 3 months. Defrost in the refrigerator. Rewarm, covered, in a warming drawer or 300°F oven.

Tip

These can be prepared in a crockpot. Place all ingredients in the crockpot, cover, and cook on low level for 7 to 9 hours or on high for 3½ to 4½ hours .

I make this as a Friday night appetizer in the winter because it's warm and comforting, just like Shabbos. The ribs are melting tender from the slow cooking, and the dish could not be easier to make. Look for the best quality short ribs you can find, with as little extra fat as possible. This can also be made with boneless short ribs or flanken (with or without the bone), as well.

makes 8 servings

¼ cup extra-virgin olive oil
1 yellow onion, chopped
2 tablespoons minced garlic
5 pounds bone-in short ribs or 4 pounds boneless
1 pound button mushrooms, sliced
1 (29-ounce) can diced tomatoes, with juice
1½ cups dry red wine
1 cup beef broth
1 teaspoon kosher salt
1 sprig fresh thyme

Heat oil in a large stockpot over medium-high heat. Add onion and garlic; cook 4 minutes, stirring occasionally. Add meat; cook until nicely browned on both sides, turning once. Take your time; this is where the flavor develops.

Add mushrooms, tomatoes with juice, wine, broth, salt, and thyme to stockpot. Bring to a boil over high heat and scrape the bottom of the pan with a wooden spoon to release any browned bits. Reduce to a low simmer and cook, partially covered, 3 to 4 hours, until meat is very tender. Serve warm.

Halibut with Tomatoes, Olives, and Capers

My friend Emuna shared this recipe with me years ago, and I've been making it ever since. The flavors are classic Mediterranean and make use of ripe tomatoes, meaty olives, and briny capers. I love the silky texture of halibut, but other white fish like cod or seabass would work equally well.

Passover

Perfect as-is!

makes 8 servings

4 tablespoons extra-virgin olive oil, divided
8 (5-ounce) halibut fillets
1 yellow onion, diced
1 cup white wine
1 (14½-ounce) can diced tomatoes, with juice
1 cup chopped pitted black olives
¼ cup capers
½ teaspoon crushed red pepper flakes
4 cups fresh baby spinach
1 teaspoon kosher salt
½ teaspoon ground black pepper

Heat 2 tablespoons of the oil in a large nonstick skillet over medium-high. When hot, add halibut and cook until golden brown. Flip and continue cooking until opaque in the center, about 5 to 8 minutes total cooking time. Transfer to a platter and tent with foil to keep warm.

Heat remaining 2 tablespoons oil in the same skillet over medium. Add onion and cook 2 minutes, stirring occasionally. Add wine and cook until reduced by half, about 5 minutes. Stir in tomatoes, olives, capers, and red pepper flakes; cook 3 minutes, stirring occasionally. Add spinach and cook until just wilted. Season with salt and pepper. Spoon vegetables over warm halibut and serve immediately.

מרקים

SOUPS

Nothing tastes and smells like Shabbos as much as Chicken Soup with Matzo Balls. Often times, whether for Yom Tov or a winter evening, however, I often crave other great soups, like Roasted Tomato with Crispy Kale or Butternut Squash Soup with Curry and Sweet Apples. Requests for my Tortilla Soup and Good-As-A-Latte Wild Mushroom Soup start at least a week before Succos, and your family will likely love them as well. Soups should be vibrant and fresh, full of color—and nutrients! Each of these soups fit the *Celebrate* mantra, easy enough for everyday and special enough for Shabbos.

Good-as-a-Latte Wild Mushroom Soup

Passover

Perfect as-is!

Make Ahead

The soup can be prepared 2 days ahead of time and stored, covered, in the refrigerator or frozen up to 3 months. Defrost in the refrigerator. Rewarm over medium heat before serving. The whipped topping is best prepared just before serving, but it can be made a day ahead of time and stored in refrigerator.

This soup is rich and flavorful and so cute to serve. It looks like a latte (especially when served in a teacup), but tastes even better. With an autumnal base of earthy mushrooms, dry red wine, port, and rich cream, it makes an ideal soup for Succot. You can use any combination of mushrooms—even button mushrooms will work—but take advantage of any wild mushrooms your grocer has. It will be worth the expense. To speed up the prep, remove any tough stems (such as those on shiitake) and pulse the mushrooms together in the food processor.

makes 8 to 12 servings

1½ ounces dried porcini mushrooms
1 cup boiling water
6 tablespoons margarine, divided
1 cup finely chopped shallots, divided
8 ounces portobello mushrooms, finely chopped, divided
8 ounces shiitake mushrooms, finely chopped, divided
8 ounces crimini mushrooms, finely chopped, divided
8 ounces oyster mushrooms, finely chopped, divided
½ teaspoon kosher salt
¼ teaspoon ground black pepper
2 cups red wine
1 cup port (or other dessert wine)
3 teaspoons chopped fresh thyme, divided
½ teaspoon dried rosemary
8 cups chicken broth or pareve chicken broth
1 cup pareve whipping cream

Place dried porcini mushrooms in a small bowl. Cover with boiling water and soak 30 minutes. Drain mushrooms and reserve liquid; chop softened mushrooms.

While porcini are soaking, melt 3 tablespoons of margarine in a large stockpot over medium heat. Add ¾ cup of the shallots; cook until tender, stirring occasionally, about 4 minutes. Add reserved porcini mushrooms and half of the assorted mushrooms to stockpot. Season with salt and pepper, and cook, stirring occasionally, until they have released their liquid and are just beginning to brown, about 10 minutes

Add wine, port, reserved mushroom liquid, 2 teaspoons of the thyme, and rosemary to stockpot. Bring to a boil over high heat; reduce heat to a simmer and cook until almost all liquid has evaporated, about 10 minutes.

Add broth to stockpot and simmer until reduced to 9 cups, about 12 minutes. Purée soup with an immersion blender or food processor until smooth. Return to pot and set over low heat.

In a medium skillet, melt remaining 3 tablespoons margarine over medium heat. Add remaining shallots and mushrooms. Season with more salt and pepper, and cook until onions are translucent and mushrooms are well softened, about 5 minutes. Add to soup. Taste and adjust the seasonings with salt and pepper as needed.

Whip cream in a large bowl until soft peaks form and fold in remaining teaspoon thyme. Serve soup in small glass mugs with pareve cream ladled on top to look like a latte.

Butternut Squash Soup with Curry and Sweet Apples

Everyone has a squash soup in their repertoire, but none as good as this one. The sweet apple complements the spiciness of the curry, and the coconut milk adds richness to the whole soup.

makes 8 servings

1 tablespoon canola oil
2 yellow onions, chopped (about 2 cups)
2 cloves garlic, minced
6 cups chicken broth or pareve chicken broth
1 (2½-pound) butternut squash, peeled, seeded, and cut into 1-inch cubes
1 Granny Smith apple, peeled and cut into 1-inch pieces
1½ tablespoons curry powder
1 teaspoon kosher salt
½ cup coconut milk, plus more for garnish
2 tablespoons honey
¼ teaspoon ground black pepper
Candied pecans, for garnish

Heat oil in a large 8-quart stockpot over medium heat. Add onions and garlic; cook until soft but not brown, 6 to 7 minutes, stirring occasionally. Add broth, squash, apple, curry powder, and salt; bring to a boil over high heat. Reduce to a simmer and cook until squash is tender, 12 to 15 minutes.

Remove stockpot from heat; stir in coconut milk and honey. Purée mixture with an immersion blender or in a food processor until smooth. Add pepper and season with additional salt if needed.

Garnish with a swirl of coconut milk and sprinkling of candied pecans and serve.

Make Ahead

Can be prepared 2 days ahead of time and stored, covered, in the refrigerator or freeze up to 3 months. Defrost in the refrigerator. Rewarm over medium heat before serving.

Roasted Tomato Soup with Crispy Kale

This soup manages to taste super creamy without any cream. The roasted tomatoes and garlic give it an amazing depth of flavor, not to mention a gorgeous color. Even better, your home will smell divine as it bubbles on the stove.

serves 6

Soup:

18 large tomatoes (about 4 pounds), stemmed and quartered

⅓ cup extra-virgin olive oil plus 3 tablespoons, divided

⅓ cup balsamic vinegar

15 large cloves garlic

1½ teaspoons kosher salt

¾ teaspoon ground black pepper

1½ cups chopped yellow onions

3 cups lightly packed fresh basil leaves

¼ teaspoon crushed red pepper (optional)

3 cups cold water

Croutons:

7 pieces thick-crusted bread, like French bread or Challah, cut into 1-inch pieces

¼ cup extra-virgin olive oil

½ teaspoon kosher salt

Kale:

4 cups curly kale leaves (stems and ribs removed)

Nonstick cooking spray

¼ teaspoon kosher salt

Preheat oven to 500°F.

Prepare the tomatoes: Grease a large sheet pan. In a large bowl, mix tomatoes, ⅓ cup of the oil, balsamic vinegar, garlic, salt, and pepper. Spread tomato mixture on prepared sheet pan and roast in oven until tomatoes are very dark in spots, 35 to 40 minutes. Remove and cool slightly.

In a large saucepan over medium heat, combine remaining 3 tablespoons oil, onions, and a pinch of salt. Cook until onions are very soft, 8 to 10 minutes, stirring occasionally. Add basil leaves and crushed red pepper, if using, and sauté for about 1 minute. Add the roasted tomato mixture and water. Bring to a simmer and cook for 10 minutes, and then purée the with an immersion blender until smooth.

Prepare the croutons: In a large bowl, toss bread with oil and season with salt. Place the cubes on a baking sheet and toast in the oven until golden brown and just beginning to crisp, about 4 minutes.

Prepare the kale, if desired: Preheat oven to 250°F. Place kale on a large roasting pan in a single layer. Spray with nonstick cooking spray. Cook in oven for 30 minutes or until crispy and dried. Sprinkle with salt.

To serve: Serve soup warm or at room temperature with croutons and kale.

Passover

Omit the croutons or substitute 5 pieces of matzo for the bread. Brush with oil and toast as described, and then break into large pieces and serve with the soup.

Make Ahead

The soup can be prepared 2 days ahead of time. Store, covered, in the refrigerator or freeze up to 3 months. Defrost in the refrigerator. Rewarm over medium heat before serving. The kale and croutons can be made up to a week ahead and stored in an airtight container.

Lighten Up

When preparing the tomatoes, reduce the olive oil and balsamic vinegar to 3 tablespoons each. When sautéing the onions, use only 1 tablespoon oil. Omit the croutons.

(Almost) My Mom's Chicken Soup

Passover

Perfect as-is!

Prep Ahead

For easy work of skimming the fat from the broth, allow time to refrigerate it overnight.

Make Ahead

This soup is best prepared 2 days ahead of time. Store, covered, in the refrigerator or freeze up to 3 months. Defrost in the refrigerator. Rewarm over medium heat before serving.

Chicken soup was one of the first recipes my mother taught me. I follow her general technique but have added additional ingredients over the years because my kids love the "meal-in-a-bowl" concept and enjoy the soup with all the veggies. (And I'm certainly not going to argue with my kids eating more vegetables!). While you'll frequently find some kind of soup simmering on my stove in the colder months, my go-to continues to be big pot of chicken soup. I love that it makes the house smell like Shabbos.

serves 10 to 12

12 carrots, peeled, and cut into 3-inch chunks
2 parsnips, cut into quarters
2 turnips, cut into 3-inch pieces
6 ribs celery and leaves, cut into 4-inch pieces, divided
½ butternut squash, cut into 4 or 5 large pieces
3 zucchini, cut into thirds
1 yellow onion, halved
1 cup flat leaf parsley (leaves only)
½ cup fresh dill
1 whole chicken
10 peppercorns
Water to cover
2 to 4 tablespoons kosher salt

In a large 12-quart stockpot, place carrots, parsnips, turnips, 4 ribs celery, butternut squash, and zucchini. In a mesh soup bag or cheesecloth, place onion, remaining celery and leaves, parsley, and dill, tie to close, and place on top of vegetables. Add chicken on top of vegetables. Add peppercorns to the pot. Fill pot with cold water until all contents are covered by 1 inch of water.

Place pot, uncovered, on stove over high heat. Bring to a boil. Reduce heat, cover, and cook for approximately 4 hours, skimming off the foam as needed. Remove from heat and let cool. Place cooled soup in the refrigerator, overnight if possible.

Skim fat from top of soup. Remove soup bag or cheesecloth and discard. Remove chicken. Remove meat from bone, discard skin, and cut meat into large pieces. Return chicken meat to pot. Add salt. Reheat and serve with fluffy matzo balls (p. 87), thin noodles, or rice.

VARIATIONS

For extra richness: Add a beef bone.

For Asian-inspired soup, which is not kosher for Passover: Cut vegetables for soup in smaller pieces. Add 1 sliced leek and 5 slices of ginger. Strain out the ginger, and garnish with thinly sliced scallions and 2 tablespoons soy sauce before serving.

For a creamy soup without the cream: Remove the celery and discard. Purée the remaining soup with an immersion blender.

For leftovers: The soup freezes well, but the broth works great in other soups, too. Strain solids and store the strained broth in the freezer for other soups.

Fluffy Matzo Balls

makes about 12 balls

4 large eggs
2 tablespoons canola oil
1 cup matzo meal
1 teaspoon kosher salt, plus more to taste
¼ teaspoon white pepper
½ cup seltzer water

In a small bowl, mix eggs well with a fork. Stir in the oil. Add the matzo meal, salt, and pepper; mix well. Gently mix in seltzer. Cover and refrigerate for at least 30 minutes or up to 12 hours.

Fill a large pot with water and salt generously. Bring to a boil over high heat. Dip your hands in cold water and gently form about 10 matzo balls slightly smaller than ping-pong balls. Place the matzo balls in the water. Cover and simmer until soft, about 30 minutes. Remove matzo balls from cooking liquid.

Passover

Use safflower or cottonseed oil for canola.

Make Ahead

Can be prepared one day ahead of time. Just before serving, place prepared matzo balls in soup broth and rewarm with soup. Alternatively, store, covered, in the refrigerator and add to soup before rewarming.

Tip

Good matzo balls need to be flavorful, round, and light. For many, this outcome is not so simple. Here are some tips for perfect matzo balls every time:

- *Do not overmix the batter.*
- *Refrigerate at least 2 hours before forming balls.*
- *Form the balls gently and with as little handling as possible.*
- *Use seltzer instead of still water in your favorite recipe.*

Albondiga Soup

Passover

Perfect as-is!

Make Ahead

Can be prepared 2 days ahead of time. Store, covered, in the refrigerator or freeze up to 3 months. Defrost in the refrigerator. Rewarm over medium heat before serving.

This exotic Spanish soup is a Passover favorite for my family, precisely because it tastes nothing like Passover. Carrots and zucchinis, fresh cilantro, wonderful rich broth, and flavorful meatballs—albondigas—make a filling first course that your family and guests will love.

makes 10 servings

Meatballs:

1 pound ground turkey
⅓ cup matzo meal
¼ cup finely chopped fresh cilantro
¼ cup chopped fresh parsley
½ teaspoon ground cumin
1½ teaspoons kosher salt
1 large egg, lightly beaten

Soup:

2 tablespoons extra-virgin olive oil
1 yellow onion, finely chopped
2 cloves garlic, minced
6 cups chicken broth
2 cups water
2 tablespoons tomato paste
2 carrots, peeled and sliced
1 large zucchini, halved lengthwise and sliced
½ cup chopped fresh cilantro or parsley
1 teaspoon dried oregano
¾ teaspoon kosher salt
½ teaspoon ground black pepper
1 avocado, pitted and chopped, for garnish
1 lime, cut into wedges, for garnish
¼ cup minced fresh cilantro or parsley, for garnish

To prepare the meatballs: Combine turkey, matzo meal, cilantro, parsley, cumin, and salt in a medium bowl. Use a wooden spoon to gently stir the mixture until blended. Add egg, mixing just until combined. Form into 1-inch balls.

To prepare the soup: Heat oil in a large stockpot over medium-high heat. Add onion and cook, stirring occasionally, until soft, about 6 minutes. Add garlic and cook until fragrant, about 1 minute. Add broth, water, and tomato paste, stirring to dissolve. Add carrots; bring to a boil over high heat. Reduce to a simmer and add meatballs; cook 15 minutes over medium-low heat. Add zucchini; cook until carrots and zucchini are tender and meatballs are cooked through, an additional 10 to 15 minutes.

Add chopped cilantro, oregano, salt, and pepper. Serve warm with avocado, lime wedges, and a sprinkle of minced cilantro.

Strawberry Mango Soup with Fruit Salsa

A few years back, Chef Jeff Nathan, from Abigael's in New York City, served a fruit soup with a fruit salsa spooned into the center of the soup. His dish inspired this one. Get creative with this recipe and add jalapeño for spice to the soup or herbs like cilantro to the salsa. Replace the mangoes with peaches or try another combination of frozen fruits. Here, the salsa is sweet, but it's quite nice with a savory salsa as well. You won't go wrong with this refreshing summer soup.

makes 12 or more servings

Soup:

1 (16-ounce) bag frozen strawberries, thawed
1 (16-ounce) bag frozen mangoes, thawed
¼ cup sugar
1 teaspoon ground cinnamon, or to taste
2½ cups orange juice

Fruit Salsa:

1½ cups chopped strawberries
1 cup blueberries
1 cup chopped pineapple
Zest of 1 lemon
2 tablespoons balsamic vinegar
2 tablespoons sugar
1 teaspoon fresh ginger, minced (optional)

To prepare the soup: Combine strawberries, mangoes, sugar, and cinnamon in a large bowl; add enough orange juice to cover the mixture. Using an immersion blender, purée the mixture. Cover and refrigerate until ready to serve.

To prepare the fruit salsa: Combine strawberries, blueberries, and pineapple in a medium bowl and toss gently. Add lemon zest, balsamic vinegar, sugar, and ginger (if using). Toss and refrigerate until ready to use.

Serve soup chilled in individual bowls with a dollop of fruit salsa in the center.

Passover

Perfect as-is!

Make Ahead

The soup can be prepared 2 days ahead of time. Store, covered, in the refrigerator or freeze up to 3 months. Defrost in the refrigerator. Serve chilled. Make the salsa just before serving.

Red Lentil Soup with Dried Apricots

Make Ahead

Can be prepared 2 days ahead of time. Store, covered, in the refrigerator or freeze up to 3 months. Defrost in the refrigerator. Rewarm over medium heat before serving.

This soup has a hint of sweetness and richness from the apricots and a nice savory kick from cumin and thyme. The red lentils lend the soup a beautiful color, perfect for fall.

serves 6

3 tablespoons extra-virgin olive oil
1 yellow onion, chopped
⅓ cup dried apricots, chopped
2 cloves garlic, minced
1½ cups dried red lentils, rinsed
5 cups chicken or vegetable broth
3 tomatoes, seeded and chopped
½ teaspoon cumin
½ teaspoon thyme
½ teaspoon kosher salt
¼ teaspoon ground black pepper
3 tablespoons red wine (optional)
2 tablespoons fresh lemon juice

In an 8-quart stockpot, heat olive oil over medium heat. Add onion, apricots, and garlic and cook until softened but not browned, about 5 minutes. Add lentils and broth. Bring to a boil, reduce heat to low, and simmer uncovered for 30 minutes, stirring occasionally.

Add tomatoes, cumin, thyme, salt, pepper, and red wine, if using. Simmer for 10 minutes. Stir in lemon juice and remove from heat for 5 minutes. Pour half of the soup into a separate bowl and purée with an immersion blender. Return to stockpot, and stir to combine. Reheat and serve warm.

Velvety Corn Soup

Corn has a naturally sweet flavor and, when puréed, has the texture of a cream soup—but without the cream. The dish can be served warm or cold, and the garnish is restaurant-quality fabulous.

serves 8

Soup:

2 tablespoons extra-virgin olive oil

1 yellow onion, chopped

2 leeks, sliced (white and light green parts only)

2 parsnips, peeled and chopped

7 cups fresh, canned, or frozen corn kernels (from 8 ears of corn)

6 to 8 cups chicken broth or vegetable broth (or water)

1 teaspoon kosher salt

1 teaspoon white pepper

¼ cup soy milk, pareve whipping cream, or non-dairy creamer (optional)

½ teaspoon chili powder (optional)

½ teaspoon cumin (optional)

Garnish:

3 tablespoons chopped tarragon, parsley, or microgreens (optional)

3 tablespoons pinenuts, toasted (p. 335)

1 teaspoon crushed red pepper, or to taste

Drizzle of truffle oil or extra-virgin olive oil

Drizzle of Sriracha sauce or hot sauce (optional)

To make the soup: Heat oil over medium-high heat in a 6-quart stockpot. Add onion, leeks, and parsnips and sauté for 6 minutes, until soft. Add corn and cook for 5 additional minutes. Add chicken broth and bring to a boil. Reduce heat to medium-low and cook for 20 minutes. Add salt and pepper, and purée until smooth or slightly chunky with an immersion blender. Add soy milk, chili powder, and cumin, if using.

To serve: Pour warm or room temperature soup into bowls. Garnish with herbs, pinenuts, crushed red pepper, a drizzle of oil, and hot sauce, if using.

Make Ahead

Can be prepared 2 days ahead of time. Store, covered, in the refrigerator or freeze up to 3 months. Defrost in the refrigerator. Rewarm over medium heat before serving or serve at room temperature.

Tip

This soup can be made 2 days ahead of time and stored in the refrigerator.

Pumpkin and Black Bean Soup

Make Ahead

Can be prepared 2 days ahead of time and stored, covered, in the refrigerator or freeze up to 3 months. Defrost in the refrigerator. Rewarm over medium heat before serving.

I've made this soup hundreds of times to rave reviews. Black beans and pumpkin, both hearty ingredients, get terrific seasoning from cumin, tomatoes, and beef broth. You can make it pareve with pareve beef broth or pareve chicken broth, but hold off on seasoning the soup with salt until the very end. The broths may have provided ample salt without adding more.

makes 10 to 12 servings

¼ cup extra-virgin olive oil
1 medium-size yellow onion, chopped
4 cloves garlic, chopped
1 tablespoon ground cumin, or more to taste
1 teaspoon kosher salt
1 teaspoon ground black pepper
3 (15-ounce) cans black beans, drained
1 (29-ounce) can diced tomatoes
6 cups beef broth or pareve beef broth
1 (29-ounce) canned pumpkin purée
½ cup dry red wine
Toasted pumpkin seeds and Tofutti sour cream, for garnish

Heat oil in a large stockpot over medium-high heat. Add onion, garlic, cumin, salt, and pepper; cook until softened, stirring occasionally, about 7 minutes.

Add black beans and tomatoes to stockpot; cook an additional 2 minutes. Add broth, pumpkin, and wine; bring to a boil over high heat. Reduce to a simmer and cook, uncovered, about 25 minutes.

Remove from heat and let mixture cool, uncovered. Purée with an immersion blender or in a food processor until smooth. Serve warm.

Garnish with toasted pumpkin seeds and sour cream before serving.

Rich Red Pepper Soup with Basil Drizzle

The gorgeous soup gets its rich flavor from the fruits and vegetables, not from cream. It makes for a healthy and beautiful choice year round and works equally well, whether served warm, cold, or my favorite, room temperature.

serves 8

Soup:

2 tablespoons extra-virgin olive oil

8 large red peppers, seeded and coarsely chopped

3 carrots, peeled and cut into ¼-inch-thick slices

3 shallots, chopped

2 cloves garlic, chopped

6 cups pareve chicken broth or chicken broth

1 ripe pear, peeled, cored, and chopped

1 teaspoon kosher salt

⅛ to ¼ teaspoon cayenne pepper

¼ to ½ cup orange juice

Basil Drizzle:

½ cup homemade pesto (p. 335) or store-bought

2 tablespoons extra-virgin olive oil

To make the soup: Heat a large skillet over medium heat. Add oil to pan. When oil is hot, add red peppers, carrots, shallots, and garlic. Cover and cook for about 15 minutes, stirring occasionally, until vegetables are soft but not browned. Add broth and pear and simmer for 20 to 30 minutes. Let cool and then purée soup until creamy with an immersion blender or food processor. Add salt and cayenne pepper. Add orange juice until soup reaches desired consistency.

For the drizzle: Mix pesto with olive oil in a small bowl.

To serve: Ladle soup—warm, cold, or room temperature—into soup bowls. Add basil drizzle and serve.

Passover

Perfect as-is!

Make Ahead

Can be prepared 2 days ahead of time. Store, covered, in the refrigerator or freeze up to 3 months. Defrost in the refrigerator. Rewarm over medium heat before serving or serve at room temperature.

Tip

This soup freezes well. Defrost in refrigerator. Basil drizzle can be made 2 days ahead of time and stored in the refrigerator.

Italian Pumpkin and Amaretto Soup

This soup has incredible depth of flavor and texture from the crumbled amaretti, and the amaretto warms and soothes. Most people will not be able to identify the flavor exactly, but will love the taste. Choose cookies without extra sugar on top. If you can't find amaretti or almond cookies, use graham crackers with ⅛ teaspoon of almond extract mixed in.

serves 6

- ⅓ cup extra-virgin olive oil
- 1 large yellow onion, chopped
- ½ teaspoon kosher salt
- ¼ teaspoon ground black pepper
- 1 (28-ounce) can pumpkin purée or 1 (2-pound) butternut squash, cut in 1-inch pieces
- 7 cups pareve chicken broth or chicken broth
- 1 cup soy milk, non-dairy creamer, or pareve cream
- ⅓ cup amaretto liqueur
- ⅓ cup amaretti cookies or almond cookies, crushed (or graham crackers plus ⅛ teaspoon almond extract
- ½ teaspoon kosher salt
- ¼ teaspoon ground black pepper
- 1 sheet of puff pastry shapes, for garnish (optional)

Heat a large pot over medium-high heat. When pot is hot add oil. Add onion, salt, and pepper and cook until wilted and soft, about 7 minutes. Add pumpkin purée and broth, stirring to combine, and cook about 5 minutes. Reduce heat to low, and stir in soy milk, amaretto, and amaretti. Taste and adjust the seasonings if needed. Remove from heat, let cool for 15 minutes, and purée soup with an immersion blender.

For garnish: Preheat oven to 375° and line a baking sheet with parchment paper. Roll out puff pastry to ¼-inch thick. With a cookie cutter shape of your choice (for fall I love to use leaves), cut out 8 - 16 pieces, depending on size of cookie cutter. Place cut dough on parchment. Bake until lightly browned and puffed up, 15 to 25 minutes.

Serve soup warm with baked puff pastry shapes floating in the center.

Make Ahead

The soup can be prepared 2 days ahead of time. Store, covered, in the refrigerator or freeze up to 3 months. Defrost in the refrigerator. Rewarm over medium heat before serving. The puff pastry can be prepared 2 days ahead of time ahead and stored in an airtight container.

Tip

If using butternut squash, preheat oven to 450°F. Grease a foil-lined baking sheet And add squash in a single layer. Roast in oven for 20 minutes, add the cooked squash to broth, and proceed with recipe instructions.

Tortilla Soup

This is my husband's all-time favorite soup. Truth is, guests, family, friends—we all love it. The unique technique of adding soft corn tortillas to the soup adds both a rich masa flavor and a thickness that would otherwise be missing. Feel free to use canned corn in lieu of fresh. You can roast the kernels in a hot oven and get the same semi-charred effect.

serves 8

2 tablespoons canola oil
1 yellow onion, thinly sliced
6 small soft corn tortillas, torn into pieces
6 cloves garlic, minced
1 tablespoon chili powder
1 tablespoon ground cumin
5 tomatoes, quartered
5 cups chicken broth or pareve chicken broth
2 cups packed fresh cilantro leaves
1 jalapeño pepper, seeded and chopped
1 bay leaf
Kosher salt and black pepper, to taste
½ pound smoked turkey, cubed
¾ cup roasted corn kernels (from 2 to 3 ears of corn)
Fresh cilantro, for garnish

Heat oil in a large stockpot over medium-high heat. Add onion; cook until just browned, about 5 minutes, stirring occasionally. Add tortillas, garlic, chili powder, and cumin; cook 1 minute, stirring frequently. Add tomatoes, broth, cilantro, jalapeño, and bay leaf. Bring to a boil over high heat; reduce to a simmer and cook 30 minutes, uncovered.

Remove from heat and let mixture cool, uncovered. Remove bay leaf and discard. Purée the soup with an immersion blender or food processor until smooth. Season with salt and pepper to taste.

Stir turkey and roasted corn into soup; ladle into serving bowls and top with cilantro leaves.

Make Ahead

Can be prepared 2 days ahead of time and stored, covered, in the refrigerator or freeze up to 3 months. Defrost in the refrigerator. Rewarm over medium heat before serving.

Tip

Roasting Corn: Preheat broiler. Cut kernels from cobs. Place kernels on a baking sheet pan coated with nonstick cooking spray. Broil approximately 5 minutes, watching carefully to prevent burning, until kernels are lightly charred. For canned corn, drain kernels and pat dry. Roast 8 minutes, watching carefully to prevent burning.

סלטים

SALADS

I have a houseful of salad lovers and we eat fresh greens with every meal. The secret to good salads are simple: Use a variety of lettuce types, including romaine, mesclun, arugula, kale, and anything crisp, colorful, and fresh. Dress the salad just before serving and don't overdress. (You can always add more dressing, but you can't take too much away.)

Balance the ingredients well: Pair bitter arugula with sweeter dressings, zippy vinaigrettes with romaine or blander greens. Contrast flavors, textures, and ingredients. Add crunch and texture with nuts or toasted ramen and seeds. Combine raw ingredients with cooked. Salty with sweet. Crunchy with tender. Move beyond the expected lettuce and croutons with roasted vegetables, pomegranate seeds, sugar snap peas, quinoa, avocado, fresh fruit, cooked beans, shredded raw beets, or wasabi peas.

Romaine Salad with Quinoa, Edamame, and Pomegranate Seeds

My friend Yenny made me this salad when I visited her beach house one summer. I've made it over and over since that beautiful day. I love the combination of lettuce and spicy arugula with hearty quinoa, protein-rich edamame, and crunchy, ruby-red pomegranate seeds. If pomegranates aren't in season, you can use dried cranberries or craisins.

serves 8

Salad:

4 cups romaine lettuce
2 cups baby arugula
1 cup cooked quinoa
1½ cups cooked, shelled edamame
¼ cup chopped or sliced red onion
1 red pepper, thinly sliced
½ cup pine nuts (or other nuts), toasted (p. 335)
¼ cup pomegranate seeds (optional)

Dressing:

2 teaspoons Dijon mustard
1 teaspoon kosher salt
2 to 3 tablespoons sugar (optional)
¼ cup red wine vinegar
½ cup extra-virgin olive oil

For the salad: Combine all ingredients in a large salad bowl. Set aside.

For the dressing: Combine all the ingredients in a jar with a tight-fitting lid. Shake well until fully incorporated.

To serve: Pour the dressing over the salad. Toss and serve immediately.

Choosing, Cutting, and Storing Pomegranates

How to choose: Select pomegranates that are heavy for their size, as they'll be the juiciest. Don't worry too much about the color of the rind: It can vary from completely red to reddish-brown without it affecting the quality. Do look for deep color though.

How to store: Pomegranates will last 3 or 4 weeks if refrigerated. Once they've been seeded, the seeds can be refrigerated for several days or frozen in a tightly sealed plastic bag.

How to seed: Score the skin in quarters and quarter the fruit. Fill a large bowl with cool water. Working under water, use your fingers to remove the seeds from each quarter. The lightweight pith will float to the top; the heavier, seedy fruit will release from the rind and sink. Discard the pith as it comes to the top and drain the water after seeding all the quarters.

Passover

Omit edamame and substitute with chopped jícama, if desired. Substitute Passover mustard for Dijon mustard.

Make Ahead

Dressing can be prepared up to 3 days ahead of time. Store, covered, in the refrigerator. Dress salad just before serving. Edamame and quinoa can be made 2 days ahead of time and stored separately in the refrigerator.

Tip

I usually make 1 cup uncooked quinoa and a full bag of shelled edamame and reserve the extra for a second salad. To prepare the quinoa, heat 2 cups water, 1 cup quinoa, and ½ teaspoon salt In a 2-quart saucepan. Bring to a boil, cover, and reduce heat to low. Simmer for 15 minutes or until water is absorbed. Cool completely before storing. For the edamame, fill a 1½-quart saucepan halfway with water and add ½ teaspoon salt. Bring water to a boil over high heat, and then add edamame. Reduce heat to medium and cook until slightly tender, 4 to 5 minutes. Drain and rinse with cold water to stop the cooking.

Asian Spinach Salad with Sliced Steak and Wasabi Crunch

Make Ahead

Dressing and steak can be prepared 2 days ahead of time. Store, covered, in the refrigerator. Bring dressing to room temperature before using, and dress salad just before serving.

Tip

Always let meat rest about 10 minutes before slicing. This allows the juices to redistribute throughout the meat, ensuring moist slices and keeping the juice from running all over your cutting board.

When wasabi peas first started showing up in delis and markets, I got hooked on this crunchy, spicy snack. They ended up in my salad one day, and they've been making regular appearances ever since. Who needs croutons when you've got wasabi peas? For a complete meal, include the meat. For a lighter salad course, serve alone.

serves 8

Dressing:

½ cup rice vinegar
2 tablespoons soy sauce
¼ cup mirin (sweet rice wine) or sake
2 teaspoon orange juice
2 tablespoon sugar
1 teaspoon kosher salt
½ teaspoon ground black pepper
¼ cup sesame oil

Steak:

2 pounds minute steak, split and deveined (ask your butcher to do this)
2 tablespoons soy sauce
2 tablespoons sesame oil

Salad:

6 cups baby spinach leaves
2 cups arugula
1 cup sliced mushrooms
1 cup snow peas, sliced in half
¼ cup sliced scallions
¼ cup wasabi peas

To prepare the dressing: Combine vinegar, soy sauce, mirin, orange juice, sugar, salt, and pepper in a small bowl. Slowly add oil, whisking continuously until emulsified.

To prepare the steak: Preheat the broiler, grill, or grill pan. Sprinkle both sides of meat with soy sauce and sesame oil and massage into the meat.

Broil 6 inches from the heat for 5 to 7 minutes per side, until meat reaches an internal temperature of 134°F for rare, 145°F for medium, and 155°F for well done meat. Remove from oven and let rest before slicing. Slice thin. For grill, preheat grill to 375°F, grease the grates, and grill over direct medium heat for 4 minutes each side. For grill pan, preheat pan. When hot, place meat on the diagonal in pan and cook undisturbed for about 4 to 6 minutes. Turn and cook on the other side an additional 4 to 6 minutes.

To prepare the salad: Combine all ingredients in a large bowl, reserving some of the wasabi peas for garnish. Add the dressing and toss gently. Distribute among 8 salad plates (or transfer to a serving bowl.) Top with sliced steak, and garnish with wasabi peas.

Citrus Salad with Toasted Seeds and Pinenuts

I love recreating favorite dishes from my travels. On my latest trip to Israel, I had a wonderful citrus salad while overlooking the beautiful scenery of Jerusalem. Israeli chefs often use crunch to add an extra layer of flavor and texture in their cooking. Such is the case here, with a lovely combination of bright citrus, bitter greens, and crunchy seeds, all dressed in apricot-sweetened dressing. (Toast the nuts in a 350°F oven until they begin to smell nutty. Each type will toast at different rates, so be careful not to burn!) This salad is my best attempt at recreating that lunch, and I'm thrilled with the results.

makes 10 servings

Salad:

2 heads Boston lettuce, torn

1 cup arugula, torn into pieces or whole if using baby leaves

½ cup sliced fennel (optional)

3 tablespoons toasted sunflower seeds

3 tablespoons toasted sesame seeds

3 tablespoons toasted walnuts, hazelnuts, pecans, or pine nuts

1 avocado, pitted and sliced

1 navel orange, trimmed of peel and pith, and cut into sections without membranes

1 pink grapefruit, trimmed of peel and pith, and cut into sections without membranes

Dressing:

2 tablespoons white wine vinegar

1 tablespoon fresh lemon or orange juice

1 tablespoon grated shallot

2 teaspoons apricot preserves or honey

1 teaspoon Dijon mustard

⅓ cup extra-virgin olive oil

½ teaspoon kosher salt

¼ teaspoon ground black pepper

To prepare the salad: Combine lettuce, arugula, and fennel (if using) on a large platter. Sprinkle evenly with seeds and nuts, reserving 1 tablespoon; top with avocado, orange slices, and grapefruit slices. Sprinkle with remaining nut mixture. Set aside.

To prepare the dressing: Combine vinegar, juice, shallot, preserves, and Dijon in a small bowl; whisk well. Slowly add oil to mixture, whisking to blend. Season with salt and pepper.

Pour dressing evenly over salad and serve.

Passover

Omit sunflower and sesame seeds. Use toasted quinoa and additional type of toasted nut as substitute for seeds. (Toast dry quinoa in a skillet until it starts to pop, about 4 minutes.) Use Passover mustard instead of Dijon mustard.

Make Ahead

Dressing, toasted nuts, and seeds can be prepared 2 days ahead of time. Store dressing, covered, in the refrigerator and bring to room temperature before serving. Store nuts and seeds in an air-tight container. Dress salad just before serving.

Tip

Add drained canned tuna or cooked flaked salmon and serve this salad for Shalosh Seudos or as an appetizer. Scatter the fish with the seeds and nuts on the top of the lettuce, and proceed with the recipe.

Fresh Kale Salad with Lemon Vinaigrette and Roasted Sweet Potato

Kale's popularity continues to rise—and for good reason. It's both nutritious and delicious. This salad is perfectly balanced with roasted sweet potatoes, healthful kale, earthy nuts, and bright, beautiful pomegranate seeds. Make sure you don't skip the step of rubbing the kale leaves with a bit of olive oil. Just like we relax with a bit of a massage, so does kale. Its flavor becomes less harsh and the leaves less stiff, turning a bright green hue after working with your fingers. This step can be done hours in advance, but don't over-oil.

serves 8

Salad:

6 to 8 cups fresh kale leaves, ribs removed

3 to 4 tablespoons extra-virgin olive oil, divided

2 sweet potatoes, peeled and cut into ½-inch cubes

½ cup walnuts, toasted (p. 335)

½ cup pomegranate seeds (p. 104)

Dressing:

Juice from 2 lemons

Zest from 1 lemon

3 teaspoons honey

1 clove garlic, minced

1 teaspoon Dijon mustard

¾ teaspoon kosher salt

¼ teaspoon ground black pepper

½ cup extra-virgin olive oil

To prepare the salad: Start with kale that is clean and dry. Drizzle with 2 to 3 tablespoons of olive oil. With your fingers, gently rub the olive oil on the kale leaves, massaging them to make them more tender. Refrigerate until ready to use.

Preheat oven to 400°F. Toss sweet potato cubes with remaining tablespoon olive oil. Bake in the oven for approximately 30 minutes, or until cooked through and a little toasted on top. Remove from oven and let cool.

In a large bowl, combine kale, roasted sweet potato, walnuts, and pomegranate seeds.

For the dressing: In a small bowl, whisk lemon juice, zest, honey, garlic, Dijon, salt, and pepper. Slowly add oil, whisking continuously until emulsified.

To serve: Pour dressing over salad. Toss and serve immediately.

Passover

Substitute Passover mustard for Dijon mustard.

Make Ahead

The dressing and sweet potatoes can be prepared 2 days ahead of serving, and the salad can be made a day ahead of time without the dressing. Store, covered, in the refrigerator. Bring dressing to room temperature before using, and dress salad just before serving.

Portobello Mushroom and Slow-Roasted Tomato Salad with Basil

My friend Rachel shared this terrific salad with me. It has a sweet-meets-savory dressing that enhances the slow-roasted tomatoes and the meaty portobellos. The secret to the success of this dish are the frozen basil cubes in the dressing, which are available in the freezer section of most Kosher markets. If you are short on time, use fresh grape tomatoes in the salad.

serves 8

Tomatoes:

1 pint cherry or grape tomatoes, sliced in half

1 tablespoon balsamic vinegar

3 tablespoons extra-virgin olive oil

¼ teaspoon kosher salt

Mushrooms:

2 tablespoons extra-virgin olive oil

1 tablespoon red wine vinegar

½ teaspoon kosher salt

¼ teaspoon ground black pepper

4 portobello mushrooms, stems removed

Dressing:

¼ cup rice vinegar

¼ cup honey

2 tablespoons fresh lemon juice

¼ teaspoon kosher salt

¼ teaspoon garlic powder

5 frozen basil cubes or 1½ tablespoons chopped fresh basil

¾ cup extra-virgin olive oil

Salad:

6 cups romaine lettuce, torn into bite-size pieces

½ cup sliced hard salami or other deli meat, sliced in 1-inch sticks (optional)

¼ cup pine nuts, toasted (p. 335)

To prepare the tomatoes: Preheat oven to 250°F. Place cherry tomato halves, cut-side up, on a baking sheet. In a small dish, whisk together balsamic vinegar, oil, and salt. Drizzle over tomatoes. Bake for 2 to 3 hours, or until tomatoes look shriveled and slightly dry but are still moist.

To prepare the mushrooms: Preheat oven to 350°F. Line a baking sheet with aluminum foil. In a small bowl, whisk together oil, vinegar, salt, and pepper. Brush both sides of mushrooms with oil mixture and place on prepared baking sheet; bake 15 to 20 minutes until mushrooms have released their liquid and are cooked through. Let cool and then slice into strips.

To prepare the dressing: Combine all ingredients in a jar with a tight lid. Shake well until fully combined.

To prepare the salad: Combine all ingredients in a large bowl and add the roasted tomatoes and sliced mushrooms; toss gently. Pour with dressing, toss again, and serve immediately.

Passover

Use apple cider vinegar in place of rice vinegar in the dressing.

Make Ahead

The dressing, mushrooms, and tomatoes can be prepared 2 days ahead of time. Store, separately, covered, in the refrigerator. Bring dressing to room temperature before using, and dress salad just before serving.

Passover

For the tomatoes, use only 1 tablespoon olive oil. For the dressing, reduce the honey to 3 tablespoons and the olive oil to ⅓ cup, and add ⅓ cup water. Omit the salami from the salad.

Wild Mushroom and Arugula Panzanella Salad

I love mushrooms pretty much any which way. You can use any combination in this salad, but make sure you give them time to caramelize before you stir them while cooking. The combination of rich mushrooms, zesty arugula, and the sweet creamy dressing makes for a perfect salad.

serves 8

Mushrooms:

¼ cup extra-virgin olive oil

1½ pounds fresh wild or button mushrooms, thickly sliced or quartered

1 tablespoon finely minced fresh thyme leaves or 1 teaspoon dried

2 tablespoons finely minced garlic

½ teaspoon kosher salt

¼ teaspoon ground black pepper

Dressing:

¼ cup red or white wine vinegar

1 tablespoon Dijon mustard

1 tablespoon honey

½ teaspoon kosher salt

1 small clove garlic, minced

½ cup canola oil

2 tablespoons extra-virgin olive oil

Salad:

8 cups baby arugula or other lettuce

¼ red onion, very thinly sliced

1 cup homemade croutons (p. 334) or store-bought

For the mushrooms: Heat a 16-inch skillet over high heat. When hot, add olive oil. When oil begins to smoke, add mushrooms. Don't stir! Let them sizzle until they have caramelized on the bottom, about 2 minutes. If you toss them too soon, they will release their liquid and begin to steam. When the bottoms are browned and caramelized, stir mushrooms, reduce heat to medium, and cook until well browned, about 5 minutes. Stir in thyme and garlic and cook for an additional minute. Stir in salt and pepper.

For the dressing: In a small bowl, whisk vinegar, Dijon, honey, salt, and garlic. With an immersion blender, drizzle in both oils and mix until emulsified. Alternatively, you can drizzle in the oils while whisking continuously.

Assemble the salad: Combine arugula, onions, mushrooms, and croutons in a large salad bowl. Pour on desired amount of dressing and toss to coat. Serve immediately.

Passover

Use 1 cup toasted farfel or broken matzo in place of croutons. Toss in farfel just before serving. For the dressing, use Passover mustard in place of Dijon mustard and safflower or cottonseed oil for canola.

Make Ahead

Dressing can be made 2 days ahead of time and stored in the refrigerator. Whisk dressing before using. Mushrooms can be prepared 2 days ahead of time and stored, covered, in the refrigerator. Bring dressing to room temperature before using, and dress salad just before serving.

Roasted Beet and Asparagus Salad

Gorgeous and delicious roasted beets and asparagus layer this salad with color. I like to serve it on a platter instead of a bowl to really showcase the vegetables. You can prepare the dressing and all ingredients ahead of time, but wait to mix them together just before serving. Beets tend to turn everything pink, so store them separately.

serves 8

Salad:

2 beets, peeled and cut into ½-inch cubes
½ teaspoon kosher salt
3 tablespoons extra-virgin olive oil, divided
8 spears green or white asparagus
6 cups chopped romaine lettuce
½ cup sliced hearts of palm
1 cup honey-glazed pecans

Dressing:

⅓ cup balsamic vinegar
¼ cup sugar
1 teaspoon kosher salt
1 clove garlic, minced
¾ cup canola oil

To prepare the salad: Preheat oven to 425°F. Line a large baking sheet with aluminum foil.

Toss beets with salt and 2 tablespoons of olive oil; place on prepared baking sheet. Roast until softened, about 40 minutes. Let cool.

Arrange asparagus on a separate baking sheet; drizzle with remaining tablespoon olive oil. Roast just until crisp, 5 to 7 minutes for green asparagus or 8 to 9 minutes for white. Let cool, and then cut into 2-inch pieces or leave whole.

Arrange lettuce on a large platter. Scatter with hearts of palm, pecans, roasted beets, and asparagus.

To prepare the dressing: Whisk together vinegar, sugar, salt, and garlic in a small bowl. Slowly add oil, whisking continuously until emulsified. Pour dressing over salad; toss and serve immediately.

Passover

Use safflower or cottonseed oil in place of canola in dressing.

Make Ahead

Dressing, beets, and asparagus can be made 2 days in advance. Store each separately in the refrigerator. Bring dressing to room temperature before using, and dress salad just before serving.

Tip

Use gloves or a paper towel when cutting cooked or uncooked beets. Their beautiful color stains not only the counter but also your fingers.

Lighten Up

Substitute ⅓ cup toasted, chopped pecans for the honey-glazed pecans. Omit the 3 tablespoons olive oil used for roasting the beets and asparagus. Instead, spray the vegetables with olive oil cooking spray. For the dressing, reduce the balsamic vinegar to ¼ cup, the sugar to 2 tablespoons, and the canola oil to ⅓ cup. Add 2 tablespoons water.

Sweet Spinach Salad

Spinach tastes spectacular with this sweet dressing. The recipe calls for persimmon, but use whatever looks ripe at the grocery store—mango, papaya, or blood oranges would all work well. The orange color of any of these fruits will look beautiful with the dark green spinach leaves.

serves 8

Salad:

8 cups baby spinach
2 ripe persimmons, finely chopped
½ cup dried cranberries
½ red onion, thinly sliced
½ cup slivered almonds, toasted (p. 335), or any honey-roasted nut

Dressing:

⅓ cup sugar
¼ cup plus 2 tablespoons apple cider vinegar
2 tablespoons raspberry or red wine vinegar
2 teaspoons fresh orange juice
1 teaspoon fresh lemon juice
1 teaspoon grated onion
1 teaspoon celery seeds
1 teaspoon kosher salt
1 teaspoon dry mustard
½ teaspoon paprika
¾ cup canola oil

To prepare the salad: Combine all ingredients in a large bowl and toss.

To prepare the dressing: Whisk together sugar, vinegars, juices, onion, celery seeds, salt, mustard, and paprika in a small bowl. Slowly add oil, whisking continuously to emulsify.

Pour dressing over salad; toss gently and serve.

Passover

For dressing, omit celery seeds, use Passover mustard for dry mustard and safflower or cottonseed oil for canola.

Make Ahead

The dressing can be made 3 days in advance and stored in the refrigerator. Bring to room temperature before using, and dress salad just before serving.

Crunchy Asian Cabbage Salad in Wonton Cups

Make Ahead

Dressing can be prepared up to 3 days in advance. Store, covered, in the refrigerator. Bring to room temperature before serving. Nuts, seeds, ramen, and wonton cups can be made 2 days ahead of time. Store nuts, seeds, and ramen together in air-tight container and wonton cups separately. Dress salad just before serving.

I've been making this salad for 20 years and never tire of it. I love the crunchy ramen noodles toasted with the nuts and seeds, and the clean, fresh taste of the cilantro. It's a great coleslaw-style salad for a Shabbos Day. Dress it shortly before serving so that everything stays crisp. The wonton cups make a beautiful presentation for the salad, but don't hesitate to skip that step if you're short on time.

makes 48 mini cups or 24 muffin-size cups

Salad:

1 tablespoon margarine or canola oil

2 (2.8-ounce) packages uncooked ramen noodles, broken into small pieces (flavor package discarded)

½ cup sliced almonds

¼ cup sunflower seeds

¼ cup sesame seeds

1 head green cabbage, shredded, or 2 (16-ounce) bags shredded cabbage

2 Persian cucumbers, thinly sliced

2 carrots, julienned

3 scallions, chopped

½ cup chopped fresh cilantro

Dressing:

⅓ cup canola oil

¼ cup sugar

¼ cup red wine vinegar

3 tablespoons soy sauce

2 teaspoons sesame oil

1 teaspoon chopped fresh ginger

Wonton Cups:

48 to 60 wonton wrappers

About ¼ cup toasted sesame oil, as needed

To prepare the salad: Melt margarine in a large skillet over medium heat; add ramen noodles, almonds, and seeds. Cook about 6 minutes, stirring, until lightly browned. (Alternatively, you can roast these without margarine in 350°F oven for 12 to 14 minutes.) Let cool.

In a large bowl, combine cooled ramen-nut mixture with cabbage, cucumbers, carrots, scallions, and cilantro. Toss gently.

To prepare the dressing: Whisk all ingredients together in a small bowl until smooth. Just before serving, pour dressing over salad; toss and serve in wonton cups.

To prepare the wonton cups: Preheat oven to 350°F.

Place one wonton wrapper in a mini muffin tin, or use 2 to 3 wrappers in a regular muffin tin. If using a regular-sized muffin tin, press the edges of several wonton wrappers together with your fingers, using a little water as glue. Push the wrappers into the edges of the muffin cups, with their pointed corner coming up out of the tin. Brush each cup with a little sesame oil and bake until golden brown and crisp, 5 to 7 minutes. Remove from oven, and let cool 5 minutes. Gently lift cups out of pan and use as little edible baskets for serving the salad.

Romaine Salad with Sweet Roasted Onions and Pinenuts

Passover

Substitute Passover mustard for Dijon mustard, or just omit mustard altogether.

Make Ahead

Onions and dressing can be prepared up to a week in advance and stored in the refrigerator. Bring dressing to room temperature before using, and dress salad just before serving.

The onions are the star of this salad. While you're roasting these, go ahead and slice a few more to use on pizzas, burgers, or omelets. The onions keep well in the refrigerator for at least a week.

serves 10

Onions:
3 red onions, cut into ¼-inch slices
¼ cup balsamic vinegar
¼ cup extra-virgin olive oil
1 teaspoon kosher salt
½ teaspoon ground black pepper

Dressing:
1 small shallot, minced
2 tablespoons balsamic vinegar
2 tablespoons white wine vinegar
2 teaspoons Dijon mustard
½ teaspoon kosher salt
¼ teaspoon ground black pepper
⅔ cup extra-virgin olive oil

Salad:
6 cups torn romaine lettuce
4 small cucumbers, sliced
1 cup cherry tomatoes, halved
½ cup pitted green olives
¼ cup pine nuts, toasted (p. 335)

To prepare the onions: Preheat oven to 375°F. Combine onions with balsamic vinegar, oil, salt, and pepper in a large bowl; toss well. Arrange evenly on a large baking sheet; place in oven and cook until the onions are tender, at least 25 minutes.

To prepare the dressing: Whisk together shallot, vinegars, Dijon, salt, and pepper in a small bowl. Slowly add oil, whisking continuously to emulsify.

Assemble the salad: Combine lettuce, cucumbers, tomatoes, and olives in a large bowl; add roasted onions and pine nuts. Add dressing; toss gently to coat and serve.

Is Your Lettuce Lifeless?

In my house, we use a lot of lettuce and keeping it crisp is crucial. No one wants unappetizing, limp and wrinkled lettuce. Proper storage is key. Follow these tips to keep your lettuce crispy and delicious for days:

1. In the store, choose lettuce with leaves that look crispy and bright in color. Avoid wilted leaves that are shriveled at the edges. Wash and dry lettuce just before using.

2. Wrap the lettuce in damp paper towels and seal in a large, resealable plastic bag. Store in the crisper drawer.

3. Do not pile other vegetables on top of the lettuce. It's tender leaves will become bruised and wilted.

4. Store leftover lettuce with a damp paper towel on top of the salad. Do not cover it with plastic wrap. Undressed salad will stay surprisingly well for a day or two when stored this way.

Kale Caesar Salad

Make Ahead

Kale can be prepped and dressing can be made a day ahead of time. Store, covered, in the refrigerator. Bring dressing to room temperature before using, and dress salad just before serving.

Tip

If you have any concerns with uncooked eggs, you can purchase pasteurized eggs at most groceries.

I enjoyed a version of this salad at Ditmas restaurant in Los Angeles and was immediately inspired to try my own version. The pareve Caesar dressing in this recipe has been a big hit for years and can be used on any type of lettuce or as a dip, but it makes for a more unique and chic salad paired with thinly sliced kale.

serves 8 to 10

Salad:

6 to 8 cups fresh kale leaves, ribs removed, sliced in long, thin strands

1 tablespoon extra-virgin olive oil

1 cup sliced cherry tomatoes (optional)

2 cups homemade croutons (p. 334) or store-bought

Dressing:

½ cup extra-virgin olive oil

1½ tablespoons red wine vinegar

2 teaspoons fresh lemon juice

¼ teaspoon ground dry mustard

1 teaspoon Worcestershire sauce, non-fish variety

2 cloves garlic, minced

½ teaspoon Dijon mustard

¼ teaspoon ground black pepper

5 drops Tabasco sauce, or to taste

1 egg yolk or 1 tablespoon mayonnaise

½ teaspoon kosher salt

For the salad: Place kale in a large salad bowl and drizzle with olive oil. With your fingers, gently massage kale with olive oil to break down any toughness in the leaves. Add tomatoes.

For the dressing: In a food processor or with an immersion blender, blend all ingredients together until fully combined and mixture is slightly thickened. Store in the refrigerator until ready to use.

Pour desired amount of dressing on salad. Toss. Add croutons and toss again, adding more dressing if necessary.

Field Greens with Sweet-Creamy Balsamic Dressing and Edible Flowers

Balsamic dressings can be earth-shatteringly good. Or cloyingly sweet and downright awful. In developing this recipe, I bought ten different versions to taste-test, and then created my own creamy version with the perfect balance of sweet, garlic, and vinegar. This can be used on everyday salads, atop fish or grilled chicken, or as a dipping sauce for veggies.

serves 8 to 10

Salad:

6 to 8 cups romaine lettuce or arugula or a mixture
1 cup sliced hearts of palm
½ cup thinly, sliced carrots
1 avocado, cut in chunks
¼ cup sliced red onion
¼ cup uncooked quinoa (optional)
Edible flowers (optional)

Dressing:

2 cloves garlic, grated
3 tablespoons mayonnaise
2 tablespoons fresh lemon juice
1 tablespoon Dijon mustard
3 tablespoons packed light brown sugar
¾ teaspoon garlic powder
2 teaspoons kosher salt
¾ teaspoon ground black pepper
½ cup balsamic vinegar
¾ cup extra-virgin olive oil

For the salad: Mix romaine, hearts of palm, carrots, avocado and red onion in a large salad bowl. If using the quinoa, toast the quinoa over low heat in a small skillet, stirring frequently until it's crunchy and starts to pop, about 5 minutes. Let cool.

For the dressing: Whisk together garlic, mayonnaise, lemon juice, Dijon, brown sugar, garlic powder, salt, and pepper until well combined. Add balsamic vinegar and whisk well. Using an immersion blender, slowly pour in olive oil to emulsify.

To assemble: Add toasted quinoa to salad. Top with desired amount of dressing and toss to combine. Garnish with edible flowers, if desired, and serve immediately.

Passover

Use Passover mustard in place of Dijon mustard.

Make Ahead

Dressing can be made up to 3 days before serving. Store, covered, in the refrigerator. Quinoa can be toasted 2 days ahead of time. Store in an airtight container. Bring dressing to room temperature before using, and dress salad just before serving.

Tip

Toasted quinoa has a nutty crunchy taste, similar to sesame seeds. It is great atop salads and as a garnish to meat, especially for people allergic to nuts.

Mexican Chicken Salad

Make Ahead

Dressing can be prepared up to 3 days ahead of time. Store, covered, in the refrigerator. Bring to room temperature before using, and dress salad just before serving.

My sister Allison shared her recipe for this delicious salad. Most of the time I send recipes her way, so when she takes the time to send me one, I know it'll be good. This one's easy as well, and the best Mexican salad I have ever had. Don't worry about the long list of dressing ingredients: it comes together quickly and the flavors are fantastic.

serves 8

Salad:

6 cups chopped romaine lettuce

2 cups cubed smoked chicken or smoked turkey

¼ cup chopped red onion

1 (15-ounce) can chickpeas, rinsed and drained

1 (15-ounce) can corn, drained, or 4 ears fresh corn, cooked and cut from cob

1 avocado, pitted and sliced

Dressing:

¼ cup sugar

2 tablespoons ketchup

2 tablespoons apple cider vinegar

1½ tablespoons ground cumin

1 tablespoon fresh lemon juice

2 teaspoons kosher salt

1½ teaspoons Worcestershire sauce, non-fish variety

1 teaspoon ground black pepper

1 teaspoon minced garlic

½ teaspoon dry mustard

¼ teaspoon crushed red pepper flakes

⅓ cup canola oil

3 tablespoons extra-virgin olive oil

Tortilla chips, for serving

To prepare the salad: Combine all ingredients in a large bowl; toss well and set aside.

To prepare the dressing: Combine sugar, ketchup, vinegar, cumin, lemon juice, salt, Worcestershire, pepper, garlic, mustard, and pepper flakes in a medium bowl; whisk well to mix. Add canola and then olive oil in a slow stream, whisking vigorously until fully combined.

Pour dressing over salad and toss well. Serve immediately with tortilla chips coarsely crumbled on top.

עוף

POULTRY

Chicken, turkey, and other poultry are some of the most versatile, affordable meats available for our families. But poultry gets a bad rap when we overcook it or underseason it. With good techniques and a few fresh ingredients, you'll be able to upgrade your weeknight chicken dishes into Shabbos-worthy meals. All recipes for flavorless, dry poultry have been banned from this chapter. Look forward to moist, delicious birds from here on out.

Apple Cider Spiced Roast Chicken

Make Ahead

Can be prepared 2 days ahead of time. Store, covered, in the refrigerator or freeze up to 3 months. Defrost in the refrigerator. Rewarm, covered, in a warming drawer or 300°F oven.

This dish can make a curry lover out of anyone. Many people think curry is a single spice when, in fact, all curries are a mixture of any variety of spices, and the combinations can range from subtle and sweet to pungent and spicy. For this recipe, I call for simply "curry powder," which is a pre-made mixture you can find in any grocery store. Don't go to an Indian market for this—they may not even know what you're talking about! Serve the chicken over steamed basmati rice to soak up the delicious sauce.

serves 8

2 (3- to 4-pound) chickens, each cut into eighths
1 teaspoon kosher salt
½ teaspoon ground black pepper
1 cup all-purpose flour
2 tablespoons extra-virgin olive oil
2 yellow onions, diced
4 shallots, chopped
5 cloves garlic, chopped
2 tablespoons peeled, chopped fresh ginger
1 cup dry red wine
1 cup apple cider
4 cups chicken broth
2 tablespoons curry powder
2 teaspoons chili sauce

Preheat oven to 350°F.

Season chicken pieces with salt and pepper. Place flour in a large bowl and dredge each piece of chicken, tapping gently to remove any excess flour.

Heat oil in a large stockpot over high heat. Add chicken; brown well, 2 to 3 minutes per side. Remove chicken pieces and place in a large roasting pan. To the original stockpot, add onions, shallots, garlic, and ginger; cook 2 minutes, stirring. Add wine and cider; cook over high heat until reduced by about half, about 8 minutes. Add broth, curry powder, and chili sauce, and bring to a boil over high heat. Simmer for 10 minutes, and then pour sauce over chicken. Cover roasting pan tightly with foil and bake 1 hour and 15 minutes. Remove cover and cook an additional 15 minutes or until top is lightly browned and skin is beginning to crisp. Serve the individual pieces of chicken topped with sauce or with the sauce served on the side.

Pretzel-Crusted Chicken with Sweet and Sour Sauce

The crunchy pretzels, fried onions, and cornflake crumbs create a coating you won't soon forget. The humble chicken tender comes to life with this crunchy outside, and the accompanying sweet-and-sour sauce plays off the Asian flavors in the chicken marinade. For a more grown-up presentation, pound a full breast to an even thickness and serve the cutlet with rice, glazed carrots, stir fried asparagus, and the sweet and sour sauce.

serves 8

Chicken:

⅓ cup soy sauce

3 tablespoons water

3 tablespoons mirin (sweet rice wine), sake, or other white wine

1 tablespoon plus 2 teaspoons packed light brown sugar

3 tablespoons sugar

2 cloves garlic, minced

1½ teaspoons minced fresh ginger

3 pounds (18 to 24 pieces) chicken tenders or boneless breast of chicken

½ cup plus 2 tablespoons coarsely chopped small twist pretzels

½ cup coarsely chopped packaged fried onions (like French's)

½ cup cornflake crumbs

1 teaspoon onion powder

1 teaspoon minced dried garlic

½ teaspoon kosher salt

Nonstick cooking spray

Skewers (optional)

Sweet and Sour Sauce:

1 cup ketchup

½ cup rice vinegar

¼ cup packed light brown sugar

2 tablespoons soy sauce

2 teaspoons grated fresh ginger

For the chicken: Position an oven rack on the upper third of the oven and preheat to 425°F. Grease a large baking sheet.

In a small bowl, whisk together soy sauce, water, mirin, brown sugar, sugar, garlic, and ginger for the marinade. Place chicken and marinade in a resealable plastic bag and refrigerate, 30 minutes to 1 hour.

In a shallow dish, mix pretzels, onions, corn flake crumbs, onion powder, minced dried garlic, and salt. Remove chicken from marinade (letting excess drip off) and dredge in the pretzel mixture. Place the chicken on greased baking sheet and then spray chicken generously with cooking spray. Bake until golden brown, about 12 minutes for tenders and 18 minutes for cutlets. Insert skewers into each chicken, if serving as appetizers.

For the sweet and sour sauce: In a small saucepan, heat ketchup, vinegar, sugar, soy sauce, and ginger over medium-high heat. Mix well and bring to a boil. Lower heat to simmer and cook until slightly thickened, about 10 minutes. Serve chicken warm or at room temperature with dipping sauce.

Make Ahead

This can be made 1 day ahead of time. Store, covered, in the refrigerator. Rewarm, uncovered or serve at room temperature.

Lighten Up

For the marinade, replace soy sauce with 3 tablespoons lite soy sauce plus 2 tablespoons water. Reduce the sugar to 1 tablespoon.

For the coating, omit the fried onion and add 3 tablespoons dried minced onion plus ½ cup wheat germ.

Roasted Chicken with Shiitake Mushrooms and Artichokes

Passover

Perfect as-is! If you cannot find artichoke bottoms for Passover, use thickly sliced zucchini instead.

Make Ahead

Can be prepared 2 days ahead of time. Store, covered, in the refrigerator or freeze up to 3 months. Defrost in the refrigerator. Rewarm, covered, in a warming drawer or 300°F oven.

Your house will smell amazing when you make this chicken. Wine, chicken, shallots, garlic, lemons, mushrooms—Whoa! Good! Artichoke bottoms are available in both the freezer section and in a can. If using frozen artichokes, thaw before using. You can also use marinated artichoke hearts from a jar in place of the artichoke bottoms, just be sure to drain them before using. This must be served warm.

serves 8

- 2 (3- to 4-pound) chickens, cut into eighths
- 5 tablespoons extra-virgin olive oil, divided
- 1 teaspoon kosher salt
- ½ teaspoon ground black pepper
- Zest and juice of 2 lemons
- 1 pound artichoke bottoms
- ¼ pound shiitake mushrooms, sliced
- 10 large cloves garlic
- 8 shallots, peeled and halved
- 2 teaspoons fresh thyme leaves or ½ teaspoon dried
- 1 cup dry white wine
- 1 cup pitted green olives

Preheat oven to 500°F.

Place chicken in a shallow roasting pan. Drizzle with 2 tablespoons of oil, and season with salt and pepper.

Zest each lemon into long strips; squeeze juice into a separate small bowl. Set juice aside.

Combine lemon zest, artichokes, mushrooms, garlic, shallots, and thyme in a medium bowl. Add remaining 3 tablespoons oil; toss to coat. Arrange mixture in pan around chicken. Roast until chicken is golden brown, about 40 minutes.

Remove chicken from oven. Pour reserved lemon juice, wine, and olives over chicken. Return to oven and cook an additional 10 to 15 minutes. Serve warm with vegetables and pan juices.

Skewered Chicken Yakitori

No matter how hard I try, I never seem to make enough of these. People love them! I shape them like torpedoes and serve them on skewers for fun, but you can omit the skewers or serve them as sliders, too. They taste good warm or at room temperature, drizzled with the glaze.

serves 10

Skewers:

40 bamboo skewers (optional)
2 pounds ground chicken
2 eggs
1 bunch scallions, finely chopped (about 1 cup)
8 cloves garlic, minced
1 cup panko breadcrumbs
¼ cup soy sauce
2 tablespoons sesame oil
1 tablespoon fresh lime juice
4 teaspoons grated fresh ginger
1 teaspoon kosher salt
½ teaspoon ground black pepper
¼ teaspoon cayenne pepper (optional)
⅓ cup chopped cilantro
Nonstick cooking spray, as needed

Dipping Sauce:

¼ cup honey
⅓ cup soy sauce
2 tablespoons sesame oil
1 teaspoon fresh lime juice (optional)
2 teaspoons minced fresh ginger
1 teaspoon garlic powder
1 clove garlic, minced
2 scallions, sliced

To prepare the skewers: Soak bamboo skewers in water for 20 minutes. Combine all ingredients in a large bowl. Form mixture into 40 football-shaped torpedoes made with about ½ cup of chicken mixture. If using skewers, thread each torpedo on to a single skewer. Coat a grill pan with cooking spray, and set over medium-high heat. (Or prepare a grill with medium-high heat and grease grates.) Grill chicken in batches until browned on one side, about 4 to 6 minutes, depending on thickness and shape. Turn and grill an additional 4 to 6 minutes, or until cooked through. Remove from pan.

To prepare the dipping sauce: Whisk together honey, soy sauce, sesame oil, lime juice, ginger, garlic powder, and garlic in a small bowl. Stir in scallions.

Serve chicken warm or at room temperature with dipping sauce.

Make Ahead

Chicken skewers and sauce can be prepared 2 days ahead of time. Store, covered, in the refrigerator or freeze up to 3 months. Defrost in the refrigerator. Rewarm, covered, in a warming drawer or 300°F oven.

Sabbath Chicken with Dried Fruit

I've served this chicken on Rosh Hashanah for years, and it's a go-to for a quick and easy Shabbos recipe. The chicken gets caramelized from the glossy and delicious sauce. It's best when marinated overnight, so be sure to plan ahead and start it early.

serves 8

½ cup orange juice

1 cup dried apricots, prunes, or a combination of any dried fruit

12 cloves garlic, minced

½-inch piece fresh ginger, peeled and finely chopped (about 1½ tablespoons)

2 tablespoons dried oregano

1 tablespoon dried thyme

⅓ cup red wine vinegar

3 tablespoons extra-virgin olive oil

1½ tablespoons fresh lemon juice

2 bay leaves

2 (3- to 4-pound) chickens, cut into 8 pieces

1½ teaspoons kosher salt

½ teaspoon ground black pepper

½ cup packed light brown sugar

½ cup white wine

In a small bowl, pour orange juice over dried fruit and let soak to plump the fruit, about 10 minutes. In a separate small bowl, whisk together garlic, ginger, oregano, thyme, vinegar, olive oil, lemon juice, and bay leaves.

Place chickens in two roasting pans. Pour marinade equally over each chicken and massage into chicken. Add orange juice and fruit mixture equally to each roasting pan. Cover pans and marinate in the refrigerator for 4 hours or up to overnight.

Preheat oven to 375°F. Sprinkle chicken with salt and pepper, and then drizzle equally with brown sugar and white wine. Bake until chicken is nicely browned on top and registers 165°F in the thickest part of the thigh, about 1 hour and 15 minutes.

Serve with pan juices and dried fruit.

Passover

Perfect as-is!

Prep Ahead

The chicken tastes best when marinated a minimum of 4 hours and preferably overnight.

Make Ahead

Can be prepared 2 days ahead of time. Store, covered, in the refrigerator or freeze up to 3 months. Defrost in the refrigerator. Rewarm, covered, in a warming drawer or 300°F oven.

Cornish Hens with Smothered Onions and Balsamic Glaze

This dish comes to the table looking like it could be photographed for a magazine. Perfectly browned Cornish hens, surrounded by glossy wine-soaked onions and sprinkled with pomegranate seeds. It's gorgeous, delicious, and perfect for Rosh Hashanah or any time of year. I also make this with small whole chickens or chicken pieces. Serve it warm.

makes 8 to 10 servings

Cornish Hens:

6 small Cornish hens or 5 pounds chicken pieces
2 tablespoons extra-virgin olive oil
1 teaspoon onion powder
1 teaspoon garlic powder
1 teaspoon kosher salt
1 teaspoon ground black pepper

Glaze:

¼ cup balsamic vinegar
3 tablespoons sugar
1½ cups chicken broth
2 tablespoons margarine
2 tablespoons all-purpose flour
Kosher salt and black pepper, to taste
½ cup pomegranate seeds (p. 104)

Onions:

3 tablespoons extra-virgin olive oil
4 yellow onions, sliced
3 tablespoons sugar
1 cup red wine
Kosher salt and pepper to taste

To prepare the hens: Preheat oven to 450°F. Place hens in two large baking pans. Drizzle each hen with oil. Sprinkle onion powder, garlic powder, salt, and pepper all over tops and sides of hens. Bake for 30 minutes, and then pour 1 cup glaze (reserving the rest) over hens and bake an additional 10 to 15 minutes, until browned on top and an internal temperature registers 165°F in the thickest part of the thigh. (Alternatively, simply pour the glaze over the finished hens before serving.)

To prepare the glaze: In a large skillet, heat balsamic vinegar and sugar over medium-high heat. Bring to a boil. Whisk in broth, margarine, and flour; cook until lumps are dissolved. Boil until slightly thickened, about 6 to 10 minutes, whisking frequently. Season with salt and pepper.

To prepare the onions: Heat oil in a large skillet over medium-high heat. Add onions and sugar; cook until golden brown, stirring often, about 15 minutes. Reduce heat to medium-low, and add wine. Cook until onions are tender and mixture is reduced to jam-like consistency, about 30 minutes. Season with salt and pepper.

Serve glazed hens on a platter surrounded by onions and sprinkled with pomegranate seeds. Drizzle with reserved glaze.

Passover

For the glaze, substitute potato starch for the flour.

Make Ahead

Hens, glaze, and onions can be prepared 2 days ahead of time. Store, covered, in the refrigerator or freeze up to 3 months. Defrost in the refrigerator. Rewarm, covered, in a warming drawer or 300°F oven.

Everything Bagel Chicken

I replicated the delicious seasonings used on everything bagels to create a marinade for simple grilled chicken that I think you'll love.

serves 8

- 1¼ teaspoons onion powder
- 1 teaspoon garlic powder
- 1 teaspoon kosher salt
- ¼ teaspoon ground black pepper
- 1 teaspoon Dijon mustard
- 1 heaping teaspoon minced dried onion
- 2 teaspoons minced dried garlic
- ¾ tablespoon poppyseeds
- 1 tablespoon sesame seeds
- 2 tablespoons red wine vinegar
- ¼ cup extra-virgin olive oil
- 8 boneless, skinless chicken breasts or thighs, pounded thin

Combine onion powder, garlic powder, kosher salt, pepper, Dijon, minced onion, minced garlic, poppyseeds, sesame seeds, and vinegar in a small bowl to make a marinade. Whisk well. Slowly add oil, whisking continuously until emulsified. Place chicken in a resealable plastic bag, Pour marinade over chicken, seal bag, and refrigerate for 2 hours, or up to overnight.

Bring chicken to room temperature before cooking. Heat a grill pan or grill to medium-high heat. Remove chicken from marinade and add to pan. Cook until cooked through and lightly browned, about 3 to 4 minutes per side. Serve this with Honey Mustard Sauce (p. 328), Grainy Mustard Sauce (p. 328), or Zesty Ketchup (p. 329).

Passover

Omit the poppyseeds and sesame seeds. Substitute Passover mustard for the Dijon mustard.

Prep Ahead

The chicken tastes best when marinated a minimum of 2 hours and preferably overnight.

Make Ahead

Can be prepared 1 day ahead of time. Store, covered, in the refrigerator. Serve at room temperature or rewarm, covered, in a warming drawer or 300°F oven.

Citrus-Marinated Chicken

Citrus can bring almost any dish to life, and the same is true here. The combination of orange and lemon zest with tarragon make this grilled chicken dish extraordinary. I love this with Citrus Aïoli (p. 329), but the mustard sauces (p. 328) work well, too.

serves 8

- 2 teaspoons orange zest
- ¼ cup fresh or bottled orange juice
- 2 teaspoons lemon zest
- ¼ cup fresh lemon juice
- ¼ cup extra-virgin olive oil
- ½ teaspoon kosher salt
- ¼ teaspoon ground black pepper
- 3 sprigs fresh tarragon, leaves chopped, or 1 teaspoon dried
- 2 cloves garlic, minced
- 8 boneless, skinless chicken breasts or thighs, pounded thin

Combine orange zest and juice, lemon zest and juice, olive oil, salt, pepper, tarragon, and garlic in a shallow dish and whisk well. Coat chicken in marinade; cover and refrigerate at least 15 minutes and up to 2 hours.

Heat a grill pan or grill to medium-high heat. Remove chicken from marinade, shaking off any excess liquid. Place chicken in pan and cook until cooked through and lightly browned, about 3 minutes per side. Serve warm or at room temperature, accompanied by Citrus Aïoli (p. 329).

Passover

Perfect as-is!

Prep Ahead

The chicken tastes best when marinated a minimum of 2 hours and preferably overnight.

Make Ahead

Can be prepared 1 day ahead of time. Store, covered, in the refrigerator. Serve at room temperature or rewarm, covered, in a warming drawer or 300°F oven.

Tip

Grill an orange half or lemon half until caramelized and then squeeze the juices over the finished chicken for added flavor.

Citrus-Marinated Chicken
So often grilled chicken recipes do not inspire—every recipe seems to come out tasting the same. These two are delightful exceptions, yielding moist and flavorful chicken that tastes just as good at room temperature as hot off the grill.
Citrus Aïoli
Zesty Ketchup
Grainy Mustard Sauce
Everything Bagel Chicken

Teriyaki Chicken with Pineapple Maple Glaze and Seared Starfruit

The fruit in this recipe takes ordinary teriyaki chicken and makes it into an extraordinary Shabbos dish. If starfruit is not in season, use pineapple slices or any other fruit that holds its shape when seared.

serves 8

1 tablespoon sesame oil
1 tablespoon extra-virgin olive oil
8 boneless, skinless chicken breasts or thighs, pounded thin
1 starfruit, sliced, pineapple rings, or other new Rosh Hashanah fruit (optional)
1 tablespoon grated ginger
2 cloves garlic, minced
1 shallot, chopped
½ cup soy sauce
¼ cup packed light brown sugar
3 tablespoons maple syrup
½ cup orange juice
1 teaspoon kosher salt
½ teaspoon ground black pepper
1 (8-ounce) can crushed pineapple, drained

In a large, stainless steel skillet, heat both oils over medium-high heat. Sear chicken until golden brown, about 3 minutes each side. Remove chicken from pan to a plate. In same skillet, place starfruit or pineapple rings. Cook until lightly browned, about 2 minutes each side. Remove from pan and set aside. Pour off all but 1½ tablespoons liquid from skillet.

To same skillet, add ginger, garlic, and shallot and cook until softened, about 3 minutes. Add soy sauce, brown sugar, maple syrup, orange juice, salt, pepper, and crushed pineapple and stir to combine. Simmer until well blended and slightly thickened, about 5 minutes.

Return chicken to skillet, coating with sauce. Simmer chicken for 10 minutes, or until cooked through.

Transfer chicken to serving platter, arrange starfruit on top of and around chicken, and drizzle with sauce. Serve warm or at room temperature.

Make Ahead

Can be prepared 2 days ahead of time. Store, covered, in the refrigerator or freeze up to 3 months. Defrost in the refrigerator. Rewarm, covered, in a warming drawer or 300°F oven.

Tip

The chicken will not properly brown in a nonstick skillet. Use stainless steel instead.

Mixed Herb Baked Chicken

This recipe has been a huge hit on my video series that runs on AOL and Yahoo, with over 100,000 views. I'm not entirely sure why it's so popular, except that it's exceptionally easy and it's made with ingredients likely already in your pantry. Once someone watches the video and makes the dish, they inevitably tell their friends, and the word spreads. Try it for yourself and see!

serves 8

⅓ cup fresh lemon juice
5 tablespoons extra-virgin olive oil
2 tablespoons thinly sliced chives or scallions, plus more for garnish
2 tablespoons chopped fresh basil or 2 teaspoons dried
2 tablespoons fresh chopped rosemary or 2 teaspoons dried
2 tablespoons soy sauce
4 cloves garlic, minced
4 teaspoons Dijon mustard
1 teaspoon kosher salt
¼ teaspoon ground black pepper
2 (3- to 4-pound) chickens, cut into eighths
3 lemons, cut into wedges

Whisk together lemon juice, oil, chives, basil, rosemary, soy sauce, garlic, Dijon, salt, and pepper in a small bowl. Place chicken in a large resealable plastic bag. Add marinade, seal bag, and shake well to coat chicken. Refrigerate at least 2 hours and up to overnight.

Preheat oven to 425°F. Remove chicken from marinade, and reserve marinade for basting. Arrange chicken skin-side up in two shallow baking pans. Tuck lemon wedges around chicken.

Roast chicken 30 minutes, and then baste with reserved marinade. Cook an additional 15 minutes, or until deeply browned and cooked through. Garnish with roasted lemons and additional chives.

Passover

Substitute Dijon mustard with Passover mustard and use Passover soy sauce in place of regular soy sauce.

Prep Ahead

The chicken tastes best when marinated a minimum of 2 hours and preferably overnight.

Make Ahead

Can be prepared 2 days ahead of time. Store, covered, in the refrigerator or freeze up to 3 months. Defrost in the refrigerator. Rewarm, covered, in a warming drawer or 300°F oven.

Lighten Up

Reduce the olive oil to 3 tablespoons and use lite soy sauce in place of regular.

Moshe, an elderly man who lives alone in Petach Tikvah, comes to the EMUNAH Golden Age Restaurant to nourish his body as well as his soul. The elderly citizens who patronize the Ma'ayan Rivka Golden Age Restaurant come for so much more than food—they come for companionship and to be surrounded by people who care.

Cornbread-Crusted Turkey London Broil

Sheldon, both a dear friend of EMUNAH of America and a master chef in his household, created this dish. He shared it with his sister-in-law, Aviva, who then shared it with me. I love the soft and toasty taste of the cornbread atop perfectly prepared turkey. Turkey London Broil is just another term for boneless, skinless turkey breast.

serves 8

- ½ teaspoon kosher salt
- ¼ teaspoon ground black pepper
- 1 (3- to 4-pound) boneless, skinless turkey breast (Turkey London Broil)
- 2 tablespoons extra-virgin olive oil
- 2 cloves garlic, minced
- 2 large pareve cornbread muffins, crumbled
- 1 tablespoon dried ground sage
- 1 tablespoon Dijon mustard
- 1 egg yolk
- 1 tablespoon extra-virgin olive oil
- Serve with Grainy Mustard Dipping Sauce (p. 328), Honey Mustard Dipping Sauce (p. 328), or Zesty Ketchup (p. 329)

Make Ahead

Can be prepared 1 day ahead of time. Store, covered, in the refrigerator. Serve at room temperature or rewarm, covered, in a warming drawer or 300°F oven.

Preheat oven to 350°F.

Sprinkle salt and pepper all over turkey. Heat skillet over high heat. Add oil. When oil is hot, sear turkey on both sides until lightly browned, about 3 to 5 minutes on each side. Remove from heat and place turkey in a small roasting pan.

In same skillet, add garlic and cook until softened, about 1 minute over medium heat. Add crumbled corn muffins, sage, and Dijon. Cook until lightly toasted, about 4 minutes.

Brush top of turkey with egg yolk. Press crumbs on top of turkey, pressing to coat the entire top of the turkey. Drizzle with olive oil. Bake, uncovered, for approximately 45 to 60 minutes or until an internal thermometer reaches 165°F.

Remove from oven and let turkey rest 10 minutes before slicing. Slice turkey and place on serving tray. Rewarm, if desired, covered, in a warming drawer or a low heat oven. Serve warm or at room temperature with sauces.

Turkey Roast with Cumin-Spiked Berry Sauce

The berry preserves in this sauce provide a sweet background to the bite of the mustard, cumin, and horseradish. Feel free to use any combination of preserves for the sauce. Or use 1 cup of whole berry cranberry sauce in place of the preserves if preferred—it saves money and shortens your shopping list. The dish works well both warm or at room temperature.

serves 8

1 (4- to 5-pound) bone-in, skin-on turkey breast
Kitchen twine, for tying
2 tablespoons Dijon mustard
1 teaspoon kosher salt
½ teaspoon ground black pepper
½ cup strawberry preserves
¼ cup raspberry preserves
¼ cup boysenberry preserves
½ teaspoon ground cumin
2 tablespoons prepared white horseradish

Preheat oven to 400°F.

Tie turkey with kitchen twine so that it holds together. Place turkey in a large roasting pan. Spread Dijon all over turkey breast and season with salt and pepper.

Combine preserves, cumin, and white horseradish in a small bowl, and pour over turkey.

Roast 45 minutes, or until an instant-read thermometer reads at least 165°F. Remove from oven and let rest 10 minutes before slicing. Spoon slices with pan sauce to serve.

Passover

Use Passover mustard in place of Dijon mustard or omit it. I use 1 cup whole berry cranberry sauce as a substitute for the preserves because it saves money and is fewer ingredients to buy. Either way it's great.

Make Ahead

Best prepared fresh but can be prepared 1 day ahead of time. Store, covered, in the refrigerator. Serve at room temperature or rewarm, covered, in a warming drawer or 300°F oven.

Tip

The twine net often used to hold turkey breasts together tends to bind to the seasonings and take the seasonings with it when removed. For a better solution, remove the netting and tie the breasts with twine in 2 or 3 places, and then proceed with seasoning. Remove any twine before serving.

Roast Balsamic Chicken with Zucchini, Tomatoes, and Onions

Roast chicken is a staple in many kitchens—and for good reason. It's easy, reliable, and delicious. This roast chicken is outstanding, though, not only because of its perfect balsamic and garlic-glazed vegetables, but also because of its secret spice: sumac.

serves 8

Vegetables:

2 medium-size red onions (about 1 pound), sliced

2 zucchini, cut into chunks

1 cup grape tomatoes

5 cloves garlic, sliced in half

½ teaspoon dried thyme

2½ tablespoons balsamic vinegar

3½ tablespoons extra-virgin olive oil, divided

1 teaspoon kosher salt, plus more to taste

¼ teaspoon ground black pepper, plus more to taste

Chicken:

2 chickens, cut into eights

1 teaspoon onion powder

1 teaspoon garlic powder

2 teaspoons ground sumac

1 teaspoon dried thyme

1 teaspoon kosher salt

½ teaspoon ground black pepper

For the vegetables: Scatter onions, zucchini, tomatoes, and garlic on a large, low-sided baking sheet. Drizzle with thyme, balsamic vinegar, and 2½ tablespoons olive oil, and stir to combine. Season with kosher salt and pepper.

For the chicken: Generously sprinkle chicken with onion powder, garlic powder, sumac, thyme, salt, and pepper. Drizzle chicken with remaining tablespoon olive oil. Place chicken on top of vegetables.

Bake until the skin is golden and an instant read thermometer reads 165°F at the deepest part of the chicken's thighs, 50 to 70 minutes.

To serve: Make a bed of cooked vegetables on a serving platter and top with chicken, leaving some vegetables to pile on top. Pour any remaining juices all over top of chicken and vegetables. Serve warm.

Passover

Perfect as-is! If you cannot find sumac for Passover use juice and zest of one lemon mixed with ¾ teaspoon paprika.

Make Ahead

This is best prepared 1 to 2 days ahead of time. Store, covered, in the refrigerator or freeze up to 3 months. Defrost in the refrigerator. Rewarm, covered, in a warming drawer or 300°F oven.

Succulent and Crispy Five-Hour Roast Chicken

Passover

Perfect as-is!

Prep Ahead

The chicken tastes best when marinated a minimum of 5 hours and preferably overnight.

Make Ahead

Best prepared fresh.

I know this sounds totally unbelievable—how could a chicken cook for five hours and be good? Well, it can! Especially if the oven is set at a low 250°F and the chicken is slathered with herbs and spices. My friends, Carol, Bonnie, and Ronnie, all power-house women behind EMUNAH of America, shared this recipe and technique with me at one of our cookbook meetings. I'm grateful to them for the recipe, and you will be too, after one try. Feel free to experiment with your favorite herbs and spices to change the flavor profile.

serves 8

4 teaspoons kosher salt
2 teaspoons paprika
1 teaspoon onion powder
1 teaspoon dried oregano
1 teaspoon white pepper
½ teaspoon ground black pepper
¼ teaspoon cayenne pepper
½ teaspoon garlic powder
2 (4-pound) whole chickens or Cornish hens
2 yellow onions, quartered
2 heads of garlic, tops sliced off to expose cloves
½ cup fresh parsley
4 carrots, peeled and cut into large chunks
4 parsnips, cut into large chunks
3 to 4 tablespoons extra-virgin olive oil

In a small bowl, mix together salt, paprika, onion powder, oregano, white pepper, black pepper, cayenne pepper, and garlic powder.

Rinse chicken cavity, and pat dry with paper towel. Rub each chicken inside and out with spice mixture. Place half an onion, a head of garlic, and half of the parsley into the cavity of each chicken. Place chickens in resealable plastic bags or double wrap with plastic wrap. Refrigerate 5 hours or up to overnight.

Preheat oven to 250°F. Place chickens in a roasting pan, breast-side up. Surround chicken with carrots and parsnips. Drizzle chicken and vegetables with olive oil. Season carrots and parsnips with kosher salt and pepper. Bake uncovered for 5 hours, or until chicken reaches a minimum internal temperature of 165°F, and are nicely browned. Let roasted chickens stand for 15 minutes before cutting into pieces. Serve with pan drippings, carrots, and parsnips.

Alternatively, while chicken is resting, use drippings to make a pan sauce. Remove roasted garlic from inside chicken. Pour any liquid from bottom of roasting pan, scraping any browned bits from roasting pan with a wooden spoon. Squeeze the roasted garlic out from its skin into sauce. Whisk together and taste for seasoning, adding more salt or pepper if needed. Serve chicken with pan sauce, carrots, and parsnips.

Turkey Basted with Coffee Liqueur

This recipe may sound unusual to you, but trust me—you must try it! The liqueur coats the skin of the turkey with a wonderful glaze with a sweet, rich flavor—but not the coffee flavor you'd expect. It transforms while baking, creating a beautiful crispy finish to the skin. It's best served warm.

serves 8

2 (3-pound) skin-on turkey breasts, boneless or bone-in

Kitchen twine, for tying

4 tablespoons paprika

4 teaspoons garlic powder

2 teaspoons kosher salt

2 teaspoons ground black pepper

1 cup coffee liqueur, such as Coco De Java or other pareve variety

½ cup chicken broth

Preheat oven to 325°F.

Tie each breast in 2 or 3 places so that it holds together. Place each turkey breast in a roasting pan; sprinkle each with 2 tablespoons paprika, 2 teaspoons garlic, 1 teaspoon kosher salt, and 1 teaspoon pepper. Roast, uncovered, 20 minutes.

Pour ½ cup liqueur and ¼ cup chicken broth over each turkey breast; cover with heavy-duty aluminum foil and return to oven. Cook an additional 30 to 40 minutes, basting every 10 minutes. Roast until the internal temperature reaches 165°F on an instant-read thermometer, about 16 minutes per pound of turkey meat.

Remove turkey breasts from oven and let rest at least 10 minutes before slicing.

Make Ahead

Best prepared fresh but can be prepared 1 day ahead of time. Store, covered, in the refrigerator. Rewarm, covered, in a warming drawer or 300°F oven. To keep the turkey as moist as possible, cover and rewarm whole turkey breasts before slicing. Let rest for 10 minutes before slicing and serving. For extra gravy, add a little more broth or water to the roasting pan before reheating.

Tip

There are a few companies that make pareve coffee liqueur, such as Coco De Java. Do not use Godiva liqueur in this recipe, as it contains dairy. Usually Kahlúa from Mexico is pareve but check before using.

Zesty Caribbean Chicken

You read it right—twenty cloves of garlic. Don't skimp! Just trust the recipe. The garlic mellows and sweetens as it marinates and roasts. The result is seriously moist chicken with a decidedly Caribbean flavor. Stay with the spirit of the dish and serve with a tropical mixed drink. Don't forget to plan ahead—the chicken needs to marinate at least 4 hours and preferably overnight.

serves 8

20 cloves garlic, halved
½ cup orange juice
½ cup fresh lemon juice
¼ cup canola oil
3 tablespoons chili powder
2 tablespoons paprika
4 teaspoons kosher salt
1½ teaspoons ground cumin
2 (3-pound) chickens, cut in eighths
¼ cup honey

Combine garlic, orange juice, lemon juice, oil, chili powder, paprika, salt, and cumin with an immersion blender or food processor, and purée until smooth.

Place chicken, skin-side up, in two large roasting pans. Pour garlic mixture over the chicken; cover and marinate for 4 hours or up to overnight.

Preheat oven to 350°F. Bake 1 hour, covered, and then drizzle with honey and baste with pan juices. Bake an additional 45 minutes to1 hour uncovered. Serve chicken warm over plain rice and drizzled with pan sauce, or alongside one of the rice dishes on pages 204 to 207.

Prep Ahead

The chicken tastes best when marinated a minimum of 4 hours and preferably overnight.

Make Ahead

Can be prepared 2 days ahead of time. Store, covered, in the refrigerator or freeze up to 3 months. Defrost in the refrigerator. Rewarm, covered, in a warming drawer or 300°F oven.

MEATS

One of the highlights of Shabbos and Yom Tov are memorable meals with sensational dishes. Meat symbolizes the festivity and specialness of Shabbos, and I've included options from a sophisticated standing rib roast to the more economical London broil and everything in between. You'll find plenty of recipes for braising, one of the best methods for transforming tougher meat into succulent fall-off-the-bone goodness through low, slow cooking. Even better, this technique gives you plenty of time for other things, like making challah, going on a run, or enjoying a few quiet minutes with someone you love.

Grandma Tillie's Brisket

Passover

Substitute potato starch for flour.

Make Ahead

This is best prepared 2 days ahead of time. Store, covered, in the refrigerator or freeze up to 3 months. Defrost in the refrigerator. Rewarm, covered, in a warming drawer or 300°F oven.

Many years ago, my cousin Esther shared this recipe of my Great Grandmother Tillie's. Even better, she also kindly shared the very large and extra special pot my great grandmother used to make it in. Esther swears the recipe and the pan are the originals from Grandma Tillie. But a few years ago, I wrote an article for the Jerusalem Post that included this recipe, and it caused quite an uproar in the family. Dozens of cousins—who had all tasted my Grandmother Tillie's original version—piped in with letters and comments to the editor, with some claiming it was a perfect rendition, while others complained that it was not her technique at all. Whether this is her actual version, only she can verify, but it sure is good. For best results, make it a day or two ahead of serving. It becomes even more delicious the longer the flavors can meld. I like to use a first cut brisket, but a second cut brisket works well here, too.

makes 8 to 10 servings

1 (5- to 6-pound) brisket
½ cup all-purpose flour
2 tablespoons paprika
2 teaspoons garlic powder
1 teaspoon kosher salt
½ teaspoon ground black pepper
¼ cup extra-virgin olive oil
3 yellow onions, sliced
2 leeks, sliced (white parts only)
5 cloves garlic, chopped
2 tablespoons tomato paste
1 cup beef or chicken broth
1 cup red wine (Cabernet or Bordeaux)
8 carrots, sliced into rounds
6 parsnips, sliced into rounds

Preheat broiler.

Rub brisket with flour; shake off excess. Season both sides with paprika, garlic powder, salt, and pepper, and rub into meat. Set on baking sheet and place under broiler. Cook until dark brown, about 4 minutes per side, 8 minutes total, turning once. (Watch closely because the broiler works fast.)

Heat oil in a large Dutch oven or stockpot over medium-high heat. Add onions, leeks, and garlic; cook until softened, about 10 minutes, stirring occasionally. Add browned brisket, tomato paste, broth, wine, carrots, and parsnips, and bring to a boil over high heat. Reduce heat to a simmer, cover, and cook until meat is very tender, 2½ to 3 hours.

Remove meat from stockpot and allow to rest 30 minutes. Slice and return meat to sauce. Reheat and serve warm.

Overnight Veal Breast

My friend Shira shared this veal recipe with me, and it consistently turns out juicy and delicious. The trick is to use her parchment and foil method described below, as it seals in all the moisture for the long cooking time. I start the night before and serve this dish for a Shabbos lunch.

makes 8 servings

1 (5-pound) veal breast
2 teaspoons paprika
2 teaspoons onion powder
2 teaspoons kosher salt
½ teaspoon ground black pepper
5 cloves garlic, minced
6 tablespoons extra-virgin olive oil, divided

Preheat oven to 350°F.

Rub veal with paprika, onion powder, salt, pepper, garlic, and 3 tablespoons olive oil.

In a large pan, heat remaining 3 tablespoons oil over medium heat. Brown veal on both sides, approximately 5 minutes per side, and then place in a roasting pan. Roast for 45 minutes, uncovered, and then remove from oven and lower oven temperature to 225°F.

Wrap veal tightly with parchment paper, and then with aluminum foil. Place back in the roasting pan and return to oven to cook overnight, from 16 to 20 hours, or until ready to serve.

Passover

Perfect as-is!

Prep Ahead

Be sure to start this dish the day before so the veal has adequate time for low, slow cooking.

Make Ahead

The 20 hours of bake time inherently make this recipe perfect for Shabbos lunch.

Lamb Chops with Savory Pear Relish

Passover

Substitute cumin for curry powder and Passover soy sauce for soy sauce.

Prep Ahead

The lamb tastes best when marinated a minimum of 2 hours and preferably overnight.

Make Ahead

Can be prepared 1 day ahead of time. Store, covered, in the refrigerator. Serve at room temperature or rewarm, covered, in a warming drawer or 300°F oven.

My kids call lamb chops meat lollipops, and they devour this recipe. Though popular with kids, this recipe is equally popular with adults, who love the sophisticated sweet and savory chutney that goes with the delightfully seasoned lamb.

serves 8

Lamb:

16 lamb chops
3 tablespoons extra-virgin olive oil
1½ teaspoons dried rosemary
1 clove garlic, minced
1 teaspoon kosher salt

Pear Relish:

2½ tablespoons margarine
1 jalapeño pepper, seeded and chopped
1 teaspoon curry powder
3 tablespoons honey
2 tablespoons soy sauce
1 tablespoon fresh lime juice
3 pears, peeled, cored, and chopped
⅓ cup dried cranberries

To prepare the lamb: Coat lamb with olive oil, rosemary, garlic, and salt. Cover and marinate in refrigerator at least 2 hours or overnight.

Heat a grill pan over high heat. When pan is hot, add lamb in a single layer, cooking in batches if needed. Cook 3 to 4 minutes per side, depending on thickness of the chops. Set aside and tent with foil to keep warm.

To prepare the relish: Melt margarine in a small skillet over medium-high heat. Add jalapeño and curry powder; cook 2 minutes, stirring continuously. Add honey, soy sauce, and lime juice; whisk well. Add pears and stir to coat. Cover, reduce heat, and simmer until pears are softened, about 10 minutes. Fold in cranberries. Serve lamb chops warm or at room temperature, with relish on the side.

Limes

To get the most juice from limes, I cut them like a mango. First, roll the fruit on the counter to soften and release their juices a bit. Then, instead of slicing the fruit in half horizontally like most do, stand them vertically on the cutting board and slice down the side, as if there's a center pit. Repeat on the opposite side. Cut two slices off the remaining core, and discard the core. By removing the tough core, you open up the slices, which allows them to release all the more juice.

Standing Rib Roast Studded with Garlic

Save this wonderful dish for special company or a holiday. Standing rib roast can be expensive, but it is so worth the cost. It is deceptively easy to prepare, and you might be tempted to indulge more often!

makes 8 servings

1 (10- to 12-pound) standing rib roast, about 4 - 6 ribs
2 teaspoons kosher salt, divided
1 teaspoon ground black pepper, divided
6 cloves garlic, thinly sliced
3 tablespoons extra-virgin olive oil, divided
30 small red potatoes, sliced in half
3 yellow onions, chopped
16 whole cloves garlic
1 teaspoon dried thyme (optional)
2 tablespoons extra-virgin olive oil

Place a rack in the middle of oven and preheat to 450°F.

Season meat on all sides with 1 teaspoon salt and ½ teaspoon pepper. Using a small, sharp knife, make several small slits in the fat along the top of the meat; gently insert the garlic slices. Drizzle with 1 tablespoon of the olive oil. Place meat in a large roasting pan and roast 20 minutes. Without opening the oven, reduce oven temperature to 325°F; roast an additional hour.

While meat is roasting, combine potatoes, onions, garlic cloves, thyme (if using), the remaining 2 tablespoons olive oil, remaining teaspoon salt, and remaining ½ teaspoon pepper in a large bowl. After the roast has cooked 1 hour at 325°F, remove from oven and arrange vegetables around meat. Roast an additional hour, or until the internal temperature of the meat reaches 140°F for rare and 150°F for medium. Baste meat and vegetables twice during the final hour of roasting.

Remove from oven. Gently remove meat from pan and let meat rest 15 minutes on a cutting board. Place potatoes back in oven and cook an additional 20 minutes, or until cooked through and slightly crispy. Carve roast and serve warm with vegetables and pan juices.

Passover

Perfect as-is!

Make Ahead

Best prepared on the same day as serving.

Savory London Broil with Sweet Braised Shallots and Mushrooms

Passover

Use Passover soy sauce or Passover Worcestershire sauce in place of soy sauce.

Prep Ahead

Be sure to allow enough time to roast the garlic—about 45 minutes. It removes all its sharpness and yields a sweet, subtle garlic flavor.

Make Ahead

This is best prepared 1 to 2 days ahead of time. Store, covered, in the refrigerator or freeze up to 3 months. Defrost in the refrigerator. Rewarm, covered, in a warming drawer or 300°F oven.

As I put together the list of meat recipes for this book, tester after tester requested more recipes for London broil. That makes sense because it's very accessible, not too large or expensive, and if prepared well, it's delicious. I like to have my butcher "split it" and remove the vein in the center. The result is a super-soft and easy-to-slice quick roast that is full of flavor.

serves 8

London Broil:

1 (2- to 4-pound) London broil or minute steak, split, and deveined (this recipe can also be made with 2 smaller (1½- to 2-pound) London broil)
1 head garlic, roasted (p. 334)
1 tablespoon onion powder
½ teaspoon ground black pepper
1 teaspoon kosher salt
2 tablespoons packed light brown sugar

Braised Shallots and Mushrooms:

3 tablespoons extra-virgin olive oil
6 shallots, sliced
1½ pounds button or assorted mushrooms
⅓ cup balsamic vinegar
3 tablespoons soy sauce
2 tablespoons sugar
½ teaspoon kosher salt
¼ teaspoon ground black pepper

Preheat oven to 300°F.

To prepare the London broil: Place meat on a piece of parchment paper in a large roasting pan. In a small dish, mix roasted garlic, onion powder, black pepper, salt, and brown sugar. Spread all over the top of the meat. Wrap the meat tightly with parchment paper and then with foil.

Bake for 1½ to 2 hours or until meat is 150°F for medium. Remove meat from oven and allow to rest 5 to 10 minutes until cool enough to slice.

Alternatively, preheat oven to broil and set the top rack 8 to12 inches from the broiler. Spread seasoning on meat but do not wrap it. Place meat in an ovensafe dish in oven and broil for 7 to 10 minutes, or until an internal meat thermometer registers 150°F for medium. The top should be browned and the meat pink on the inside.

To prepare the shallots and mushrooms: Set a sauté pan over medium heat and add olive oil. When oil is hot, cook shallots until soft, about 6 minutes. Add mushrooms and cook an additional 4 to 6 minutes. Add balsamic vinegar, soy sauce, and sugar. Season with salt and pepper. Bring to a boil and cook for 3 to 5 minutes, until sauce is syrupy.

When meat is cool, slice and return meat to the cooking juices in the baking pan. Pour shallot and mushroom mixture over meat.

Italian Veal Stew with Breadcrumb Gremolata

This hearty stew is Italian comfort food, but the breadcrumb topping makes it company-worthy. It is extra flavorful if you make it a day ahead of time.

serves 8

- 3 pounds cubed veal
- 1 teaspoon kosher salt, divided
- ½ teaspoon ground black pepper, divided
- ¼ cup extra-virgin olive oil
- 1 Vidalia or yellow onion, chopped
- 2 medium carrots, sliced ¼-inch thick
- 2 ribs celery, sliced ¼-inch thick
- 2 tablespoons chopped thyme or 2 teaspoons dried
- 1 teaspoon dried basil
- 2 cups dry white wine
- 2 cups canned crushed tomatoes
- 2 cups chicken broth
- ¼ cup chopped fresh parsley
- 1 cup homemade breadcrumbs (p. 333) or store-bought seasoned panko

Season veal with ½ teaspoon salt and ¼ teaspoon pepper. Heat a large Dutch oven or a large sauté pan with 3-inch sides over medium heat, and add oil. When oil is hot, add veal, and brown on each side, about 12 minutes total. Remove veal from pan and pour off all but 2 tablespoons of the fat. Return pan to heat, and add onion, carrot, celery, thyme, and basil. Cook over moderate heat, stirring, until softened. Add wine and bring to a boil, scraping up any browned bits with a wooden spoon. Simmer until wine is reduced by half, about 4 minutes. Add crushed tomatoes and chicken broth and bring to a boil. Return veal to pan, cover, and simmer for 1½ hours, or until veal is very tender. Stir in remaining ½ teaspoon salt, ¼ teaspoon pepper and parsley. Let stand, covered, for 10 minutes before serving.

Transfer veal stew to a serving dish. Sprinkle breadcrumbs over the veal and serve warm

Passover

Omit breadcrumb topping. Sprinkle with toasted farfel, nuts, and a bit of lemon zest on top.

Make Ahead

Can be prepared 2 days ahead of time. Store, covered, in the refrigerator or freeze up to 3 months. Defrost in the refrigerator. Rewarm, covered, in a warming drawer or 300°F oven.

KOSHER MEATS

CUTS AND COOKING TECHNIQUES

CHUCK/NECK

Chuck eye roast/California roast *(braise)*

French roast/brick roast/Delmonico roast/shell roast *(braise)*

Club steak: first 3 steaks from the chuck *(grill, broil)*

Flanken usually 5 bone flanken *(crockpot, cholent, braise)*

Ground beef *(oven, stove top, grill)*

Pot Roast *(braise)*

Beef neck bones *(cholent, soups)*

Square cut roast/chuck roast *(braise)*

BRISKET

First cut and second cut brisket *(braise)*

Traditional corned beef *(braise, boil)*

SHANK

Stew *(crockpot, braise)*

Small kolichel *(cholent, crockpot, soup)*

Marrow bones *(soup, cholent)*

Beef osso buco *(braise, crockpot)*

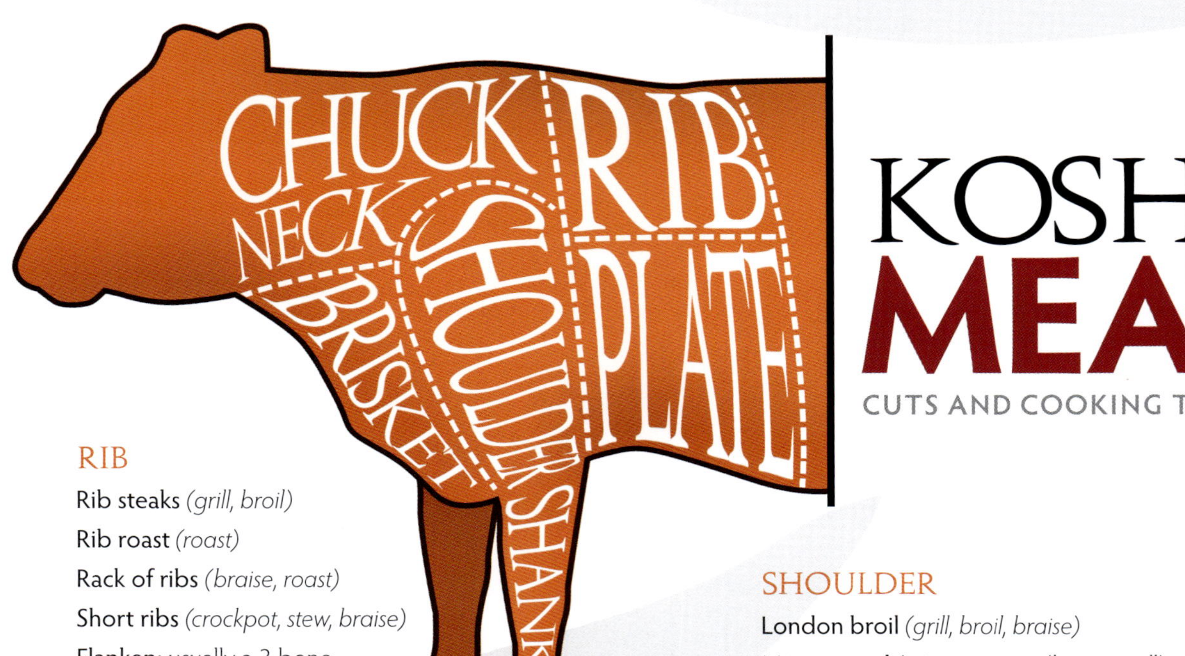

RIB

Rib steaks *(grill, broil)*

Rib roast *(roast)*

Rack of ribs *(braise, roast)*

Short ribs *(crockpot, stew, braise)*

Flanken: usually a 3 bone *(braise, crockpot, grill)*

Crescent steak/surprise steak *(grill, broil)*

Top of rib roast *(braise)*

Kosher filet mignon: sometimes from the club *(grill, broil)*

PLATE

Skirt Steak *(grill, stir fry, broil)*

Hanger steak *(grill, stir fry, broil)*

Navel pastrami *(braise, crockpot, cholent)*

SHOULDER

London broil *(grill, broil, braise)*

Minute steak/minute roast *(braise, grill)*

Silver tip roast/shoulder roast/roast beef *(braise, roast)*

Split fillet roast: London broil that's trimmed/deveined of grizzle *(broil, braise, grill)*

Flat London broil: 1½ to 2 pounds from the inside of should blade *(grill, braise)*

Mush steak/oyster steak: very tender *(grill, braise, broil)*

Shoulder steak *(grill, braise, broil)*

Pepper steak *(stir fry, crockpot)*

Large koichel *(braise)*

Shin meat: very lean *(stew, soup, cholent)*

Skirt Steak
Beef Stew Meat, Beef Chuck
First Cut Brisket
Split Minute/
Fillet Roast
Standing
Rib Roast
Beef Ribs
Veal Stew Meat
Shoulder
London Broil

Coffee-Marinated Brisket

Coffee tenderizes the brisket in this recipe, giving it strong depth of flavor without necessarily tasting like coffee. It has a great smoky barbecue sauce and comes together in just minutes. Make it a day or two ahead of time; the flavors develop well when the meat rests in the sauce.

serves 8

- 1 teaspoon chili powder
- ¼ teaspoon crushed red pepper, or more (optional)
- 3 tablespoons packed light brown sugar
- 1 teaspoon dried oregano
- 1 teaspoon cumin
- ½ teaspoon garlic powder
- 2 teaspoons kosher salt, divided
- 1 (5- to 6-pound) brisket or shoulder roast (see note)
- 1 tablespoon canola oil
- 2 yellow onions, sliced
- 4 cloves garlic, minced
- 2 cups brewed or instant coffee
- ½ teaspoon ground black pepper

In a small dish, stir together chili powder, crushed red pepper, brown sugar, oregano, cumin, garlic powder, and 1 teaspoon salt. Rub mixture all over meat on both sides. Let sit 1 hour at room temperature or up to overnight in the refrigerator.

Preheat oven to 350°F.

Heat oil in a large skillet over medium-high heat. Add meat and cook until browned on both sides, turning once. Remove from skillet and place in a roasting pan; set aside.

Add onions and garlic to skillet; cook until softened, stirring, about 10 minutes. Place mixture on top of reserved meat. Pour coffee over meat. Sprinkle with pepper and remaining teaspoon kosher salt. Cover and cook 2½ hours, until meat is very tender. (Smaller cuts of meat require shorter cooking times.)

Remove from oven and let stand 30 minutes. Remove meat to cutting board and slice as thinly as possible. Return meat to sauce. Serve warm with pan sauce drizzled over meat.

Passover

Omit chili powder. Add additional ½ teaspoon oregano and cumin.

Prep Ahead

The brisket tastes best when marinated a minimum of an hour and preferably overnight.

Make Ahead

This is best prepared 2 days ahead of time. Store, covered, in the refrigerator or freeze up to 3 months. Defrost in the refrigerator. Rewarm, covered, in a warming drawer or 300°F oven.

Note

Second-cut brisket works best here. A shoulder roast is similar to a brick roast or French-cut square roast; any of these can be used instead.

Tip

To make instant coffee, stir 1 tablespoon instant coffee granules into 2½ cups hot water until granules are dissolved.

Moroccan Lamb Stew

My friend Emuna has been making this recipe for years. She shared it with me when I lived in California and was somewhat new to Shabbos entertaining. You know a recipe is good when it's still part of your repertoire, 20 years later.

serves 12

¼ cup extra-virgin olive oil
1 large yellow onion, chopped
4 cloves garlic, minced
2½ teaspoons ground cumin
1 teaspoon ground cinnamon
1 teaspoon ground ginger
1 teaspoon kosher salt
½ teaspoon ground black pepper
3 pounds cubed lamb stew meat
3 cups beef broth
2 cinnamon sticks
1 tablespoon grated lemon zest
1 teaspoon grated orange zest
1 cup pitted prunes
½ cup dried apricots
1 cup whole blanched almonds

Heat oil in a large Dutch oven over medium-high heat. Add onion, garlic, cumin, cinnamon, ginger, salt, and pepper and cook until softened, about 4 minutes. Add meat and stir to coat. Add broth, cinnamon sticks, and lemon and orange zest. Bring to a boil, then simmer, partially covered for 30 minutes. Stir in prunes, apricots, and almonds and simmer for another 1½ hours. Serve warm with pan juices, dried fruit, and almonds.

Passover

Perfect as-is!

Make Ahead

This is best prepared 1 to 2 days ahead of time. Store, covered, in the refrigerator or freeze up to 3 months. Defrost in the refrigerator. Rewarm, covered, in a warming drawer or 300°F oven.

Brick Roast with Porcini Mushrooms and Onions

A brick roast is usually the same cut as a French-cut square roast or a Delmonico roast. It looks similar to a brisket and can be used interchangeably in those recipes too.

Passover

Perfect as-is!

Make Ahead

This is best prepared 1 to 2 days ahead of time. Store, covered, in the refrigerator or freeze up to 3 months. Defrost in the refrigerator. Rewarm, covered, in a warming drawer or 300°F oven.

serves 8

- 1 (5-pound) brick roast
- ½ teaspoon kosher salt
- ¼ teaspoon ground black pepper
- 3 tablespoons extra-virgin olive oil
- 2 yellow onions, sliced
- 2 cups sliced white button mushrooms
- 6 cloves garlic, minced
- 1½ cups beef broth
- 1 cup dry red wine
- 1 ounce dried porcini mushrooms
- 1 teaspoon fresh rosemary, plus sprigs for garnish

Preheat the oven to 350°F.

Sprinkle meat with salt and pepper on both sides. Heat oil in a large Dutch oven or 8-quart stockpot over medium-high heat. Add meat and cook until browned on all sides, turning as needed. Remove meat from stockpot; set aside.

Add onions, sliced mushrooms, and garlic to stockpot; cook until tender, scraping up the brown bits on the bottom of the pot, about 5 minutes. Add broth, wine, porcini mushrooms, and rosemary; cook 2 minutes. Return meat to pan; bring liquid to a boil over high heat. Cover and transfer to oven. Cook until meat is fork-tender, about 2½ to 3 hours.

Remove stockpot from oven; remove meat and set aside to cool. Slice.

Using an immersion blender, purée pan juices and vegetables in stockpot until smooth. Return sliced meat to stockpot; reheat until warmed through.

Arrange the sliced meat on a platter with sauce; garnish with rosemary sprigs and serve.

Root Beer Braised Beef Ribs

The sweetness of root beer (and its rooty savoriness, too) coats these short ribs and gives them amazing flavor. Do not substitute diet root beer! The recipe needs the sugar to sweeten the dish and develop the sauce (it doesn't taste like root beer by the time it's finished braising). And how much fun is it to tell your kids that the soda is already on the table?

serves 8

4 pounds boneless beef ribs (or 6 pounds bone-in ribs)
⅓ cup all-purpose flour
3 tablespoons canola oil
2 yellow onions, cut into 1½-inch chunks
2 ribs celery, cut into 1½-inch pieces
4 teaspoons finely chopped fresh ginger
6 cloves garlic, minced
1¼ cups root beer (not diet)
¾ cup beef broth
4 tablespoons tomato paste
2 tablespoons balsamic vinegar
2 bay leaves
1 teaspoon kosher salt
½ teaspoon ground black pepper
Cooked egg noodles, for serving

Preheat oven to 300°F.

Toss meat with flour in a large bowl to coat; set aside.

Heat oil in a large ovensafe stockpot over medium-high heat. Add reserved meat; cook until browned on both sides, turning once. Remove from pan; set aside.

Add onions, celery, ginger, and garlic to stockpot; cook 3 minutes, stirring occasionally. Add root beer, broth, tomato paste, vinegar, bay leaves, salt, and pepper; stir well. Bring to a boil over high heat. Return meat to stockpot and stir to coat; the meat should be partially covered with cooking liquid. Cover and place in oven; cook 2 hours. Uncover pot, stir ribs and sauce. Cover and cook an additional hour, until meat is very tender.

Serve warm over egg noodles.

Passover

Use potato starch in place of flour. Use Coca-Cola (not diet) in place of root beer.

Make Ahead

Can be prepared 2 days ahead of time. Store, covered, in the refrigerator or freeze up to 3 months. Defrost in the refrigerator. Rewarm, covered, in a warming drawer or 300°F oven.

Minute Steak with Peanut Sauce

Make Ahead

Can be prepared 2 days ahead of time. Store, covered, in the refrigerator or freeze up to 3 months. Defrost in the refrigerator. Rewarm, covered, in a warming drawer or 300°F oven.

Minute steak indeed! It requires no planning or marinating, and it can be served hot or room temperature. How much easier does it get?!

serves 8

- 3 to 4 pounds minute steak, split and deveined (ask your butcher to do this)
- 2 tablespoons soy sauce
- 2 tablespoons sesame oil
- Spicy Peanut Sauce (p. 330) or Peanut Dipping Sauce (p. 330), for serving

Preheat the broiler, grill, or grill pan. Sprinkle meat on both sides with soy sauce and sesame oil and massage into meat to season.

Broil 6 inches from the heat for 5 to 7 minutes per side, depending on desired doneness. (Alternatively, quickly grill or sear over high heat about 4 minutes per side.) Remove from oven and let rest before slicing and serving with either of the peanut sauces from page 330.

It's So Easy Anyone Can Make It Corned Beef

Passover

Substitute 2 tablespoons Passover mustard for Dijon mustard. Use Passover approved or revised sauces.

Make Ahead

Can be prepared 2 days ahead of time. Store, covered, in the refrigerator. Serve at room temperature or rewarm, covered, in a warming drawer or 300°F oven.

Everyone seems to love corned beef, but most people tell me it's too time consuming to make. Before I had this recipe, I spent years babysitting corned beef on the stovetop. Literally hours of watching it boil, adding cold water, and reboiling the meat. I've got good news for you! My local mashgiach, Rabbi Berel Wolowik, taught me this amazing method for corned beef. It is so simple, and the corned beef comes out tender and delicious. Serve it with Honey Mustard Sauce (p. 328), Zesty Ketchup (p. 329), or Sri-Rancha Sauce (p. 331).

serves 8

- ¾ cup water
- ¼ cup white wine
- 4 to 5 pounds corned beef, rinsed well and dried
- 4 tablespoons Dijon mustard
- ¾ cup packed light brown sugar
- 3 tablespoons balsamic vinegar
- Honey Mustard Sauce (p. 328), Zesty Ketchup (p. 329), or Sri-Rancha Sauce (p. 331)

Preheat oven to 375°F.

Pour water and wine into a large roasting pan. Place corned beef in pan. Coat meat with Dijon and then sprinkle with brown sugar. Drizzle balsamic vinegar on top of sugar.

Cover pan with heavy-duty aluminum foil. Bake for 2½ to 3 hours, or until the meat is fork tender. Cool completely. Store in the refrigerator in its juices. Slice when cold.

Serve at room temperature or warm with dipping sauces.

Fork-Tender Pastrami

I love events with buffets for one reason: ***inspiration****. I walk around and see what's new in food, I taste, I admire the presentation, and when I'm lucky, someone will share a tip or technique that can be useful for the home cook. Most events feature a carving station. The meat is always tender and cuts like butter. At one event, I was lucky enough to have the waiter share the technique for fork-tender meat. And after experimenting at home a few times, I am thrilled with the results. Better yet, this technique works for any deli meat, including smoked turkey or roast turkey. This pastrami can be served warm on Shabbos day because it stays heated and soft all night either in an oven or warming tray.*

serves 8

2 pounds pastrami from the deli counter, in a single piece, not sliced

Honey Mustard Sauce (p. 328) or Zesty Ketchup (p. 329), for serving

Wrap pastrami tightly in a layer of parchment paper, and then a layer of aluminum foil.

Heat a large pot of water over high heat. After the water is boiling, place the wrapped pastrami in the water. Cover pot and place in a 200°F oven or a warming drawer, until ready to serve. For a Shabbos day entrée, this is warmed overnight for 12 to 20 hours. (Alternatively, place wrapped pastrami in a 9 x 13 x 2-inch ovensafe pan, pour boiling water over and around pastrami. Cover tightly, and place in a 200°F oven or warming drawer for up to 20 hours or until ready to serve.)

To serve, carefully remove wrapped pastrami from water. (I do this with tongs over the sink.) Place pastrami on a cutting board; unwrap and discard foil and paper.

Slice pastrami and serve with Honey Mustard Sauce (p. 328) or Zesty Ketchup (p. 329).

Passover

Perfect as-is!

Prep Ahead

Be sure to start this recipe a day in advance to allow for the low, slow cooking.

Tips

I start this on Friday afternoon and serve it warm for lunch. Prepare it before Shabbos begins.

Be careful when you remove the pastrami from the water, as the liquid is very hot. This technique works for any deli meat, including smoked turkey or roast turkey.

Sweet and Savory Champagne-Braised Brick Roast

Make Ahead

Can be prepared 2 days ahead of time. Store, covered, in the refrigerator or freeze up to 3 months. Defrost in the refrigerator. Rewarm, covered, in a warming drawer or 300°F oven.

This technique and recipe can be used on any roast or on ribs. The dry rub gives a smoky depth of flavor and the Champagne makes it sweet and tender.

serves 8

Dry Rub:

½ cup packed light brown sugar

2 teaspoons paprika

1 teaspoon garlic powder

½ teaspoon ground black pepper

1 tablespoon kosher salt

1 teaspoon instant espresso powder

¼ teaspoon allspice

1 teaspoon chili powder

1 (4- to 5-pound) brick roast, Delmonico roast, brisket, or beef ribs, about 7 to 9 pounds bone-in

Glaze:

1 cup Champagne, sparkling white wine, or Prosecco

2 tablespoons apple cider vinegar

2 tablespoons Worcestershire sauce, non-fish variety

1 tablespoon honey

Make the dry rub: In a small bowl, mix brown sugar, paprika, garlic powder, pepper, salt, espresso powder, allspice, and chili powder. Rub all over the meat, coating all sides. Place in a roasting pan (for ribs, place in a single layer on 2 rimmed baking sheets) and let sit, covered, in the refrigerator for 1 hour.

For the glaze: Place the glaze ingredients in a small pot and cook over medium heat until just hot.

Remove meat from the refrigerator. Pour the glaze over the meat. Cover the pan with heavy-duty aluminum foil and cook for 3½ to 4 hours (2½ hours for ribs), or until tender.

Remove from the oven. Pour the liquid from roasting pan into a saucepan. Bring to a boil, reduce heat to a simmer, and let it cook until the liquid reduces by half and is slightly thickened, about 20 to 25 minutes.

Preheat the broiler.

Brush the glaze on the roast or ribs. Set under the broiler until the glaze caramelizes and forms a crust, 1 to 2 minutes. Watch carefully so it doesn't burn! Serve with remaining glaze. (Alternatively, serve the roast or ribs with the glaze on the side and skip the broiling step).

Spicy Grilled Brisket

If you are fortunate enough to have a gas line to your barbecue then try this terrific, flavorful brisket that my friend Sharon shared with me. I added the marinade (it can be omitted if you prefer) because it tenderizes the meat and adds some other great flavors. The spices and smoky barbecue flavors seep into the meat, creating a wonderfully rich and spicy brisket.

serves 8 to 10

1 (5- to 6-pound) first or second cut brisket

¼ cup beer

¼ cup orange juice

1 tablespoon canola oil

2 tablespoons paprika

1 tablespoon kosher salt

½ to 1 tablespoon ground black pepper (add more or less depending on how peppery you like it)

¼ teaspoon to 1 teaspoon cayenne pepper (use more or less depending on how spicy you like it)

1 teaspoon dried thyme

Zesty Ketchup (p. 329) or Sri-Rancha Sauce (p. 331)

Place brisket in a roasting pan. Pour beer and orange juice over meat. Cover and place in the refrigerator to marinate for at least 4 hours or overnight.

Preheat grill and adjust grates for indirect heat.

Remove brisket from marinade and place in a roasting pan. Discard marinade. Brush brisket with oil. In a small bowl, stir together paprika, salt, pepper, cayenne, and thyme. Rub spices all over meat.

Reduce grill heat to low. Place the roasting pan on grill over indirect heat (the burners under roasting pan should be off), and grill the meat for 3 hours or until fork tender.

Alternatively, cover and cook in a preheated 300°F oven for 2½ to 3½ hours.

Let meat rest 15 to 20 minutes before slicing. Serve warm with cooking juices or at room temperature with Zesty Ketchup (p. 329) or Sri-Rancha Sauce (p. 331).

Passover

Either omit the marinade or substitute white wine for beer.

Prep Ahead

The brisket tastes best when marinated a minimum of 4 hours and preferably overnight.

Make Ahead

Can be prepared 2 days ahead of time. Store, covered, in the refrigerator or freeze up to 3 months. Defrost in the refrigerator. Rewarm, covered, in a warming drawer or 300°F oven.

Tip

If preparing a smaller brisket, adjust cooking times: For 2 to 2½ pounds, cook about 1½ to 2 hours. For 3 to 4 pounds, cook 2 to 2½ hours.

Glazed Asian-Spiced Hanger Steak

I was inspired to create a terrific Asian marinade because so many readers and students raved about the bottled versions. I'm all for a little semi-homemade sometimes, but I love recreating great store-bought flavors at home with all-natural seasonings—plus I can control the amount of salt and sugar, one of the biggest issues with bottled sauces. This recipe was an instant winner with testers. It's easy, make-ahead, and full of all the wonderful ingredients that bottled sauces sometimes lack.

Prep Ahead

The steak tastes best when marinated a minimum of 4 hours and preferably overnight.

Make Ahead

Can be prepared 2 days ahead of time. Store, covered, in the refrigerator or freeze up to 3 months. Defrost in the refrigerator. Rewarm, covered, in a warming drawer or 300°F oven.

serves 8 to 10

3 tablespoons canola oil
3 yellow onions, thinly sliced
4 pounds hanger steak, minute steak (split), London broil (split), or any type of thin-cut roast
2 teaspoons sesame oil
7 cloves garlic, minced
2 teaspoons minced fresh ginger
⅔ cup mirin (sweet rice wine) or sweet white wine
¾ cup soy sauce
1½ tablespoons rice vinegar
⅓ cup packed light brown sugar
Pinch red pepper flakes

Heat oil in large sauté pan with 3-inch sides, over medium heat. Add onions to pan and cook until softened and lightly browned, about 15 minutes.

Place meat in a roasting pan. Spread browned onions on top of meat and set aside.

Reheat sauté pan over medium-high heat. Add sesame oil. When oil is hot, cook garlic and ginger until softened, about 1 to 2 minutes. Add mirin and bring to a boil. Reduce heat and simmer for 5 minutes, or until mirin is reduced to half. Stir in soy sauce, rice vinegar, brown sugar, and red pepper flakes. Simmer until sauce is slightly thickened and sugar is melted, about 5 more minutes.

Pour sauce over onions and meat and marinate for 1 hour or up to overnight.

Preheat oven to 350°F.

Place covered pan in the oven and cook for 1½ to 2 hours, or until fork tender. Remove from oven, and allow meat to rest 10 minutes before slicing. Serve warm with sauce.

SIDES

From simple roasted vegetables to more unique flavor combinations, side dishes should help show off the main course and complement their flavors and textures. I pair rich, savory meats with milder side dishes, and simpler main courses with some of the bolder flavored side dishes. Almost every side dish is better with a zest of citrus, sautéed onions scented with garlic, and a sprinkle of fresh herbs.

Flavors of Fall Wild Rice

Wild rice, which is not a rice at all, but a grass, has more than thirty times the antioxidants of traditional white rice and more protein than other whole grains. Sweet figs, chewy cranberries, and toasted nuts combine with a lovely homemade dressing to make this rice salad a perfect Shabbos side dish that can be prepared days in advance. For a beautiful presentation, serve in roasted squash halves.

makes 10 servings

Salad:

- 2 cups wild and long grain rice blend or 1 cup wild rice + 1 cup basmati
- ½ cup finely chopped dried figs or dates
- ¼ cup dried cranberries
- ¼ cup chopped scallions
- ¼ cup chopped red onion
- 1 rib celery, finely chopped
- ⅓ cup chopped roasted cashews (optional)
- ⅓ cup chopped toasted pecans (p. 335)

Dressing:

- ¼ cup raspberry or red wine vinegar
- 2 tablespoons lemon juice
- 2 teaspoons Dijon mustard
- 2 teaspoons sugar
- 2 cloves garlic, minced
- 1 teaspoon kosher salt
- ¼ teaspoon ground black pepper
- ½ cup canola oil
- ½ cup extra-virgin olive oil

Serving:

- 2 acorn squash, sliced and roasted (optional)
- 8 small oranges, flesh scooped out (optional)

To prepare the salad: Prepare the rice according to package instructions. Combine the cooked rice with the figs, cranberries, scallions, onion, celery, cashews (if using), and pecans in a large bowl.

To prepare the dressing: Combine vinegar, lemon juice, Dijon, sugar, garlic, salt, and pepper in a small bowl; purée using an immersion blender. Gradually add canola and olive oil in a stream to emulsify and blend well.

Pour ¾ cup dressing over salad; toss well. Check to make sure all rice is nicely coated with dressing. If dry, use additional dressing. If moist and tasty, store remaining dressing in refrigerator for a green salad or other use.

Store rice salad, covered, in refrigerator at least 1 hour and up to 3 days. Serve warm or at room temperature.

To serve: Decorate plate or platter with roasted squash rings. Top with wild rice salad. Alternatively, spoon rice into orange cups.

Passover

Use quinoa in place of wild rice. Combine 1½ cups quinoa with 3 cups water in a large pot and bring to boil. Reduce the heat, cover, and simmer 14 minutes, or until water is absorbed. Use Passover mustard in place of Dijon mustard and cottonseed or safflower oil in place of canola oil.

Make Ahead

Can be prepared 2 days ahead of time. Store, covered, in the refrigerator. Serve at room temperature or rewarm, covered, in a warming drawer or 300°F oven.

Tip

To roast the squash, brush squash rings lightly with canola oil. Roast in a 400°F oven for 20 minutes, or until tender.

Asparagus with Sesame-Soy Dressing

Make Ahead

Can be prepared a day ahead of time. Store, covered, in the refrigerator. Serve at room temperature or rewarm, covered, in a warming drawer or 300°F oven.

Tip

Many markets sell toasted sesame seeds and sometimes carry white and black together. I keep them in the pantry and use them as a garnish on chicken, salmon, and salads to make things look a little dressier.

This makes a light and tasty side dish for Shabbos lunch. The sesame and soy are a natural flavor combination and coat the asparagus well. When I can find white asparagus, I like to do a mixture of both green and white for a beautiful presentation. A sprinkling of black and white sesame seeds adds even a touch more pizzazz. Try this recipe with green beans or sugar snap peas, too.

serves 8

- ½ teaspoon kosher salt
- 3 tablespoons soy sauce
- 2 tablespoons sesame oil
- 1 tablespoon water
- 1 tablespoon sugar
- 2 tablespoons toasted white or black or mixed sesame seeds
- 1½ pounds asparagus, tough stems trimmed, cut on the diagonal into 1-inch pieces (I use a combination of green and white asparagus)

Fill a medium saucepan halfway with water, season with salt, and bring to a boil over high heat.

While the water is boiling, whisk together soy sauce, sesame oil, water, and sugar in a medium bowl until the sugar dissolves to make the dressing. Stir in sesame seeds and set aside.

Add asparagus to boiling water and cook until crisp-tender, about 2 minutes (if using white asparagus, add it first and cook for 1 minute, then add green asparagus and cook for 2 more minutes). Drain immediately, and plunge in bowl of ice water to stop the cooking and keep the asparagus bright green. Drain and pat dry, and then toss gently with the reserved dressing. Arrange in a serving dish and serve chilled or at room temperature.

Persian Spiced Meat Roll

Deli rolls are a go-to staple for Shabbos. And why not? A sandwich rolled in puffed pastry that's great for make-ahead dinners—does it get much better than this? Here's my take on the classic. I like to make an overlapping dough top for a pretty lattice effect, but you can make it "deli-roll style" too and keep it simple.

serves 8 to 10

- 1 teaspoon extra-virgin olive oil
- 1 yellow onion, finely diced
- 1 pound ground beef or turkey
- 2 cloves garlic, minced
- ⅓ cup crushed tomatoes
- 1 teaspoon paprika
- ⅛ teaspoon ground cloves
- ¾ teaspoon cinnamon
- ½ teaspoon ground cumin
- ¼ cup chopped flat leaf parsley
- ¼ cup chopped fresh mint (optional)
- ½ teaspoon kosher salt
- ¼ teaspoon ground black pepper
- 1 piece frozen puff pastry, thawed in the refrigerator
- 1 egg yolk

Preheat oven to 375°F.

Heat a large sauté pan over medium heat. Add oil. When oil is hot, add onion and cook until soft, 5 or 6 minutes. Add ground beef and garlic and cook for 7 minutes, or until meat is lightly browned. Add crushed tomatoes, paprika, cloves, cinnamon, and cumin. Stir and cook for an additional 3 minutes, or until juices are mostly reduced. Stir in parsley, mint, salt, and pepper. Remove from heat and let cool slightly.

On a piece of parchment paper, gently roll out puff pastry to a 12 x 8-inch rectangle about ¼- to ½-inch thick. Spoon the meat into the center of the puff pastry. Fold in the top and bottom piece of puff pastry. Then fold the side pieces over the meat, pressing together to seal (you may need to wet your fingertips to do this). Gently turn the roll over so that it's seam-side down and make a few diagonal slits in the top of the roll. Brush with egg yolk, and transfer parchment paper to a cookie sheet.

For the pretty lattice-work top pictured, gently roll out puff pastry to a 12 x 8-inch rectangle about ¼- to ½-inch thick. Spoon the meat into the center of the puff pastry. Fold in the top and bottom piece of puff pastry. Make 1-inch-wide by about 3-inch-long cuts in the dough on each side of the puff pastry, so that you have strips of attached dough on each side. (The base and sides of roll will be fully covered with pastry and just the top will appear latticed.) With your hands, bring pastry up to cover sides of meat, and gently pat the dough to adhere it to the meat. Then, lay one strip of pastry across the top of the meat, then another one from the opposite side over that. Layer that with another strip from the first side. Continue by alternating sides and slightly overlapping each strip in a criss-cross pattern. Brush with egg yolk, and transfer parchment paper to a cookie sheet.

Bake for 25 to 30 minutes, until top is nicely browned and puffed up. Serve warm or at room temperature.

Make Ahead

Can be prepared 2 days ahead of time. Store, covered, in the refrigerator or freeze up to 3 months. Defrost in the refrigerator. Rewarm, covered, or serve at room temperature.

Tip

If making it deli-roll style, be sure to make several slices in the top so steam can escape while baking.

Lighten Up

Substitute ground turkey for the ground beef and phyllo dough for the puff pastry. For the phyllo dough, unroll the thawed dough on a work surface and cover with a damp cloth to keep from drying out. Place 1 sheet phyllo dough on a parchment-lined baking sheet. Spray dough lightly and evenly with nonstick cooking spray. Top with another sheet of phyllo and spray. Repeat process for a total of 5 sheets. Spoon cooled turkey mixture down the center of the phyllo, leaving 5 inches on each side. Fold top and bottom of dough over filling, and then fold sides over the filling, wetting the edges to help them seal. Gently turn the roll over and place seam-side down. Make diagonal slits in the dough and brush with egg yolk. Bake for 25 to 30 minutes at 375°F.

Roasted Garlic Potatoes

I've tried many roasted potato recipes. This one seems a little richer than most, with deep flavors of roasted garlic, Dijon, and balsamic vinegar. Feel free to add some familiar favorite herbs like rosemary or thyme, but don't skip the luscious and rich roasted garlic (p. 334).

serves 8

2 teaspoons Dijon mustard
2 tablespoons balsamic vinegar
1 head roasted garlic (p. 334)
¼ cup extra-virgin olive oil
1½ teaspoons kosher salt
½ teaspoon ground black pepper
3 pounds small baby red or yellow potatoes, cut in half

Line a large rimmed baking sheet with aluminum foil. Preheat oven to 400°F.

In a small bowl, whisk together Dijon, vinegar, roasted garlic squeezed from its skin, olive oil, salt, and pepper until thick and well combined.

Place potatoes in a large bowl. Pour mustard mixture over potatoes, mixing until the potatoes are thoroughly coated. Pour potatoes and the mustard mixture onto prepared pan.

Roast potatoes in oven for 50 to 70 minutes, or until crispy on the outside but soft on the inside.

Passover

Use Passover mustard in place of Dijon mustard.

Prep Ahead

Be sure to allow enough time to roast the garlic—about 45 minutes. It removes all its sharpness and yields a sweet, subtle garlic flavor.

Make Ahead

Can be prepared a few hours before serving. Rewarm, uncovered, in a 300°F oven or a warming drawer.

Tip

It's important to roast the potatoes and vegetables on a low-sided, large baking sheet to allow ample room for air to circulate. If they're crowded or in a pan with high sides, they won't get as crispy as you like. Make use of your convection oven if you have one. It'll speed up the roasting process and make them even crispier. Watch them closely towards the end of cooking so they don't burn.

Honey-Balsamic Glazed Vegetables

The colors in this dish are a gorgeous mix of red, cream, and orange. It's perfect throughout autumn, and especially for Rosh Hashanah, when we like to infuse all our foods with sweet honey for a sweet New Year.

serves 8 to 10

4 parsnips (1¼ pounds), peeled and sliced into ½-inch pieces

5 carrots (1¼ pounds), peeled and sliced into ½-inch pieces

2 medium-sized sweet potatoes (1 pound), peeled and sliced into ½-inch pieces

3 golden or red beets (1½ pounds), peeled and sliced into ½-inch pieces

½ cup extra-virgin olive oil

½ cup honey

½ teaspoon dried thyme

1 teaspoon kosher salt

½ teaspoon ground black pepper

2 tablespoons balsamic vinegar

Preheat the oven to 425°F.

In a large bowl, toss parsnips, carrots, sweet potatoes, and beets with oil, honey, thyme, salt, and pepper. Divide between 2 large, sturdy, rimmed baking sheets. Cover with foil and roast until the vegetables are tender, about 30 minutes, shifting the pans once. Remove the foil and roast 20 minutes more, until nicely glazed and fully cooked through. Drizzle with balsamic vinegar and stir to coat the vegetables evenly. Serve warm.

Passover

Perfect as-is!

Make Ahead

Can be prepared 1 day ahead of time. Store, covered, in the refrigerator. Serve at room temperature or rewarm, uncovered, in a warming drawer or 300°F oven.

Lighten Up

Reduce the olive oil and honey from ½ cup each to ⅓ cup each.

Green Beans with Garlic and Dill

Make Ahead

Can be prepared 2 days ahead of time. Store, covered, in the refrigerator. Serve at room temperature or rewarm, covered, in a warming drawer or 200°F oven.

My kids never tire of these green beans. I prepare them a day ahead of time and rewarm them and serve with brisket or any type of roast. Prepare them as you wish—crispy and lightly cooked, or a bit shriveled.

makes 8 servings

2 tablespoons extra-virgin olive oil
1 yellow onion, chopped
1½ pounds French-cut green beans
4 cloves garlic, chopped
¼ cup chopped fresh dill
Kosher salt and ground black pepper, to taste

Heat oil in large skillet over medium heat. Add onion and cook until lightly browned, stirring occasionally, for 4 to 6 minutes. Add green beans and garlic, and cook to your desired degree of doneness—7 to 8 minutes for crisp-tender and bright green, or longer for softened and shriveled. Add dill and season with salt and pepper to taste.

Serve warm or at room temperature.

Zesty Chickpeas

If it's possible, these chickpeas are even better as leftovers. They're great both warm and served at room temperature, and they look gorgeous to boot. For ultimate deliciousness, I serve them atop basmati rice. But I also eat them as part of a big green salad or with simple chicken. My friend and recipe tester Arielle, stumbled upon a great idea during recipe testing while her child was "helping." What could've been a recipe disaster turned into a delicious salsa. Simply purée all the ingredients except for the chickpeas. She served her unexpected salsa creation alongside poached salmon and as a dip for shalosh seudos.

Make Ahead

Can be prepared 2 days ahead of time. Store, covered, in the refrigerator. Serve at room temperature or rewarm, covered, in a warming drawer or 300°F oven.

makes 8 servings

2 tablespoons extra-virgin olive oil
1 yellow onion, chopped
4 cloves garlic, minced
½ teaspoon cayenne or crushed red pepper
2 teaspoons coriander
2 teaspoons freshly grated ginger
1 teaspoon turmeric
2 teaspoons ground cumin
2 teaspoons curry powder
2 cups chopped tomato
3 (15-ounce) cans chickpeas, rinsed and drained
½ cup water
1 teaspoon kosher salt
½ teaspoon ground black pepper
2 cups fresh dill, chopped

Heat oil in a large skillet over medium heat. Add onion and cook until lightly browned, stirring occasionally, about 5 minutes. Add garlic, cayenne, coriander, ginger, and turmeric and cook 2 to 3 minutes. Add cumin, curry, and tomatoes and cook for 5 more minutes. Add chickpeas, water, salt, and pepper. Reduce heat and simmer for 10 minutes. Add dill and stir to mix. Serve warm or at room temperature.

Acorn Squash Stuffed with Jeweled Israeli Couscous

Larger than traditional couscous, Israeli couscous cooks and tastes more like a small pasta. I love the presentation of this dish, which uses squash halves as natural serving vessels for the colorful couscous. It has bursts of color from the dried fruit, parsley, and acorn squash and extra bursts of flavor from the garlic and orange zest. After you zest the orange, be sure to use the fresh juice in the recipe for its bright, clean flavor.

serves 8

Squash:

4 acorn squash (about 1½ pounds each), halved lengthwise and seeds removed

3 tablespoons canola oil

¼ cup packed light brown sugar

¾ teaspoon kosher salt

¼ teaspoon ground black pepper

Filling:

3 tablespoons extra-virgin olive oil

1 yellow onion, finely diced

3 cloves garlic, minced

1 cup sliced mushrooms

2 (8.8-ounce) packages Israeli couscous

2¾ cups pareve chicken broth or chicken broth

2 teaspoons orange zest

¼ cup orange juice

¼ cup diced dried apricots (optional)

¼ cup craisins (optional)

¼ cup chopped flat leaf parsley

¼ to ½ teaspoon kosher salt

¼ teaspoon ground black pepper

¼ cup pinenuts, toasted (p. 335)

Preheat oven to 425°F. Place acorn squash, cut-side up, on two baking sheets. Brush the flesh of the squash with canola oil, sprinkle with brown sugar, and season with salt and pepper. Roast in the oven until just fork tender, about 25 to 30 minutes.

Heat a 3-quart saucepan over medium heat. Add oil. When oil is hot, cook onion until soft, about 3 to 5 minutes. Add garlic and mushrooms and cook an additional 4 minutes. Pour in couscous and stir for 2 minutes, until it begins to smell toasty and nutty.

Add broth and bring to a boil. Reduce heat, cover, and simmer for 8 minutes, or until liquid is fully absorbed. Add orange zest, orange juice, apricots, craisins, parsley, salt, and pepper. Stir and cook an additional minute for the orange juice to absorb. Add pinenuts. To serve, spoon couscous into squash halves. Rewarm in oven if necessary. Serve warm or at room temperature.

Make Ahead

Can be prepared 1 day ahead of time. Store, covered, in the refrigerator. Serve at room temperature or rewarm, covered, in a warming drawer or 300°F oven.

Fresh Caramelized Apple and Cranberry Noodle Kugel

I make this kugel on Rosh Hashanah and often in the fall when cranberries are fresh and available. Apples and cranberries taste amazing together and give a sweet-tart contrast to the whole dish. Buy extra bags of fresh cranberries and store in the freezer so you can make this any time of year.

serves 12

Kugel:
12 ounces extra-wide noodles
4 tablespoons margarine, divided
2 Granny Smith apples, chopped
1½ cups fresh cranberries
3 tablespoons brown sugar
5 eggs
1 cup sugar
1 cup Tofutti sour cream
¾ cup vanilla soy milk
1½ teaspoons vanilla extract
1 teaspoon salt

Topping:
⅔ cup all-purpose flour
⅔ cup sugar
½ cup old-fashioned oats
½ cup canola oil
½ teaspoon ground cinnamon

To prepare the kugel: Preheat oven to 350°F. Lightly grease a 9 x 13-inch baking pan.

Bring a large pot of water to a boil over high heat. Add noodles and cook about 7 minutes, or until al dente. Drain and mix with 2 tablespoons of the margarine in a medium bowl.

Melt the remaining 2 tablespoons margarine in a large skillet over medium-heat heat. Add apples and cook 3 to 4 minutes, or until soft. Add cranberries and brown sugar; stir and cook about 4 minutes, until cranberries are cooked through but not popping open. Remove from heat and set aside.

Combine eggs, sugar, sour cream, soy milk, vanilla, and salt in a large bowl; whisk until smooth. Add reserved noodles and apple-cranberry mixture; stir to mix. Pour mixture into prepared pan.

To prepare the topping: Combine flour, sugar, oats, oil, and cinnamon in a small bowl; mix well. Sprinkle over kugel.

Bake about 1 hour, until set and cooked through. Best served warm.

Make Ahead

Can be prepared 2 days ahead of time. Store, covered, in the refrigerator or freeze up to 3 months. Defrost in the refrigerator. Rewarm, covered, in a warming drawer or 300°F oven.

Tip

If you can't find fresh cranberries, this recipe works well with frozen cranberries or 1 (15-ounce) can whole berry cranberry sauce.

Szechwan Sugar Snap Peas

This dish gets a terrific kick from the garlic and crushed red pepper. If you like a bit of heat, use the full teaspoon of red pepper. But for just a hint of flavor and a milder result, start with ½ teaspoon and increase to taste. Feel free to substitute French-cut green beans or zucchini for the sugar snaps.

Make Ahead

Can be prepared 1 day ahead of time. Store, covered, in the refrigerator. Serve at room temperature or rewarm, covered, in a warming drawer or 300°F oven.

makes 6 servings

2 tablespoons peanut oil
2 pounds sugar snap peas (about 6 cups), strings removed
4 cloves garlic, minced
1 teaspoon kosher salt
½ to 1 teaspoon crushed red pepper flakes, to taste
2 teaspoons sesame seeds, divided (optional)

Set a large skillet on high and heat the oil. Add sugar snap peas and garlic. Cook until the sugar snaps are softened, about 5 or 6 minutes, stirring occasionally. Add salt, pepper flakes, and 1 teaspoon of the sesame seeds to taste. Continue cooking until sugar snap peas begins to turn a darker green.

Serve warm or at room temperature and garnish with remaining sesame seeds.

Paprika Roasted Cauliflower

Passover

Omit smoked paprika if not available and use an additional ½ teaspoon regular paprika.

Make Ahead

Can be prepared a day ahead of time. Store, covered, in the refrigerator. Serve at room temperature or rewarm, uncovered, in a warming drawer or 300°F oven.

The cauliflower takes on a beautiful orangey-red hue from the paprika in this dish. Be sure to buy a naturally smoked paprika. Many versions use artificial smoke, which has an overly strong and unnatural flavor. Even so, you can find common national brands like McCormick and Pereg with a good smoked paprika. Just check the label—it should clearly identify if the spice is naturally smoked.

serves 8

2 heads cauliflower, cut into bite-sized florets
¼ teaspoon crushed red pepper (optional)
1 teaspoon smoked paprika
½ teaspoon paprika
½ teaspoon onion powder
½ teaspoon garlic powder
¼ teaspoon cumin
1 teaspoon kosher salt
⅓ to ½ cup extra-virgin olive oil

Preheat oven to 400°F and line a rimmed baking sheet with parchment paper.

Place cauliflower pieces in a large bowl and add red pepper, smoked paprika, paprika, onion powder, garlic powder, cumin, and salt. Toss with olive oil until coated evenly with oil and spices.

Place cauliflower and excess oil and spices on baking sheet and spread evenly into a single layer. Roast for 25 to 30 minutes, or until lightly browned. Serve cauliflower warm or room temperature.

Red and White Quinoa with Grapes and Pomegranate Seeds

Last year at Rabbi Grossman's Migdal Ohr event, I spotted this gorgeous quinoa salad served in a martini glass. The flavor combination of sweet, nutty, light, and smoky made it a clear winner. I tried and tested and retried and retested, until my version was just as wonderful. I bring this to friends often and it's always a big hit!

serves 8

Quinoa:

4 cups water
1 cup red quinoa, rinsed
1 cup white quinoa, rinsed
½ teaspoon kosher salt
½ cup chopped chives
1 cup halved red grapes
1 cup halved green grapes
½ cup pomegranate seeds (p. 104)
½ cup cubed smoked turkey, leftover roast, or grilled chicken
½ cup slivered almonds, toasted (p. 335)

Dressing:

1 shallot, minced
1 tablespoon honey
2 teaspoons Dijon mustard
1 teaspoon kosher salt
¼ cup raspberry vinegar or red wine vinegar
3 tablespoons balsamic vinegar
¾ cup extra-virgin olive oil

For the quinoa: Combine water, both types of quinoa, and salt in a large pot over medium-high heat. Bring to a boil, and then reduce heat, cover, and simmer for about 15 minutes, or until all the water is absorbed. The quinoa should look fluffy and puffed. Let cool.

For the dressing: In a small bowl, whisk shallot, honey, Dijon, salt, and both vinegars. Slowly add oil, whisking vigorously until emulsified and well blended.

In a large bowl, mix quinoa, chives, both grapes, pomegranate seeds, smoked turkey, and slivered almonds. Add half the dressing and toss. Taste and add more dressing to taste.

Passover

Use Passover mustard in place of Dijon mustard.

Make Ahead

Can be prepared 2 days ahead of time. Store, covered, in the refrigerator. Serve at room temperature.

A Rainbow of Rice:
White, Yellow, Green, and Red

White Coconut Rice

If you've never made rice with coconut milk, it's way past time to do so. The coconut milk gives the rice a rich and smooth flavor that cannot be compared to anything else. This side dish would work well with any Thai- or Indian-inspired menu, but I'm just as likely to serve it with a simple brisket. If you prefer a slightly lighter version of coconut rice, feel free to reduce the coconut milk by one cup and add one additional cup of water.

serves 8

2 cups rice
2½ cups coconut milk
1½ cups water
1 tablespoon sugar
1 teaspoon kosher salt
½ cup golden raisins (optional)

Combine rice, coconut milk, water, sugar, and salt in a medium stockpot; bring to a boil over high heat. Reduce to a simmer, cover, and cook 15 to 20 minutes over low heat, or until liquid is absorbed. Add raisins, if using, and stir to mix. Keep covered until ready to serve. Serve warm.

Make Ahead

Can be prepared a day ahead of time. Store, covered, in the refrigerator. Serve at room temperature or rewarm, covered, in a warming drawer or 300°F oven.

Red Rice

This Spanish rice has festive red color from the tomato paste and sauce, which also adds a nice foundation for the earthy spices in this dish. It goes well with any type of meat or roast chicken. For a quick weeknight meal, pair it with beans, leftover chicken, and some creamy avocado.

serves 8

2 tablespoons extra-virgin olive oil or chili oil
1 yellow onion, chopped
3 cloves garlic, chopped
2 cups long-grain white rice
2½ cups chicken or vegetable broth
3 tablespoons tomato paste
1 (8-ounce) can tomato sauce
¾ teaspoon chili powder or 1 serrano pepper, chopped
½ teaspoon paprika or smoked paprika
¼ teaspoon cayenne pepper (optional)
2 teaspoons kosher salt
¼ teaspoon ground black pepper

Heat the oil in a large saucepan over medium-high heat. Add onion and garlic and cook, stirring often, until softened, 1 to 2 minutes. Add the rice and cook, stirring often, until the grains begin to turn opaque, 2 to 3 minutes. Add the broth, tomato paste, tomato sauce, chili powder, paprika, cayenne, salt, and pepper, and stir to combine. Bring to a boil, and then reduce heat to low, cover, and simmer until the rice is tender and the liquid is absorbed, 25 to 30 minutes.

Remove the rice from heat and let stand, covered, for 5 minutes. Fluff with a fork and serve warm.

Make Ahead

Can be prepared a day ahead of time. Store, covered, in the refrigerator. Serve at room temperature or rewarm, covered, in a warming drawer or 300°F oven.

Yellow Turmeric Rice

Make Ahead

Can be prepared a day ahead of time. Store, covered, in the refrigerator. Serve at room temperature or rewarm, covered, in a warming drawer or 300°F oven.

The fragrant turmeric and saffron turn this rice a gorgeous yellow. It's beautiful on the plate and mildly flavored, so it can accompany just about anything.

serves 8

- 2 teaspoons canola oil
- 3 garlic cloves, minced
- 2 cups basmati white rice
- 2 cups chicken broth or vegetable broth
- 1¾ cups water
- 1½ teaspoons kosher salt
- ¾ teaspoon turmeric
- Pinch of saffron
- ½ cup frozen peas
- ¼ cup pinenuts or sliced almonds, toasted (optional) (p. 335)

Heat oil in medium saucepan over medium heat. Add garlic and rice. Sauté until the rice begins to turn opaque and to smell nutty and the garlic is softened and lightly browned, stirring frequently, about 2 minutes. Add broth, water, salt, turmeric, saffron, and frozen peas. Bring rice to boil. Reduce heat to low, cover, and simmer until rice is tender and liquid is absorbed, about 16 minutes. Stir in nuts. Fluff with fork and serve warm.

Herbed Green Rice

Make Ahead

Can be prepared a day ahead of time. Store, covered, in the refrigerator. Serve at room temperature or rewarm, covered, in a warming drawer or 300°F oven.

This is a seriously superb creation. I know it sounds a bit odd. Green rice? It gets its color from the spinach and fresh herbs, which also lend it a fresh flavor. Try it, and I know you will be eager to make it a staple in your repertoire.

serves 8

- 1 cup tightly packed spinach leaves
- ½ cup tightly packed basil, cilantro, flat-leaf parsley, or any combination
- 1¼ cups chicken or vegetable broth
- 1¼ cups soy milk or non-dairy creamer
- 1 teaspoon kosher salt
- 2 tablespoons canola oil
- 1 tablespoon extra-virgin olive oil
- 1½ cups basmati or long-grain white rice
- ¼ cup minced yellow onion
- 1 garlic clove, minced

In a blender or food processor, purée spinach, herbs, and broth until smooth. Add soy milk and salt and blend until combined.

In a medium saucepan, heat canola and olive oils over medium heat. When hot, add rice, onion, and garlic and cook for 2 to 3 minutes, or until the rice begins to turn opaque and smells slightly nutty and the onion is tender. Add spinach mixture, stir well, and bring to a boil. Reduce heat to low, cover, and cook for 18 to 20 minutes. Stir and recover and cook for an additional 3 to 5 minutes, or until liquid is mostly absorbed. Remove from heat and leave covered for an additional 5 minutes. Rice should be green and fluffy, with the liquid fully absorbed. Serve warm.

Ginger and Fruit-Sweetened Fried Rice

Leftover rice can get a much needed makeover with this sweet-savory side dish for chicken or beef. It calls for persimmons, which are known as the fruit of the Gods because they grow on trees that are over 70 feet tall. There many types of persimmons, but you'll probably have the best luck finding fuyu persimmons in the US. They're shaped a bit like an acorn squash and flat on the bottom, with a light-orange hue. Look for ones that are somewhat firm, yet give slightly to the touch, much like a perfectly ripe peach.

serves 6

2½ cups long-grain white rice
3⅓ cups water
¼ cup peanut or vegetable oil
1½ tablespoons peeled and grated fresh ginger
5 scallions, finely chopped
1 teaspoon kosher salt
¾ cup diced persimmon, mango, or fresh sweet pineapple
1 tablespoon soy sauce
2 teaspoons sesame oil

Place rice in a 4-quart saucepan, add water, and bring to a boil. Reduce heat to low and cook, covered, until water is absorbed, about 13 minutes. Remove from heat and let stand, tightly covered and undisturbed, 5 minutes. Fluff rice with a fork and spread in a large shallow baking pan to cool quickly, about 45 minutes. Chill, covered with plastic wrap, at least 4 hours or preferably overnight.

Once the rice has chilled, heat oil in a 12-inch skillet over moderate heat until very hot. Add ginger, scallions, and salt until fragrant, about 1 minute. Crumble rice into pan and sauté until lightly toasted, 10 to 12 minutes, stirring frequently. Remove from heat, and then add persimmon, soy sauce, and sesame oil, tossing to combine. Serve warm or at room temperature.

Persimmons

Beautiful, orange persimmons are in season from October to February. I love using them in salads, stirred into a bowl of couscous, or atop grilled salmon. (Try them in the Sweet Spinach Salad (page 117), Fruit Sweetened Ginger Fried Rice (page 207), Strawberry Mango Fruit Soup with Fruit Salsa (page 91), Seasonal Fruit and Heirloom Tomato Salad (page 316), and the Watermelon Tabbouleh (page 313).

But fair warning: don't eat persimmons until they're ripe. Instead of a sweet, aromatic flavor, you'll get an altogether bitter and unpleasant experience. Hachiya persimmons are orange-red and shaped like a Roma tomato. They'll be almost squishy when they're ripe. The other common variety, fuyus, are light orange and give only slightly to the touch when ripe.

Prep Ahead

For best results, the rice should be chilled overnight before stir-frying.

Make Ahead

For best results, make your rice a day or two ahead of time. Fresh, warm rice gets sticky and gummy in a stir fry, while cold leftovers actually work much better. The full recipe can be prepared 2 days ahead of time, as well. Store, covered, in the refrigerator. Serve at room temperature or rewarm, covered, in a warming drawer or 300°F oven.

Pumpkin Soufflé

Passover

Substitute ½ cup potato starch plus ½ cup matzo cake meal for 1 cup flour. Prepare as instructed.

Make Ahead

Can be prepared 2 days ahead of time. Store, covered, in the refrigerator or freeze up to 3 months. Defrost in the refrigerator. Rewarm, covered, in a warming drawer or 300°F oven.

This is a wonderful pudding-like soufflé for a winter night. The cinnamon, nutmeg, and cloves are a natural pairing with pumpkin and the warm spices adding depth to every bite of soufflé. Prepare in an attractive oven-safe dish, as you'll be serving it directly from the baking dish. It should have tall sides as well, so that the edges are cake-like, while the center remains a loose, warm pudding consistency. An 8 x 8-inch dish or standard loaf pan both work well. Serve warm for the most oohs and aahs.

serves 8 to 10

6 eggs or 1¼ cup egg beaters
1 cup sugar
1 (15 ounce) can pumpkin purée
1 cup whole wheat flour
1 teaspoon baking powder
1 teaspoon baking soda
1 teaspoon cinnamon
Pinch nutmeg
¼ teaspoon ground cloves
½ teaspoon salt

Preheat oven to 375°F.

Grease an oven-to-table loaf pan or 8 x 8-inch baking pan with nonstick cooking spray or canola oil.

In a large bowl, whisk eggs and sugar together. Add pumpkin and mix until combined. In a separate small bowl, whisk flour, baking powder, baking soda, cinnamon, nutmeg, cloves, and salt. Add to pumpkin mixture and stir until moistened. Pour into loaf pan and bake for approximately 22 to 25 minutes, or until the edges are set, but the center remains loose and pudding-like. Serve warm.

Garlic and Pesto Stuffed Mushrooms

Garlic, pesto, mushrooms—need I say more? Cooking the garlic in the soy milk calms and sweetens the garlic and thickens the soy milk, which makes a delicious base for the rest of this recipe.

serves 8

1 cup soy milk
12 cloves garlic, peeled
24 large button mushrooms
3 tablespoons plus 1 teaspoon extra-virgin olive oil, divided
2 large shallots, chopped
1 cup breadcrumbs
3 tablespoons homemade pesto (p. 335) or store-bought
1½ teaspoons kosher salt, divided
½ teaspoon ground black pepper, divided
½ teaspoon red wine vinegar

Combine soy milk and garlic in a small saucepan over very low heat; cook until garlic is soft enough to mash with a fork, about 45 minutes. (Soy milk will be reduced and thick.) Remove from heat and mash garlic with a fork to a rough purée.

While the garlic is poaching, remove the stems from the mushrooms and chop the stems to use in the stuffing. Reserve the mushroom caps for stuffing. Heat 2 tablespoons of the olive oil in a large skillet over medium; add shallots and chopped mushroom stems. Cook until softened, stirring occasionally, about 5 minutes.

Combine the mashed garlic with the breadcrumbs, pesto, 1 teaspoon of the salt, ¼ teaspoon of the pepper, and shallot-mushroom mixture and mix thoroughly.

Preheat oven to 450°F. Lightly grease a large baking sheet.

In a large bowl, whisk together 1 tablespoon of the olive oil, vinegar, remaining ½ teaspoon salt, and ¼ teaspoon pepper. Add the mushroom caps and toss to coat. Arrange mushroom caps on prepared baking sheet and fill centers evenly with reserved garlic-breadcrumb mixture. Drizzle tops with remaining teaspoon of olive oil.

Bake until just browned, about 12 to 15 minutes. Remove from oven and let sit 5 to 10 minutes before serving.

Passover

Substitute non-dairy creamer for soy milk and matzo meal for breadcrumbs.

Make Ahead

Can be prepared 2 days ahead of time. Store, covered, in the refrigerator. Serve at room temperature or rewarm, covered, in a warming drawer or 300°F oven.

Zucchini with Basil and Garlic

Passover

Perfect as-is!

Make Ahead

Can be prepared 2 days ahead of time. Store, covered, in the refrigerator or freeze up to 3 months. Defrost in the refrigerator. Rewarm, covered, in a warming drawer or 300°F oven.

This dish says summer through and through and makes a great side dish for Friday night or any weeknight. The flavors improve each day as the flavors meld together, so make it a day or two ahead of time and warm it before serving.

serves 8

- 3 tablespoons extra-virgin olive oil
- 6 cups (about 8 medium) zucchini, chopped into 3/4-inch pieces
- 3 cloves garlic, minced
- 2 tablespoons tomato paste
- ¾ teaspoon dried basil
- 1½ teaspoons kosher salt
- ¼ teaspoon ground black pepper

In a large skillet, heat oil over medium-high heat. Add zucchini and garlic and cook until soft, about 10 to 15 minutes. Add tomato paste, basil, salt, and pepper and stir to coat. Cook an additional 2 to 4 minutes to blend the flavors.

Roasted Spiced Broccoli

Passover

Perfect as-is!

Make Ahead

Can be made a few hours before serving. Rewarm, uncovered, in a warming drawer or a 300°F oven.

Tip

If you have a convection oven, use it when you roast vegetables to take advantage of its hot, even cooking. For this recipe, preheat convection oven to 375°F (bake or roast) and cook for approximately 15 minutes. All ovens heat a bit differently, so always watch vegetables carefully to avoid burning

I roast vegetables almost every night to serve with dinner, so I'm always looking for fresh approaches. This one comes out crispy on the outside and soft on the inside. It's a great way to lure your kids to green vegetables, and it works well with cauliflower, too.

serves 8

- ¼ cup extra-virgin olive oil
- 1 teaspoon brown sugar
- 1 teaspoon ground coriander (optional)
- 1 teaspoon ground cumin
- 1 teaspoon kosher salt
- ⅛ to ¼ teaspoon cayenne pepper (optional)
- ⅛ teaspoon ground cinnamon
- 4 heads broccoli, broken into florets (or 1 (32-ounce) bag frozen broccoli florets, defrosted)

Preheat oven to 400°F.

Combine oil, brown sugar, coriander, cumin, salt, cayenne, and cinnamon in a large bowl; whisk well. Add broccoli and toss to coat.

Arrange broccoli in a single layer on a large rimmed baking sheet. Bake 20 to 35 minutes, or until the tops of the broccoli are crisp.

Serve warm.

Vegetable Carbonata

My mom gave me this recipe more than 20 years ago and I still make it almost every week. I love the effect of cooking fresh summer vegetables with good quality olive oil, garlic, and tomatoes. I serve it as a side dish, warm or at room temperature. But I also make it because days later we still love it as leftovers on pasta, omelettes, or atop toasty garlic baguettes.

serves 8

3 tablespoons extra-virgin olive oil
1 yellow onion, cut into 1-inch chunks
3 zucchini, cut into ½-inch-thick slices
3 yellow squash, cut into ½-inch-thick slices
2 red peppers, cut into 1-inch chunks
2 yellow peppers, cut into 1-inch chunks
1 eggplant, peeled and cut into 1-inch chunks just before using
3 cloves garlic, minced
1 (28-ounce) can whole tomatoes
2 tablespoons tomato paste
2 tablespoons sugar
¼ cup red wine vinegar
2 teaspoons dried basil
2 teaspoons salt
½ teaspoon ground black pepper

Heat a large Dutch oven or an 8-quart pot over high heat. Add oil. When oil is hot, add onion, zucchini, squash, bell peppers, eggplant, and garlic. Cook until softened, about 12 minutes, stirring often. Add whole tomatoes, tomato paste, sugar, red wine vinegar, basil, salt, and pepper. Cover, reduce heat, and simmer for 20 minutes, or until vegetables are cooked through but not mushy. Serve warm or at room temperature.

Passover

Perfect as-is!

Make Ahead

Can be prepared 2 days ahead of time. Store, covered, in the refrigerator. Serve at room temperature or rewarm, covered, in a warming drawer or 300°F oven.

קינוחים

DESSERT

Desserts, as you may notice from the large collection here, hold a special place in my heart. It's not just because I have a sweet tooth (though I do), but I love the way a good dessert brings a smile to everyone at the table. What a (sweet) treat! Let your festive and creative spirit add personality to any meal and finish the evening off in grand fashion.

Chocolate Angel Pie

This is called an angel pie because the meringue looks simply angelic as a pie shell: white and glorious. That is also what makes it so unique. I garnish it with lots of chocolate and white shavings. This is easy and delicious for Passover too. Make sure to start this recipe ahead of time. The layers need to be cooled completely and the meringue takes time to cook. This recipe uses the whites and yolks of 4 eggs. I recommend separating the eggs before you start the recipe so the egg whites can come to room temperature before whipping. Reserve the yolks until ready to use.

makes 10 servings

Meringue Crust:

4 egg whites, at room temperature
1 cup plus 2 tablespoons sugar
2 teaspoons cornstarch
1 teaspoon distilled white vinegar
¾ teaspoon vanilla extract

Filling:

2 ounces unsweetened chocolate, chopped
4 egg yolks
½ cup sugar
2 tablespoons water
⅛ teaspoon salt
2 cups pareve whipping cream, whipped until soft peaks form, divided
Generous amount of chocolate and pareve white chocolate shavings, for garnish

Preheat oven to 450°F. Grease a 9-inch deep-dish pie pan.

To prepare the meringue crust: With an electric mixer, beat egg whites in a large bowl until soft peaks form. Gradually add sugar and cornstarch, constantly beating. Stir in vinegar and vanilla; beat until stiff peaks form and meringue is thick and glossy. Spoon meringue into prepared pie pan; press against sides to form a crust. Place in oven and turn off heat. Leave meringue in oven for 3 hours; remove pan to cool. The meringue can be stored up to 2 days, covered, in a dry place.

To prepare the filling: Melt chocolate in a medium saucepan over low heat, stirring until smooth. Cool to lukewarm.

Using an electric mixer, beat egg yolks, sugar, water, and salt until frothy. Stir into pan of melted chocolate. Cook mixture over low heat, whisking constantly until thick, about 4 minutes. Cool completely. Fold chocolate mixture into half of the prepared whipped cream. Pour into cooled shell; chill in refrigerator until mousse is set.

Top with remaining half of whipped cream; garnish with chocolate and white chocolate shavings. Store in refrigerator until ready to serve.

Passover

Use 1 teaspoon potato starch in place of cornstarch. Use Passover vanilla extract.

Prep Ahead

The meringue needs time to dry and the mousse needs time to chill. Plan accordingly.

Make Ahead

You need to start this recipe ahead of time. Pie can be prepared up to 2 days in advance. Store, lightly covered, in the refrigerator. Do not freeze. I like to whip the cream for topping and prepare the chocolate shavings in advance, storing in the refrigerator. Garnish before serving.

Easy Creamy Lemon Tart

Make Ahead

The tart can be made 1 day ahead. In fact, the lemon flavors develop well with a little time in the refrigerator. Cover loosely with plastic wrap or aluminum foil, being careful not to press on the filling, and refrigerate. Will keep for about 3 days. Shortly before serving, garnish with fruit.

This tart looks like artwork on a plate. The key is to decorate the top with an unusual variety of fruits, cut in all different shapes and sizes. I use champagne grapes, kumquats, pomegranate seeds, lady apples, whole and cut strawberries, starfruit, or anything that is seasonal and looks great. Don't place them on the tart in an organized way, just place pretty groupings and individual pieces on the tart for a truly artistic presentation. For a simpler version of this dish, make the lemon filling and serve in decorative cups with the Balsamic Berries and the Caramel Crunch (both on page 241) sprinkled on top.

serves 10

Crust:

½ cup (1 stick) unsalted margarine, melted

2 cups graham cracker crumbs (about 14 crackers ground)

⅓ cup sugar

¼ teaspoon ground cinnamon

Filling:

¼ cup pareve whipping cream

2 (8-ounce) packages Tofutti cream cheese, at room temperature

1½ cups lemon pie filling or lemon curd (see pantry)

Zest of 2 lemons

Topping:

2 bunches champagne grapes

5 kumquats

3 small apples, halved

1 cup strawberries, halved

1 cup blueberries

Any other decorative fruits of choice

Preheat oven to 350°F.

To prepare the crust: Combine margarine, graham cracker crumbs, sugar, and cinnamon in a large bowl; mix well. Pour into a 10-inch tart pan with a removable bottom; press evenly into the sides and bottom. Bake10 minutes; cool to room temperature.

For the filling: Using an electric mixer, beat whipping cream until soft peaks form. Add cream cheese, lemon pie filling, and lemon zest; mix until fully incorporated. Spread into chilled tart pan, covering the base evenly. Chill for at least 2 hours, so that the filling firms up, before decorating with fruit.

To assemble: Arrange the fruit gently (so it doesn't sink in too much) on top of the lemon filling in a decorative manner, leaving some of the fruits whole. Refrigerate until serving.

I Can't Get Enough S'mores So You Get S'mores Three Ways

S'mores three ways: is it redundant, you ask? No way! We seriously cannot get enough s'mores and all of these recipes are cookbook worthy! We make the pie for dessert and, admittedly, I pick at all the leftovers. The cupcakes are a great go-to recipe when you have a lot of kids over. The kids love them and they're so gorgeous that you'll get supermom points. If these are not enough for you, check out the S'mores Blondies on page 227, too.

S'mores Pie

makes 10 servings

Crust:

1½ cups graham cracker crumbs (from about 10 to 12 graham crackers ground in a food processor)

⅓ cup unsalted margarine, melted

4 tablespoons sugar

⅛ teaspoon salt

Chocolate Filling:

1 cup pareve whipping cream

7 ounces good-quality bittersweet chocolate (not more than 70% cacao), finely chopped

1 large egg

Pinch of salt

Topping:

1 (16-ounce) container of marshmallow fluff (or less, as desired)

Put oven rack in middle position and preheat oven to 350°F.

To make the crust: Lightly grease a 9- to 9½-inch pie pan or a 9-inch tart pan with removable bottom. Stir together graham cracker crumbs, margarine, sugar, and salt in a medium bowl; press evenly on bottom and up the sides of pie plate. Bake until crisp, 10 to 12 minutes; cool on a rack to room temperature. Leave the oven on.

To make the filling: Place whipping cream in a small saucepan and bring just to a boil over medium-high heat. Add chocolate and remove from heat. Let stand 1 minute, and then gently whisk until chocolate is melted and mixture is smooth. Gently whisk in egg and salt until combined. Pour into graham cracker crumb crust (crust will be about halfway full). Bake until filling is softly set and jiggles slightly in center when gently shaken, about 22 to 25 minutes. Cool to room temperature on a wire rack (filling will firm as it cools), about 1 hour.

To make the topping: Melt marshmallow fluff in a small saucepan over medium-low heat until soft and spreadable, about 4 minutes. Pour over cooled chocolate filling. Use as much fluff as desired, but cover chocolate layer completely.

Preheat broiler and place oven rack a few inches under the broiler. Broil assembled pie about 30 seconds, watching closely, or until the topping is slightly browned and looks like toasted marshmallows. Store at room temperature until ready to serve.

Passover

Make a Passover crust: Preheat oven to 350°F. Melt 4 tablespoons margarine and mix with 2 cups ground nuts (from about 4 cups whole nuts; I use a mixture of walnuts and almonds), ¼ cup packed light brown sugar, and ½ teaspoon Passover vanilla extract. Stir until combined. Gently press into the bottom and up the sides of a pie pan or tart pan. Bake as directed and proceed with recipe.

Make Ahead

This can be made a day ahead of time. Do not use aluminum foil or plastic wrap on top, as it will stick and ruin the toasty appearance. Cover with a cake dome or tented foil for storage. Do not freeze.

Note

Broiling the marshmallow creates a crispy toasty topping that's soft and gooey underneath. Before slicing, spray a knife with nonstick spray or dip in hot water between slices.

S'mores Cupcakes

Make Ahead

Cupcakes can be made a day or two ahead of time and stored, covered, on the counter. They can also be frozen before adding the garnish. Garnish after defrosting and before serving.

makes 12 cupcakes

Cupcakes:

1½ cups graham cracker crumbs (from about 10 to 12 graham crackers ground in a food processor)

½ cup all-purpose flour

2½ teaspoons baking powder

¾ cup sugar

½ cup (1 stick) margarine, at room temperature

2 large eggs

1 teaspoon vanilla extract

¾ cup non-dairy creamer

Ganache:

½ cup pareve whipping cream

8 ounces bittersweet chocolate, chopped

Filling:

¾ cup marshmallow fluff

Garnish:

12 large marshmallows

Broken graham crackers

Preheat oven to 350°F. Line 12 standard muffin cups with paper liners.

To prepare the cupcakes: Combine graham cracker crumbs, flour, and baking powder in a large bowl. Set aside.

With an electric mixer, cream sugar and margarine in a separate large mixing bowl until light and fluffy. Add eggs, one at a time, beating after each addition. Stir in vanilla. Add reserved graham cracker mixture alternately with non-dairy creamer, beginning and ending with graham cracker mixture. Divide batter among muffin cups.

Bake about 22 minutes, or until a tester inserted into the center come out with moist crumbs. Transfer cupcakes to rack to cool completely.

To prepare the ganache: Place whipping cream in a small saucepan and bring just to a boil over medium-high heat. Add chocolate and remove from heat. Let stand 1 minute, then gently whisk until chocolate is melted and mixture is smooth. Cool until lukewarm.

To assemble: Use a teaspoon to scoop out a small piece from the middle of each cooled cupcake, reserving the small pieces for another use (or eat them!). Fill each hole with 1 to 2 teaspoons marshmallow fluff. Spread 2 teaspoons cooled ganache over each cupcake.

For garnish: Toast marshmallows over an open flame until browned. Drop one marshmallow on top of each cupcake. Cool slightly and garnish with graham cracker pieces, if desired.

S'mores Blondies

S'mores have finally made the move from the campfire to restaurants, with variations showing up on menus everywhere. I wanted to find a way to get this combination of great flavors into one of my favorite desserts, the blondie. My spin includes all the great flavors of s'mores with the same great soft and chewy texture of a traditional chocolate chip cookie. The finished bars freeze well.

Make Ahead

Can be prepared 2 days ahead of time. Store, covered, in the refrigerator or freeze up to 3 months. Defrost in the refrigerator. Serve at room temperature.

makes about 14 bars

- 1 cup graham cracker crumbs (about 7 graham crackers, ground)
- 1¼ cups all-purpose flour
- ½ teaspoon baking soda
- ½ teaspoon salt
- ½ cup (1 stick) margarine, at room temperature
- ½ cup packed light brown sugar
- ⅓ cup granulated sugar
- 1 egg
- 1 teaspoon vanilla extract
- 1¼ cups mini chocolate chips
- 3 cups mini marshmallows, divided
- 1 tablespoon soy milk, or as needed
- ½ cup coarsely chopped graham cracker pieces (from about 3 to 4 full graham crackers)
- 1 cup chocolate chips

Preheat oven to 350°F. Grease a 13 x 9 x 2-inch baking pan.

In a large bowl, whisk together the graham cracker crumbs, flour, baking soda, and salt. Set aside.

In a mixer, beat margarine, brown sugar, and granulated sugar until creamy and smooth, about 3 minutes. Add the egg and vanilla and mix until combined. Slowly add dry ingredients and mix.

Stir in chocolate chips and 2 cups of the marshmallows. The batter will be dry and thick. If it is falling apart, add soy milk to moisten.

Press batter into prepared pan. Bake for 17 minutes, until lightly toasted on top and just set, and tester inserted has moist crumbs. Meanwhile, mix remaining 1 cup marshmallows, the coarsely chopped graham cracker pieces, and chocolate chips in a small bowl. Remove pan from oven. Evenly sprinkle blondies with marshmallow mixture, gently pressing into the dough. Bake for 5 to 7 more minutes, or until marshmallows are lightly toasted. Cool in refrigerator before cutting.

Chocolate Caramel Pecan Pie

The pecan pie that appears on every Thanksgiving table has nothing on this souped-up chocolate caramel version. In fact, you may never go back to that boring plain pecan pie again! To make cookie crumbs, grind approximately 40 chocolate cookies, like tea biscuits or chocolate sandwich cookies in a food processor, using on and off pulses. If using sandwich cookies, reduce the margarine to 3 tablespoons. This pie freezes well.

serves 8

Crust:

1½ cups chocolate tea biscuit cookie crumbs or chocolate sandwich cookie crumbs (see above)

5 tablespoons margarine, melted

½ teaspoon vanilla extract

Filling:

¾ cup (1½ sticks) margarine

¾ cup packed light brown sugar

6 tablespoons light corn syrup

3 cups pecan halves

3 tablespoons pareve whipping cream

2 ounces unsweetened chocolate, chopped

Pareve whipped cream or pareve vanilla ice cream, for serving

Homemade caramel sauce (p. 338) or store-bought, for serving

Preheat oven to 350°F.

For the crust: In a food processor, blend cookie crumbs, margarine, and vanilla. Press crumb mixture into bottom and sides of 9-inch pie dish. Bake crust for 5 minutes. Cool completely.

For the filling: Combine margarine, brown sugar, and corn syrup in saucepan. Bring to a boil, stirring often. Boil 1 minute. Stir in nuts and whipping cream. Boil until mixture thickens just slightly, about 3 minutes. Remove from heat and add chocolate. Stir until chocolate melts and mixture is well blended. Pour hot filling into crust and distribute evenly.

Bake for 10 minutes, or until filling bubbles all over. Let cool.

Serve with pareve whipped cream or pareve vanilla ice cream. Drizzle caramel sauce over pie or on the dessert plate under the pie.

Make Ahead

Pie can be made 2 days in advance. Store, covered, in the refrigerator but remove from refrigerator 30 minutes before serving so that it softens slightly. Freeze up to 3 months. Defrost in the refrigerator.

Apple Galette

This is a family favorite recipe during Rosh Hashanah and Succot or a beautiful fall dessert. It's great any time of year but I love to use the apples we pick ourselves on Succot in this pie. I use shortening in this recipe (the Earth Balance brand that is made from canola oil). It adds a flakiness and texture to the crust that makes a pie special. You can substitute margarine for the shortening if you prefer. Serve with the Red Wine Caramel Sauce (p. 338), if desired.

serves 10

Crust:

2½ cups all-purpose flour, divided

2 tablespoons sugar

1 teaspoon salt

¾ cup (1½ sticks) cold margarine, cut into ¼-inch pieces

½ cup cold shortening, cut into ¼-inch pieces

¼ teaspoon imitation butter extract (optional)

¼ cup chilled vodka

¼ cup cold water

Crunch Topping:

¾ cups all-purpose flour

¾ cup packed dark brown sugar

½ cup old-fashioned oats

6 tablespoons margarine, melted

Apple Filling:

¾ cup sugar

3 tablespoons all-purpose flour

1 teaspoon cinnamon

⅛ teaspoon salt

2 medium-sized McIntosh apples, or any sweet apple of your choice, peeled, cored, and sliced (approximately 4 cups sliced)

2 medium-sized Granny Smith apples, peeled, cored, and sliced (approximately 4 cups sliced)

3 tablespoons apricot preserves

1 egg yolk beaten with 1 teaspoon water

To prepare the crust: Combine 1½ cups of the flour, sugar, and salt in a food processor; blend. Add margarine, shortening, and butter extract (if using). Pulse a few times, until dough starts to pull together in clumps. Scrape sides of bowl and redistribute dough around blade. Add remaining 1 cup flour; pulse 4 to 6 times, until evenly distributed.

Transfer dough to a medium bowl. Gently mix in vodka and water. Do not over mix. Divide dough into 2 balls; flatten each into a 4-inch disc. Wrap in plastic wrap; refrigerate at least 1 hour and up to 2 days. Use half of the dough for this pie and store the rest for future use.

To prepare the crunch topping: In a medium bowl, combine flour, brown sugar, oats, and melted margarine. Stir to combine and set aside.

To prepare the apple filling: In a large bowl combine sugar, flour, cinnamon, and salt. Add apple slices and toss to coat.

Preheat oven to 375°F.

Make Ahead

Can be prepared 2 days ahead of time. Store the finished galette, covered, in the refrigerator or freeze up to 3 months. Defrost in the refrigerator. Rewarm, covered, in a warming drawer or 300°F oven. Dough can be prepared up to 3 months ahead of time, wrapped tightly in plastic wrap and then foil, and then stored in the freezer. Defrost in the refrigerator before rolling.

Lighten Up

Substitute 8 sheets phyllo dough for the traditional crust. To use the phyllo dough, unroll the thawed dough onto a work surface and cover with a damp cloth to keep from drying out. Place 1 sheet phyllo dough on a parchment-lined baking sheet. Spray dough lightly and evenly with nonstick cooking spray. Top with another sheet of phyllo and spray. Repeat process for a total of 8 sheets.

Leaving a 3 to 4 inch border, brush apricot preserves over the dough and top with ¼cup crunch mixture. Starting at the outer edge of the preserves, lay the apple slices in concentric circles and proceed with the rest of the recipe as directed. Bake 20 minutes uncovered, and then cover loosely and bake an additional 20 minutes, or until apples are cooked through.

To assemble: Remove dough from refrigerator. On a lightly floured piece of parchment paper, roll the dough into 14- to 15-inch circle. Leaving a 3- to 4-inch border, brush apricot preserves over center of dough. Place three-quarters of crunch mixture over apricot preserves. Starting at outer edge of apricot, and working your way towards the center, lay the apple slices in concentric circles, going around and adding layers until all apples are used up. Using the parchment paper to help, fold the dough border over apples. The dough will cover 2 to 3 inches of the filling. Sprinkle the top with remaining crunch.

Carefully slide the parchment paper with galette onto a rimless baking sheet. Brush the exposed dough with beaten egg yolk. Bake for 25 minutes. Remove from oven and carefully cover dough with foil to prevent burning. Return to oven and bake an additional 30 minutes.

Serve with Red Wine Caramel Sauce (page 338), if desired.

Shaved Chocolate Pound Cake

This is a classic, delicious, and great cake to have around anytime. My friend and piano teacher, Minda, shared it with me. She lived in Italy for many years and became an amazing cook there. We both love music and cooking and always have so much to chat about. Flouring the pan in addition to greasing it ensures that it will come out in one beautiful piece and present perfectly.

serves 8

Cake:

6 eggs
2 cups sugar
1 cup canola oil
1 teaspoon vanilla extract
1½ cups all-purpose flour
1 teaspoon baking powder
7 ounces good-quality bittersweet chocolate, shaved or grated

Optional Glaze:

1 cup semisweet chocolate chips
2 tablespoons canola oil

Preheat oven to 350°F.

Grease and flour a Bundt pan.

To make the cake: Beat eggs until light and fluffy with an electric mixer, about 3 minutes. With the mixer running, slowly pour in sugar, and then slowly add in oil and vanilla. Mix on low just until blended. Add flour and baking powder and mix until just combined. Do not overmix. Fold in grated chocolate. Pour batter into prepared pan.

Bake for 55 minutes or until a tester inserted comes out with a few crumbs on it. Cool in pan for 10 minutes. Remove from pan and cool completely.

Prepare the glaze, if using: In a small saucepan, over very low heat, melt chocolate chips and oil, stirring while heating. Pour glaze decoratively over cake.

Make Ahead

Can be prepared 2 days ahead of time. Store, covered, in the refrigerator or freeze up to 3 months. Defrost in the refrigerator.

Chocolate Cookies and Cream Cake

Make Ahead

The frosted cake freezes well. Place uncovered in the freezer until frozen solid, at least 4 hours. Once frozen, wrap with plastic wrap and then with foil. Freeze for up to 1 month. Or freeze the cake unfrosted, and then frost it while it's still frozen. Allow to defrost in the refrigerator fully before serving. Alternatively, the cake can be prepared 1 day in advance. Store, covered, in the refrigerator.

This cake is a big hit with kids: moist cake with lots and lots of cookies throughout the cake and frosting. Truth is, adults love it just as much because sandwich cookies are a secret comfort food for everyone. I like to freeze the cake layers for at least 2 hours before frosting. This cake decorating trick makes frosting easy by keeping crumbs to a minimum.

makes 10 servings

Cake:

2 cups all-purpose flour
¾ cup unsweetened cocoa powder
1½ teaspoons baking powder
1 teaspoon salt
½ teaspoon baking soda
3 large eggs
1 egg yolk
2 cups sugar
1 cup (2 sticks) margarine, melted
1 cup non-dairy creamer
2 tablespoons distilled white vinegar
1½ cups finely crumbled chocolate sandwich cookies

Frosting:

2 (8-ounce) packages Tofutti cream cheese
¾ cup (1½ sticks) margarine, at room temperature
3¾ cups confectioners' sugar
2 teaspoons vanilla extract
1½ cups crumbled chocolate sandwich cookies, divided

Preheat oven to 350°F. Grease two 9-inch cake pans.

For the cake: Combine flour, cocoa, baking powder, salt, and baking soda in a large mixing bowl. Set aside.

With an electric mixer, beat eggs, egg yolk, sugar, and melted margarine in a separate large mixing bowl until fluffy. Set aside.

Whisk together creamer and vinegar in a small bowl. Add to egg mixture alternately with flour, beginning and ending with dry ingredients. Fold in crumbled cookies until incorporated.

Pour batter evenly into prepared pans. Bake about 25 to 30 minutes, or until a tester inserted in the center comes out with moist crumbs. Let rest in pans 5 minutes. Turn the cakes out onto a rack and cool completely.

To prepare the frosting: With an electric mixer, cream together cream cheese and margarine in a large bowl. Beat in confectioners' sugar and vanilla until smooth.

To assemble: Place one cake layer, dome-side down, on a cake platter. Cover flat surface with frosting. Sprinkle with ½ cup of crumbled sandwich cookies. Top with second cake layer, right-side up. Spread remaining frosting over top and sides. Sprinkle sides or top of cake with remaining 1 cup crumbled cookies, pressing into frosting. Store in refrigerator, lightly covered until ready to serve.

Peach and Blueberry Crisp with Cinnamon Crumble Topping

This is one of my favorite desserts anytime. I admit, I even eat the leftovers for breakfast, lunch, or even a snack (shhh, don't tell my kids). The crumbly topping (there is a lot of it, because that's how I like it) with the sweet fruit filling is really sublime. I make it with apples instead of peaches when they are not in season, and sometimes with apples and pears when blueberries are hard to find. Just replace the existing peaches and blueberries with equal amounts of peeled, sliced apples and pears—or any combination of fruits you like. Only blueberries, strawberries, and other tender berries would need any pre-cooking, but you should increase the baking time for apples or pears and bake until the fruits are tender.

serves 10

Filling:

3 cups blueberries

¼ cup granulated sugar

7 peaches, peeled, cored, and sliced (about 5 cups)

2 tablespoons all-purpose flour

Topping:

1 cup all-purpose flour

1¼ cups old-fashioned oats

1 cup chopped walnuts

½ cup packed light brown sugar

4 tablespoons granulated sugar

1 teaspoon cinnamon

¼ teaspoon nutmeg

½ teaspoon salt

¾ cup margarine, melted, or canola oil

Pareve whipping cream or pareve ice cream, for garnish (optional)

Preheat oven to 350°F.

For the filling: Combine 1½ cups blueberries with ¼ cup sugar in a large saucepan over low heat. Cook until berries soften and release their juices a little, stirring frequently, about 5 minutes. Remove from heat and cool slightly. Add peaches, remaining blueberries, and flour and stir until combined. Transfer mixture to an ungreased 13 x 9 x 2-inch baking dish.

For the topping: In a large bowl, mix flour, oats, walnuts, brown sugar, granulated sugar, cinnamon, nutmeg, and salt. Gradually add melted margarine or oil and mix until small moist clumps form. Sprinkle crumble over fruit, covering the whole top.

Bake for about 45 minutes, until topping is crisp and golden. Cool slightly. Serve with pareve whipping cream or pareve ice cream.

Passover

For the filling, use 1½ tablespoons potato starch in place of 2 tablespoons flour. For the topping, use 1½ cups potato starch in place of flour, and 1 cup matzo cake meal in place of oats.

Make Ahead

Can be prepared 1 day ahead of time. Store, covered, in the refrigerator. Serve at room temperature or rewarm, covered, in a warming drawer or 300°F oven.

Banana Cake with Warm Praline Topping

Feel free to make this banana cake with or without the topping. It's delicious on its own but I like to serve this on Friday nights when the banana pecan topping can be kept warm on a warming tray or in a warming drawer. It's also a winter favorite. The cake can be made a day or two ahead of time or stored in the freezer for a great make-ahead option. The banana-pecan topping needs to be made the same day it is served.

serves 8

Cake:

1⅓ cups granulated sugar

½ cup (1 stick) margarine, at room temperature

2 eggs

2 to 3 overripe bananas

2 cups all-purpose flour

1 teaspoon baking powder

1 teaspoon baking soda

½ teaspoon salt

½ cup vanilla soy milk

1 tablespoon distilled white vinegar

1 teaspoon vanilla extract

Topping:

¾ cup packed light brown sugar

6 tablespoons margarine

3 tablespoons non-dairy creamer

½ cup chopped toasted pecans (p. 335)

3 ripe but firm bananas, sliced

1 cup pareve whipping cream, whipped to soft peaks, for serving

Preheat oven to 350°F. Grease an 8½ x 4½-inch loaf pan.

To prepare the cake: With an electric mixer, beat sugar and margarine in a large mixing bowl until light and fluffy. Add eggs, one at a time, beating after each addition. Add bananas and mix until incorporated. Stir in flour, baking powder, baking soda, and salt. Beat in soy milk, vinegar, and vanilla.

Pour batter into prepared pan; let rest 10 minutes. Bake 55 to 60 minutes, or until a tester inserted in the center comes out with moist crumbs. Remove from oven and cool 10 minutes. Invert onto a wire rack to cool completely.

To prepare the topping: Melt sugar and margarine in a large saucepan over medium heat. Stir until smooth. Whisk in creamer until fully incorporated. Add pecans and bananas; toss to coat with sauce. Turn off the heat. Keep warm until ready to serve.

To serve, spoon warm banana pecan topping over individual slices of cake. Top with freshly whipped cream.

Make Ahead

Cake can be prepared 2 days ahead of time. Store, covered, in the refrigerator or freeze up to 3 months. Defrost in the refrigerator. Rewarm, covered, in a warming drawer or 300°F oven. Make topping shortly before serving.

Simply the Best Babka Ever

Make Ahead

This freezes well. Wrap tightly in plastic wrap and store in freezer. Defrost in the refrigerator and serve at room temperature.

This recipe first appeared in the EMUNAH cookbook, Chef's Confidential. *The recipe was such a hit that we had to include it in this book, too. No one can possibly say whether chocolate, cinnamon, or vanilla is the best filling, so we decided to include them all! This recipe makes enough for you to make some with each filling. Instant or rapid rise yeast does not require proofing in warm water. It works best in this recipe.*

makes 4 loaves

Babka:

7 cups all-purpose flour plus 1 additional cup, as needed, divided

6 (¼-ounce) packages or 4½ tablespoons instant or rapid rise yeast

¾ cup granulated sugar

1 tablespoon vanilla sugar

1½ cups margarine, melted

1¾ cups warm water

2 eggs

2 egg yolks

2 teaspoons salt

Crumb Topping:

4 tablespoons margarine, at room temperature

1 cup all-purpose flour

¾ cup granulated sugar

To make the babka: Combine flour, yeast, sugar, vanilla sugar, margarine, water, eggs, egg yolks, and salt in a large bowl. Turn out on floured board and knead 5 minutes, adding up to 1 cup of flour if dough is sticky. Allow to rise in a large bowl covered with plastic wrap for 1½ hours.

For the crumb topping: Crumble margarine with flour and sugar in a small bowl, using fingertips.

Spray 4 (10-inch) loaf pans with nonstick cooking spray.

Divide dough into 8 pieces. Using a rolling pin, roll each piece into a ½-inch-thick rectangle, the length of the loaf pan. Spread filling of choice (see measurement on filling recipe) onto each rectangle, within 1 inch of borders. Roll from long side, like a jelly roll. Twist 2 rolls around each other and place a twist in each pan. Using all the crumbs, sprinkle a quarter of crumb topping on of each babka. Let rise for 30 minutes.

Preheat oven to 350°F.

Bake for 30 minutes. Cool for 15 minutes in pan, then remove and cool completely on wire rack.

Chocolate Babka Filling

makes enough for 4 babkas

1 cup margarine, melted
1 (4.1-ounce) box instant chocolate pudding
1 egg
½ cup water
2 cups sugar
1 cup unsweetened cocoa powder

In a small bowl, combine margarine, chocolate pudding, egg, water, sugar, and cocoa. Use an eighth of this recipe for each section of dough.

Cinnamon Babka Filling

makes enough for 2 babkas

1 cup packed dark brown sugar
4 tablespoons cinnamon
½ cup margarine, melted, or ¼ cup coconut oil, melted

In a small bowl, combine brown sugar, cinnamon, and melted margarine. Use a quarter of this recipe for each section of dough.

Vanilla Babka Filling

makes enough for 2 babkas

½ cup canola oil
½ cup granulated sugar
½ cup confectioners' sugar
2 tablespoons vanilla sugar

In a small bowl, mix oil, sugar, confectioners' sugar, and vanilla sugar. Stir until fully blended. Use a quarter of this mixture for each section of dough.

Hazelnut-Mocha Mousse with Caramel Crunch

Meringue Mousse with Balsamic Berries

Meringue Mousse with Balsamic Berries

No need for homemade meringues here, as they get crumbled into the mousse. You can replace the meringues with chocolate sandwich cookies for a delicious cookies-and-cream mousse.

serves 10

Mousse:

½ cup berry jam of choice

12 meringue cookies, coarsely crumbled

2 cups pareve whipping cream, whipped to soft peaks

Balsamic Berries:

1½ cups sliced strawberries

1 cup blueberries

3 tablespoons sugar

2 tablespoons balsamic vinegar

To prepare the mousse: Heat jam in microwave until just melted; cool slightly. Fold jam and meringues into whipped cream in a large bowl until they are swirled but not completely mixed. Spoon into individual dishes and refrigerate until ready to serve.

To prepare the berries: Combine strawberries, blueberries, sugar, and balsamic vinegar in a medium bowl; mix well. Let mixture sit 10 minutes before spooning over mousse.

Passover

Perfect as-is!

Prep Ahead

The mousse needs a minimum of 4 hours to chill before serving.

Make Ahead

Meringue mousse can be prepared a day ahead of time and stored, covered, in the refrigerator. Top with berries before serving.

Tip

Serve this in store-bought chocolate cups for a nice presentation. Mash the berries slightly for a more rustic feel.

Hazelnut-Mocha Crunch Mousse

This recipe uses what I refer to as pareve Nutella cream, that luscious and delicious chocolate hazelnut spread. Many Israeli companies make a pareve version that work perfectly well here. Top with the balsamic berries above for a lovely fruit-nut-chocolate combination.

serves 8

Mousse:

1 cup pareve whipping cream

⅓ teaspoon instant espresso powder or instant coffee

½ cup hazelnut chocolate spread

Caramel Crunch:

9 whole graham crackers, coarsely crushed

1 cup old-fashioned oats

1 teaspoon vanilla extract

¼ cup canola oil

¾ cup caramel or butterscotch chips

To prepare the mousse: Using an electric mixer, beat cream on high until soft peaks form. Sprinkle in instant espresso powder and mix until dissolved into cream. Add chocolate spread and mix just until blended. Spoon into decorative cups or chocolate shells so that they set nicely with smooth tops. Alternatively, chill in bowl and assemble later. Refrigerate at least 4 hours or overnight.

To prepare the caramel crunch: Preheat oven to 350°F. Line a baking sheet with parchment paper. Combine the graham crackers, oats, vanilla extract, and canola oil. Bake for 8 minutes. Remove from oven and immediately stir in the caramel chips. The heat of the hot crumbs will help melt the chips and distribute the flavor. Let cool completely and sprinkle with the caramel crunch and balsamic berries if desired.

Passover

Mousse is Passover perfect as-is. For Caramel Crunch, use 1 cup matzo farfel and, ¾ cup of any type of Passover cookies, macaroons, or chocolate chips in place of graham crackers and oats.

Prep Ahead

The mousse needs a minimum of 4 hours to chill before serving.

Make Ahead

Mousse can be prepared 2 days ahead of time and stored, covered, in the refrigerator. Garnish with berries before serving.

Cherry-Almond Coffee Cake

This is a delicious cake to serve to sleepover guests. I love it as a pre-Shabbos treat or as a morning coffee sweet. Make it a day ahead of time: the vinegar and extracts meld better after a day or two. The cake just gets better and better. It works great with any pie filling. Try apple for Rosh Hashanah or raspberry, just because.

Make Ahead

This cake is best made a day or two ahead of serving.

Tip

Ideally, the cake should be made in an 8-inch springform pan. The high sides give it plenty of room for the rising when it bakes. It can, however, be made in a 9-inch springform—just spread the batter more thinly.

serves 10

- ½ cup (1 stick) margarine, at room temperature
- 3 tablespoons confectioners' sugar
- 1 cup plus 2 teaspoons granulated sugar, divided
- 2 eggs
- 1 teaspoon vanilla extract
- ½ teaspoon almond extract
- 2 cups all-purpose flour
- 1 teaspoon baking powder
- 1 teaspoon baking soda
- ½ teaspoon salt
- 1 cup vanilla soy milk or almond milk
- 1 tablespoon distilled white vinegar
- 1 (21-ounce) can cherry pie filling
- ½ cup sliced almonds, toasted (p. 335)
- ½ teaspoon ground cinnamon

Preheat oven to 350°F. Grease an 8-inch (3-inch deep) springform pan.

With an electric mixer, beat margarine with confectioners' sugar and 1 cup granulated sugar in a large bowl until creamy. Add eggs, one at a time, beating after each addition. Stir in vanilla and almond extracts.

Whisk together flour, baking powder, baking soda, and salt in a small mixing bowl. Mix half of the flour mixture into the egg mixture. In a small dish, stir soy milk and vinegar together. Beat soy milk and vinegar into egg mixture, and then add the remaining flour mixture. The batter will be thick. Spread 2 cups of the batter into prepared pan; spoon cherry filling on top. Spread remaining batter over filling. Sprinkle with almonds, cinnamon, and 2 remaining teaspoons sugar.

Bake 55 to 60 minutes, or until a tester inserted in the center comes out with moist crumbs.

Sweet Apple Cake with Orange Essence

Everyone must have an apple cake to serve on Rosh Hashanah. I've made and tasted dozens over the years. This one is my favorite. I especially love it because it freezes well and it's even better made in advance. Let it sit on the counter for 24 hours, covered, with a cake dome. The flavors are delicious.

Make Ahead

Can be prepared 2 days ahead of time. Store, covered, on the countertop or in the refrigerator. Freeze up to 3 months. Defrost in the refrigerator. Serve at room temperature.

serves 10

Filling:

6 Granny Smith apples, peeled, cored and cut into 1-inch chunks

5 tablespoons sugar

2 teaspoons cinnamon

Cake:

3 cups all-purpose flour

2 cups sugar

1 teaspoon baking powder

1 teaspoon kosher salt

4 eggs

1 cup canola oil

¼ cup orange juice

2½ teaspoons vanilla extract

⅓ cup craisins (optional)

Crumb Topping:

1 cup all-purpose flour

¾ cup sugar

¼ cup (½ stick) margarine, melted

1 teaspoon cinnamon

½ teaspoon orange zest (optional)

Preheat oven to 350°F. Grease a 10-inch tube pan and line the bottom with a ring of parchment paper.

For the filling: In a large bowl, toss the apples with the sugar and cinnamon and set aside.

For the cake: In a medium bowl, whisk together flour, sugar, baking powder, and salt. With an electric mixer, beat eggs, oil, orange juice, and vanilla. Gradually beat in the dry ingredients, mixing until combined. Stir in craisins and apple mixture with all of its juices. Do not overmix. Pour batter into prepared pan.

Make the crumble topping: In a small bowl, mix flour, sugar, margarine, cinnamon, and orange zest. Sprinkle over the top of the cake.

Bake for 1 hour 15 minutes. Cool completely.

Run a knife around the sides and center tube of pan and remove from pan. Cake will keep, well wrapped and refrigerated, for several days.

Meringue-Crusted Chocolate Cake

Passover

See below.

Make Ahead

Can be prepared 1 day ahead of time. Store, covered, in the refrigerator. Serve at room temperature. Do not freeze.

Tip

You can make your own cake flour by sifting together 2 cups all-purpose flour with ¼ cup cornstarch. Measure out 1⅔ cups of this mixture for this recipe and reserve the rest for another time.

The rustic appearance of this cake makes it gorgeous and irresistible. The outside is crispy with a swirled appearance and the inside is soft and rich. It's one of my oldest recipes that I cherish and make over and over again.

serves 10

1½ cups cake flour (don't have cake flour? see tip)

½ cup unsweetened cocoa powder

1 tablespoon baking powder

½ teaspoon salt

¾ cup plus 2 tablespoons non-dairy creamer

1½ tablespoons distilled white vinegar

1 teaspoon vanilla extract

2 teaspoons espresso or strong brewed coffee

4 eggs, 3 separated and 1 left whole

2 cups sugar, divided

½ cup (1 stick) margarine, at room temperature

1 cup mini chocolate chips

Preheat oven to 325°F. Grease a 9-inch springform pan.

Stir together flour, cocoa, baking powder, and salt in a small bowl; set aside. Mix non-dairy creamer, vinegar, vanilla, and espresso in a separate small bowl; set aside.

With an electric mixer, beat the 3 egg whites in a large mixing bowl until soft peaks form. Gradually add ¾ cup of the sugar, beating until stiff and glossy. Set aside.

In a separate large bowl, beat remaining 1¼ cups sugar, margarine, the 3 egg yolks, and the 1 whole egg until blended. Add reserved flour mixture, alternating with creamer mixture, beginning and ending with dry ingredients. Mix in chocolate chips. Set aside.

Spread two-thirds of the reserved egg white mixture (meringue) around the sides of the prepared pan (the inside perimeter should be covered in meringue, leaving the center empty). Spoon chocolate batter into the center. Top with the remaining egg white mixture. Using the tip of a knife, swirl the top, mixing chocolate and meringue.

Bake about 1 hour and 10 minutes, or until a toothpick comes out with moist crumbs (it should not be loose but very moist and fudgy on the tester). Cool completely. Run a sharp knife around pan to release sides.

Passover variation:

1 cup safflower or cottonseed oil
4 whole eggs
2¾ cups sugar, divided
1 cup potato starch
1 cup unsweetened cocoa powder
2 teaspoons espresso or strong brewed coffee
1½ teaspoons Passover vanilla extract
1½ cups mini chocolate chips
3 egg whites

Grease a 9-inch springform pan. Preheat oven to 325°F.

In a large bowl, stir together oil, 4 whole eggs, 2 cups sugar, potato starch, cocoa powder, coffee, vanilla, and chocolate chips. Mix until smooth.

With an electric mixer with whisk attachment, beat 3 egg whites until soft peaks form. Gradually add remaining ¾ cup sugar, and beat until stiff peaks form and meringue is glossy.

Spread two-thirds of the meringue around the sides of the prepared pan (the inside perimeter should be covered in meringue, leaving the center empty). Spoon chocolate batter into the center. Top with the remaining meringue. Using the tip of a knife, swirl the top, mixing chocolate and meringue.

Bake about 45 minutes to 1 hour until a toothpick comes out with moist crumbs (it should not be loose but very moist and fudgy on the tester). Cool completely. Run a sharp knife around pan to release sides.

Berry Custard Tart

This tart is delicious and so easy to make, but it will make you look like a pastry chef. Get creative with the fruit topping. I usually make the blueberries and then top with a variety of sliced fruit like strawberries, kiwi, and more blueberries. Want to make it even dressier? Add a layer of Lemon Curd (p. 338) on top of the cooked custard, and then top with cooked berries and garnish with fresh fruit.

makes 12 servings

Crust:

10 to 12 graham crackers, ground in a food processor (about 1½ cups)

⅓ cup unsalted margarine, melted

4 tablespoons sugar

⅛ teaspoon salt

Custard:

3 eggs

1½ cups Tofutti sour cream

½ cup sugar

1½ teaspoons vanilla extract

Topping:

1 tablespoon cornstarch

2 tablespoons water, divided

4 cups fresh or frozen berries (blueberries, strawberries, or a combination)

½ cup sugar

Garnish:

Fresh strawberries, blueberries, or other fruit (optional)

Put oven rack in middle position and preheat oven to 350°F.

To prepare the crust: Lightly grease a 10-inch tart pan with removable bottom. Stir together graham cracker crumbs, margarine, sugar, and salt in a medium bowl; press evenly on bottom and up the sides of tart pan. Bake until crisp, 10 to 12 minutes; cool on a rack to room temperature.

Reduce oven temperature to 325°F.

To prepare the custard: Whisk eggs, sour cream, sugar, and vanilla in a medium mixing bowl until smooth. Pour over prepared crust. Bake about 35 minutes, or until set. Cool to room temperature.

To prepare the topping: Dissolve cornstarch in 1 tablespoon of the water in a small bowl; set aside. Cook berries with sugar in a medium saucepan over medium heat. Add cornstarch mixture and remaining 1 tablespoon water. Simmer until thickened, stirring, about 10 minutes. If mixture is too thick, add an additional tablespoon water and stir. Cool slightly. Spoon over prepared custard.

Garnish with decorative fruit on top (optional). Refrigerate until ready to serve.

Make Ahead

This can be made a day or two ahead of time. Garnish just before serving. Store in the refrigerator

Tip

Short on time? Use canned blueberry pie filling on top. Use about ¾ cup to replace the cooked berries, though, because it is sweeter than the homemade version and will overwhelm the tart.

Chocolate Raspberry Cake

My friend Audrey gave me this cake recipe years ago and I've been enjoying it ever since. It has a sophistication and romance to it: rich chocolate mixed with sweet raspberries is an amazing combination. I often make it in a special shape like a flower or a heart for Sheva Brachos.

serves 8

Cake:

2 cups sugar

1 cup plus 2 tablespoons unsweetened cocoa powder

1¼ cups (2½ sticks) margarine

½ cup plus 3 tablespoons raspberry jam, divided

4 eggs

1 teaspoon vanilla extract

1 cup all-purpose flour

¼ teaspoon salt

Ganache:

½ cup pareve whipping cream

¾ cup chocolate chips

Passover

Use ¾ cup potato starch plus ¼ cup matzo cake meal in place of flour. Use Passover vanilla extract in place of pure vanilla extract and follow instructions.

Make Ahead

Can be prepared 1 day ahead of time. Store, covered, in the refrigerator or freeze up to 3 months. Defrost in the refrigerator.

Preheat oven to 350°F. Grease a 9-inch round cake pan.

To prepare the cake: Combine sugar and cocoa in a large mixing bowl; set aside.

Melt margarine and ½ cup of the jam in a small saucepan over low heat. Add to cocoa mixture; mix until well combined. Cool 5 minutes. Add eggs one at a time, beating after each addition. Stir in vanilla. Mix until smooth and satiny. Add flour and salt; mix until just combined. Do not over mix.

Pour batter into prepared pan; bake 15 minutes. Reduce heat to 325°F. Bake an additional 30 to 40 minutes, or until a tester inserted in the center comes out with moist crumbs. Cool for 15 minutes in pan then remove and cool completely.

When cool, spread remaining 3 tablespoons jam over top of the cake.

To prepare the ganache: Heat cream and chocolate chips in a small saucepan over low heat. Stir until smooth; pour over cooled cake. Cool.

Store in refrigerator until ready to serve. Take out 1 hour before serving. Serve at room temperature.

Hot Chocolate Pudding Cake

I love to serve this dessert in the Succah. It comes out of the oven warm and oozing with chocolate. It's delicious with pareve vanilla ice cream or whipped cream. The sides and top are cake-like while the center has a very soft chocolate pudding texture. Scoop it out and serve it in bowls. I also make it on Friday nights and keep it on a warming tray or in a warming drawer until serving time.

serves 8 to 10

- 2 cups all-purpose flour
- 4 teaspoons baking powder
- 1 teaspoon baking soda
- ⅛ teaspoon salt
- 2 teaspoons cinnamon
- ½ teaspoon chili powder (optional)
- 2 cups superfine sugar (see tip)
- 1 cup unsweetened cocoa powder, divided
- 2 teaspoons vanilla extract
- 1 cup non-dairy creamer or soy milk
- ½ cup canola oil
- 1 cup packed dark brown sugar
- 1¼ cups water
- 2 tablespoons dark rum

Preheat oven to 350°F. Grease a 2½-quart soufflé dish, oven-to-table bowl, or Pyrex dish (I like to use an old-fashioned charlotte dish). This can also be made in an 8 x 8-inch baking dish.

In a small bowl, combine flour, baking powder, baking soda, salt, cinnamon, chili powder, superfine sugar, and ½ cup cocoa. In another bowl, mix vanilla, non-dairy creamer, and oil. Pour wet mixture into dry ingredients and mix until just combined. Pour into prepared dish and smooth top.

In a small bowl, stir remaining ½ cup cocoa and brown sugar. Sprinkle over the entire top of batter in pan.

Bring water to a boil in microwave or in a small pot. Gently pour water over the top of cake. Then pour rum on top of the water. Do not mix or stir.

Bake for 30 minutes. The top of the cake should be puffy and the sides set. The middle of the cake should jiggle when you shake the pan and appear loose.

Make Ahead

Best served fresh and warm. Can be prepared 1 day ahead of time and rewarmed before serving.

Tip

Superfine sugar is finer and dissolves faster than regular granulated sugar. It's available in supermarkets on the baking aisle. If you would like to make it at home, place 2¼ cups granulated sugar in a food processor and blend for 1 to 2 minutes until the sugar feels like fine sand, letting the sugar dust settle before opening your food processor to check. Remeasure the correct amount for the recipe before using.

Sorbet, Every Which Way

Sorbet is the perfect finale to a rich meal, or the ideal snack in the summertime and so easy to make! My kids bought me a sorbet maker for Mother's day a few years ago, and we make tons of flavors. These are a few of our favorites. It's easiest in a sorbet maker, but I've included a great technique for anyone who does not own one.

Pomegranate Sorbet with Mini Chocolate Chips

Pomegranate juice makes this sorbet a stunning red, but lends a more sophisticated flavor over sweeter berry sorbets.

makes 1 quart

1 cup sugar
½ cup water
2 cups pure pomegranate juice (like POM)
½ cup orange juice
¾ cup sliced strawberries
½ cup mini chocolate chips (optional)
½ cup pomegranate seeds (p. 104)

Heat sugar and water in a saucepan over low heat. Stir until sugar has melted, about 3 minutes. Add pomegranate juice and orange juice and bring to a simmer. Remove from heat. Chill mixture for ½ hour in the refrigerator. Add strawberries. With an immersion blender, purée until smooth.

Pour the pomegranate mixture in an ice cream maker and freeze according to the manufacturer's instructions. During the last 10 minutes of churning, add the mini chocolate chips.

Alternatively, freeze mixture for 45 minutes. With immersion blender purée it again and refreeze for another 45 minutes. Repeat this process 4 times. Add mini chocolate chips after the final blending. Then freeze until ready to serve.

Scoop the sorbet into dessert bowls and garnish with pomegranate seeds.

Passover

Perfect as-is!

Make Ahead

This must be made numerous hours in advance. Store, covered, in the freezer for up to 3 months. Best stored in a glass container.

Chocolate Sorbet with Salted Pretzels and Chocolate Ribbons

Passover

Use Passover vanilla extract in place of vanilla extract. Omit pretzels.

Make Ahead

This must be made numerous hours in advance. Store, covered, in the freezer for up to 3 months. Best stored in a glass container.

The icy palate of chocolate sorbet is a much better end after an already-rich meal. For extra deliciousness, fold in some crunchy, salty pretzels and ribbons of melted chocolate.

makes 1 quart

- 2¼ cups water, divided
- 1 cup sugar
- ¾ cup unsweetened cocoa powder
- Pinch of salt
- 6 ounces bittersweet or semisweet chocolate, finely chopped
- ½ teaspoon vanilla extract
- ½ cup chopped salted pretzels (optional)
- ½ cup chocolate chips, melted (optional)

In a large saucepan, whisk together 1½ cups water with the sugar, cocoa powder, and salt. Bring to a boil, whisking frequently. Let it boil, continuing to whisk for 1 minute.

Remove from the heat and stir in the chocolate until it's melted, then stir in the vanilla and the remaining ¾ cup water. Whisk until smooth.

Chill mixture completely in the refrigerator, then freeze it in your ice cream maker according to manufacturer's instructions. This sorbet tends to take a few extra minutes to thicken. If using the pretzels and chocolate ribbons: Sprinkle in chopped pretzels and drizzle in melted chocolate during the final 5 minutes of churning. The chocolate strands will freeze while the sorbet mixes.

Alternatively, freeze the mixture for 45 minutes. With immersion blender purée it again and refreeze for another 45 minutes. Repeat this process 4 times. Fold in pretzels and chocolate ribbons, and then freeze until ready to serve.

Mango Sorbet

Passover

Perfect as-is!

Make Ahead

This must be made numerous hours in advance. Store, covered, in the freezer for up to 3 months. Best stored in a glass container.

Like a delicious tropical get-away.

makes 1 quart

- 3 ripe mangos, peeled and chopped (reserve as much pulp and juice as possible)
- ⅔ cup sugar
- ⅔ cup water
- 4 teaspoons fresh lime juice
- Pinch of salt
- Shredded coconut, for garnish

Using an immersion blender or a standard blender, purée mangos, sugar, water, lime juice, and a pinch of salt. Chill for 30 minutes in refrigerator, and then freeze it in your ice cream maker according to manufacturer's instructions.

Alternatively, freeze mixture for 45 minutes. With immersion blender purée it again and refreeze for another 45 minutes. Repeat this process 4 times. Then freeze until ready to serve. Garnish with coconut, if desired.

Chocolate Sorbet with Salted Pretzels and Chocolate Ribbons

Mango Sorbet with Coconut

Pomegranate Sorbet with Mini Chocolate Chips

עוגיות

COOKIES

I am a cookie monster, and I rarely meet a homemade cookie that I do not like. I have dozens of cookie recipes that I make and store in the freezer. Frozen cookies are my favorite, and all these recipes for cookies and bars freeze well. They are the best treat, any time, day or night. I think I turned my whole family into cookie monsters too. I often hear the rustling of plastic storage bags full of cookies from the kitchen, late at night—but who can resist? Selecting cookie recipes for this book was tough. It's so hard to choose!

TROUBLESHOOTING COOKIE CHART

I get lots and lots of questions about baking issues. There is nothing more frustrating than putting effort into baking, only to have the results not turn out as expected. I've created a chart to help with all the possible causes of the misbehaving cookies. Always make sure your oven is calibrated correctly and keep a thermometer inside the oven to double check the cooking temperature accuracy.

PROBLEM	POSSIBLE CAUSES	SOLUTIONS
DOUGH		
Dough too sticky to roll	Dough is not thoroughly chilled or has too little flour.	Cover and chill dough.
Dough is too dry	Dough has too much flour.	Dribble in vegetable oil until the dough reaches desired consistency.
Dough cracks when rolling	Dough is too cold.	Cover dough and let sit at room temperature to warm slightly.
COOKIES		
Cookies crumble and taste dry and hard	The dough has been overmixed.	Stop mixing when the dough is just mixed. Do not overdo it.
	The dough has been overbaked.	Remove the cookies from the oven a few minutes earlier, when they're a bit softer.
	Dry fruits or coconut give the cookies a dry texture.	Soak dry fruit in water a few minutes to absorb some moisture so it won't pull it from the cookie.
	Excessive salt.	Measure salt accurately with measuring spoons and level the top.
	Too much water.	When substituting margarine for butter in a recipe, use a brand that has the least amount of water. The water in margarine prevents the fat from coating the flour.
	Not enough fat.	Measure fat accurately. ½ cup is 1 whole stick, not ½ stick
Cookies stick to baking pan	Cookie sheets not properly prepared according to the recipe.	Use parchment paper or Silpats to line pans or lightly grease pan before using. (Cookies spread more on greased sheets so parchment paper is preferred.)
	Cookies are still too hot from the oven to be moving.	Let the cookies cool on the pans for a few minutes before transferring to wire racks.
Cookies break when removed from baking sheets	Cookies are still too hot from the oven to be moving.	Let the cookies cool on the pans for a few minutes before transferring to wire racks.
Cookies bake unevenly	Dough was not rolled or portioned to a consistent thickness or size.	Use spring-release scoops for forming equal portions for drop cookies quickly and easily. They're available in a variety of sizes at kitchenware or restaurant supply stores.
	Oven bakes unevenly.	Rotate pans midway through baking.
Cookies are oily	Type of fat used.	Do not substitute shortening, stick butter, or margarine for vegetable oil. Margarine is softer and more oily than butter, switch to shortening if you're getting oily cookies.
	Cookie dough was not chilled adequately before baking.	Chill longer.
	Too much fat.	Add flour.
Cookies fall apart	Used diet or whipped spreads, which are full of air and water.	Use stick butter, margarine or shortening.

COOKIES CONTINUED

Problem	Cause	Solution
Cookies too flat and spread while baking	Dough was not properly chilled.	Chill dough, form cookies, and then chill on pans again before baking.
	Pans were greased too much.	Use parchment paper to line your cookies sheets for less spread than greased cookies sheets.
	Dough was placed on warm baking sheets	Use room temperature baking sheets or, even better, chilled ones.
	Used a low-fat margarine.	Low-fat margarine has excess water in it. Use Earth-Balance margarine sticks that are made from canola oil.
	Butter/margarine was not properly chilled.	Use fully chilled butter/margarine in the batter and chill the cookies before baking.
	Wrong type of flour.	Use cake flour instead of all-purpose. It has more moisture and will therefore puff more. (Note that the cookies will be softer and paler, too.) Additionally, adding 1 to 2 tablespoons flour can sometimes help cookies puff more.
	Dough not acidic enough.	Acidic doughs and batters (such as those made with baking powder) set faster and yield puffier cookies, but do not brown as well. Use 1 teaspoon baking powder to 1 cup flour.
	Too much butter in the recipe.	Use shortening instead of butter (or a combo). Butter melts faster than solid shortening and cookies will spread more if made with all butter. Margarine does not melt as fast as butter. A combination of margarine and shortening yields a soft but crunchy cookie.
	Over-crowding on cookie sheet.	Make smaller cookies, they'll puff better than larger ones.
Cookies too puffy	Used shortening as the only fat in the cookies, which can make them puffy.	Use all butter/margarine or half shortening+half butter/margarine.
	Dough too cold.	Bring the dough to room temperature before baking, which will make them spread and be thinner.
Cookies not chewy	Baked too long.	Remove the cookies a few minutes before they are done, while their centers are still soft and not quite cooked through. The edges should be slightly golden but the middle will still look slightly raw.
	Didn't have enough moisture or fat in the dough.	Use 2 egg yolks instead of one whole egg to add moisture and fat to the cookie for a chewier texture.
	Used only granulated sugar, which yields a crispier cookie.	Substituting half brown sugar for the white sugar will make a chewier cookie. Dark brown sugar has more molasses and will yield a chewier cookie than light brown sugar.
Cookies aren't crispy	Didn't bake long enough.	Bake cookies a few minutes longer than suggested and immediately remove them to wire racks to cool.
	Type of fat used.	Make with all butter.
	Used too much fat.	Replace the egg called for in the recipe with milk for a crispier cookie.
	Brown sugar makes cookies chewier.	Use more white sugar than brown to give more crispiness.
	The dough was too acidic.	A less acidic batter spreads more, yielding crispier cookies. Substitute ½ teaspoon baking soda per cup of flour for the baking powder called for in the recipe. The cookies will also brown better.
	The dough didn't have enough moisture.	Use a little bit more liquid in the batter to help the cookies to spread more.
	Type of sugar used.	Substitute 1 tablespoon of corn syrup for 1 tablespoon of the sugar called for in the recipe; it will make the cookies crispier and browner.

Cinnamon and Chocolate Chip Mandelbrot

Make Ahead

Can be prepared 2 days ahead of time. Store, covered, or freeze up to 3 months. Serve at room temperature.

This is my friend Emuna's famous Mandelbrot recipe. She makes them often and gives them as gifts, only sharing the recipe with special friends like me. (And now you!) Make sure the toasted nuts are not warm when you add them to the batter, as they could melt the chocolate chips.

makes 2 dozen

1 cup canola oil

1 cup plus 5 tablespoons sugar, divided

3 eggs

3 cups all-purpose flour

2 teaspoons baking powder

1 cup chocolate chips

1 cup finely chopped toasted pecans (p. 335)

1 teaspoon ground cinnamon

Preheat oven to 375°F. Lightly grease two baking sheets.

With an electric mixer, beat oil, 1 cup of the sugar, and eggs until thick. Add flour and baking powder; mix well. Fold in chocolate chips and pecans. Divide dough into four loaves, about 12-inches by 3-inches; place on prepared sheets and set aside.

Combine remaining 5 tablespoons sugar with cinnamon in a small bowl; sprinkle over loaves. Bake 15 to 18 minutes. Cool for 5 minutes.

Cut loaves into ½-inch-thick slices. Turn cookies on their sides and continue to bake until golden, an additional 5 to 7 minutes.

Variation

White Chocolate–Cranberry Mandelbrot: Substitute 1 cup white chocolate chips for the semisweet chocolate chips. Substitute 1 cup dried cranberries for the pecans. Sprinkle with 2 tablespoons sugar instead of sugar-cinnamon mixture.

Apricot, White Chocolate, and Pecan Oatmeal Cookies

Marbled Chocolate Chip Cookies

Ballpark Cookies

Ballpark Cookies

I call these "ballpark" cookies because they include chocolate chips, salty pretzels, and peanuts—all flavors that remind me of the baseball park. I love the pretzels and the nuts together. It's an awesome contrast in flavor: salty pretzels and nuts to sweet batter with chocolate. I use pareve chocolate lentils, which are similar to M&M's and sold in most kosher markets to make these cookies non-dairy. I use the small twist mini pretzels in this recipe. They have the perfect thickness to add a real pretzel crunch to the cookie. These cookies freeze well.

Make Ahead

Can be prepared 2 days ahead of time. Store, covered, or freeze up to 3 months. Serve at room temperature.

makes 3 dozen

1 cup (2 sticks) margarine, at room temperature
1 cup packed light brown sugar
½ cup granulated sugar
1 egg
1 teaspoon vanilla extract
2¼ cups all-purpose flour
1 teaspoon baking soda
½ cup pareve M&M's (chocolate lentils), chocolate chips, white chocolate chips, or any combination
¾ cup coarsely chopped pretzels
½ cup roasted salted peanuts or chopped pecans

Preheat oven to 350°F.

With an electric mixer, cream together margarine, brown sugar, and granulated sugar until fluffy, about 4 minutes. Beat in egg and vanilla. On low speed add flour and baking soda. Fold in M&M's, pretzels, and peanuts.

Drop by rounded tablespoonfuls onto 2 ungreased baking sheets. Bake 10 to 12 minutes until lightly browned. Let cool on baking sheet for 1 to 2 minutes before removing to wire rack to finish cooling.

Marbled Chocolate Chip Cookies

Make Ahead

Can be prepared 2 days ahead of time. Store, covered, or freeze up to 3 months. Serve at room temperature.

This cookie is a cookie mashup: regular chocolate chip cookies mixed with chocolate cookie dough studded with white chocolate chips. The two doughs are made together until the last step, and are then rolled side by side to make a yin-yang, marbled effect on the cookie. It's the best of both worlds all in one cookie, and they are quite impressive to look at too. These freeze well.

makes 2½ dozen

- 2¼ cups all-purpose flour
- 1 teaspoon baking soda
- ¾ teaspoon salt
- 1 cup (2 sticks) unsalted margarine, melted and cooled slightly
- 1 cup packed light brown sugar
- ½ cup granulated sugar
- 2 large eggs
- 1 teaspoon vanilla extract
- ¼ cup unsweetened cocoa powder
- 1 cup white chocolate chips
- 1 cup semisweet chocolate chips

Preheat oven to 375°F.

Combine flour, baking soda, and salt in a medium bowl; set aside. Using an electric mixer, beat margarine, brown sugar, and granulated sugar in a large bowl until well blended. Add eggs and vanilla; beat until smooth. Stir in flour mixture until just incorporated.

Spoon half of the dough into a separate mixing bowl; stir in cocoa powder. Add white chocolate chips and set aside. Stir chocolate chips into bowl with plain dough. If the dough is too sticky, place both bowls in the refrigerator, covered, for 10 minutes (or up to 6 hours).

To shape the cookies, take a rounded teaspoonful of one dough and a rounded teaspoonful of the other dough; roll them together between your palms to form a single ball. Place on 2 ungreased baking sheets, leaving about 2 inches between each cookie.

Bake until golden around the edges but still soft on top, about 10 minutes. Cool 5 minutes on pan before removing to wire racks.

Apricot, White Chocolate, and Pecan Oatmeal Cookies

These cookies are sweet, crunchy, and chunky: all of my favorites things in a cookie. Substitute any type of nut or dried fruit and use chocolate chips if you prefer, but the combination of apricots, white chips, and pecans is spectacular. Like most cookies, these freeze well.

makes 2½ to 3 dozen

- ¾ cup plus 2 tablespoons margarine, at room temperature
- ½ cup packed light brown sugar
- ½ cup granulated sugar
- 1 egg
- 1 teaspoon vanilla extract
- 1¼ cups all-purpose flour
- 1 teaspoon baking powder
- 2½ cups old-fashioned oats
- ½ cup chopped dried apricots
- ½ cup chopped toasted pecans (p. 335)
- ¼ cup white chocolate chips

Preheat oven to 375°F. Grease two baking sheets or line with parchment paper or Silpats.

With an electric mixer, cream together margarine, brown sugar, and granulated sugar until light and fluffy, about 4 minutes. Beat in egg and vanilla. On low speed, add flour and baking powder. Add oats, apricots, pecans, and chocolate chips; mix until completely incorporated.

Drop dough by rounded tablespoonfuls onto prepared baking sheets. Bake until just brown around the edges, about 9 to 12 minutes. Cool 2 minutes before removing to wire racks.

Make Ahead

Can be prepared 2 days ahead of time. Store, covered, or freeze up to 3 months. Serve at room temperature.

Dipping our cookies in chocolate was as much fun for me as it was for the children at Bet Elazraki Children's Home.

Hermits

Make Ahead

Can be prepared 2 days ahead of time. Store, covered, or freeze up to 3 months. Serve at room temperature.

"Hermits" have been popular since the 1800s and no one seems to know where the name came from. The various recipes include a nice spice blend, nuts, and raisins or dates, a combination that bursts with fall flavors. This recipe is well-balanced and delicious. Use any type of molasses in the recipe, and stash finished cookies in the freezer for later.

makes 3 dozen

1 cup sugar
¾ cup (1½ sticks) margarine, at room temperature
¼ cup molasses
1 egg
2¼ cups all-purpose flour
2 teaspoons baking soda
1 teaspoon ground cinnamon
½ teaspoon ground ginger
½ teaspoon ground cloves
½ cup chopped walnuts
¼ cup golden raisins
¼ cup dark raisins

Preheat the oven to 350°F. Line two baking sheets with parchment paper or Silpats.

With an electric mixer, cream together sugar, margarine, molasses, and egg until fluffy, about 4 minutes. Add flour, baking soda, cinnamon, ginger, and cloves; mix well. Stir in walnuts and both raisins.

Drop by tablespoonfuls onto prepared baking sheets. Bake 8 to 10 minutes, until just brown around the edges. Cool 3 minutes before removing to wire racks. Store in an airtight container.

Mocha Chip Cookies

Passover

Use ¾ cup potato starch plus ¼ cup matzo cake meal in place of flour. Use Passover vanilla extract instead of pure vanilla extract.

Make Ahead

Can be prepared 2 days ahead of time. Store, covered, or freeze up to 3 months. Serve at room temperature.

Chocolate and coffee mixed together in this great cookie makes it dark and delicious. Oh, and it doesn't require a mixer either! Make sure to use instant espresso powder or dark instant coffee so that the granules dissolve in the batter. Regular coffee grounds will stay grainy and not dissolve. The cookies freeze well.

makes 2 dozen

⅔ cup packed light brown sugar
¼ cup granulated sugar
1 cup all-purpose flour
3 tablespoons unsweetened cocoa powder
1 teaspoon baking soda
½ teaspoon salt
1½ tablespoons instant espresso powder
1 cup cappuccino chips or chocolate chips
½ cup (1 stick) margarine, melted
1 egg
1 teaspoon vanilla extract
½ cup espresso beans or chocolate covered espresso beans

Preheat oven to 325°F. Line two baking sheets with parchment paper or Silpats.

In a large bowl, stir brown sugar, sugar, flour, cocoa powder, baking soda, salt, espresso powder, and cappuccino chips. Mix until combined.

In a small bowl, whisk melted margarine, egg, and vanilla extract. Pour into dry mixture and stir until a dough forms.

Drop tablespoons of batter about 3 inches apart on prepared baking sheets. Press one or two espresso beans decoratively into top center of cookie, pressing just to adhere. Bake for 9 to 11 minutes or until edges and tops are just firm. Cool fully on baking sheets (they are too soft to move when warm).

Mocha Chip Cookies

Hermit Cookies

Best Ever Crispy Chip Cookies

Make Ahead

Can be prepared 2 days ahead of time. Store, covered, or freeze up to 3 months. Serve at room temperature.

Tip

To bring a cold egg to room temperature quickly, simply place in a bowl of warm water for 5 minutes.

These cookies are crispy and crunchy from the Rice Krispies cereal and are lighter in texture than standard chocolate chip cookies. Kids love these. I think a cookie with Rice Krispies and oats qualifies as a comfort food. The kids at Bet Elazraki in Israel loved making them with me too. And—you guessed it—these are great for the freezer.

makes 4 dozen

- ½ cup (1 stick) margarine, at room temperature
- ½ cup canola oil
- ½ cup packed light brown sugar
- ½ cup granulated sugar
- 1½ cups all-purpose flour
- 1 egg, at room temperature
- 1 teaspoon vanilla extract
- ½ teaspoon salt
- ½ teaspoon cream of tartar
- 1 cup Rice Krispies cereal
- ¾ cup old-fashioned oats
- ½ cup coconut flakes
- ½ cup chocolate chips
- ½ cup butterscotch chips

Preheat oven to 350°F. Line two baking sheets with parchment paper or Silpats.

With an electric mixer, cream together margarine, oil, brown sugar, and granulated sugar until fluffy, about 4 minutes. Beat in flour, egg, vanilla, salt, and cream of tartar. Stir in cereal, oats, coconut, chocolate chips, and butterscotch chips.

Drop dough by rounded tablespoonfuls onto prepared baking sheets. Bake until just brown around the edges, about 10 to 12 minutes. Cool 2 minutes before removing to wire racks.

Scooping out the delicious cookie dough together with the children at Bet Elazraki Children's Home gave me a chance to bond with these precious children. They come to Bet Elazraki to be loved and nurtured, often for the first time in their young lives.

Peanut Butter Cookies

Peanut butter cookies are a huge fan favorite: classic, kid-friendly, and just plain addictive. Even better—they're easy! You probably have all the ingredients in your kitchen already. This cookie recipe is quick and delicious, and they're great for the freezer. You will make them over and over again. Feel free to add chopped chocolate or chopped roasted peanuts for extra chunks and bumps throughout each cookie.

Make Ahead

Can be prepared 2 days ahead of time. Store, covered, or freeze up to 3 months. Serve at room temperature.

makes 3 dozen

- 1 cup (2 sticks) margarine, at room temperature
- 1 cup granulated sugar
- 1 cup packed light brown sugar
- 2 eggs, at room temperature
- 1½ cups creamy peanut butter
- 2 teaspoons vanilla extract
- 3⅓ cups all-purpose flour
- 1½ teaspoons baking soda

Preheat oven to 300°F. Line two baking sheets with parchment paper.

Using an electric mixer, cream together margarine, granulated sugar, and brown sugar until fluffy, about 4 minutes. Beat in eggs, peanut butter, and vanilla. Add flour and baking soda; mix well.

Drop by tablespoonfuls onto prepared baking sheets; flatten with a fork. Bake until brown on the edges, about 15 to 18 minutes. Do not overbake. Cool 2 minutes before removing to wire racks.

Coconut and Macadamia Nut Biscotti

Make Ahead

Can be prepared 2 days ahead of time. Store, covered, or freeze up to 3 months. Serve at room temperature.

I love dunkable biscotti because, since they are usually made with oil, they can be a breakfast treat or a late-night snack. I officially give you permission to eat cookies in the morning. This one is especially good because it uses decadent macadamia nuts. You can substitute another type if you prefer, but I love the combination with coconut. This cookie base is a great one for any kind of add-in, so change up any of the ingredients as you like: you can substitute or add lemon zest or orange zest, different types of chips, or other dried fruits. It comes out great every time—plus they freeze well.

makes 2 dozen

1 egg plus 1 egg white
½ cup canola oil
¾ cup sugar
¾ cup white chocolate chips
⅔ cup chopped macadamia nuts
½ cup shredded sweetened coconut
1 teaspoon vanilla extract
½ teaspoon salt
1½ cups all-purpose flour
1½ teaspoons baking powder

Whisk egg, egg white, and oil in a large bowl. Add sugar, white chocolate chips, nuts, coconut, vanilla, and salt; mix well. Set aside.

Combine flour and baking powder in a small bowl; gradually add flour mixture to egg mixture. Stir until combined. Cover and chill dough in the freezer for 20 minutes, or in the refrigerator for an hour or up to overnight (the dough should be chilled before shaping so it isn't too sticky).

Preheat oven to 325°F. Line two baking sheets with parchment paper or Silpats.

Divide dough in three equal parts. Flour a board or the counter and your hands. Form each piece of dough into a log about 1 inch thick and 3 inches wide. Press down a little so that the top is all level. Place on prepared sheets.

Bake 25 minutes. Cool 5 minutes, and then cut logs into diagonal slices. Turn slices on their sides, and return baking sheets to oven. Bake an additional 10 minutes. Cool 2 minutes before removing to wire racks.

Dark Chocolate Mint Chip Cookies

These cookies remind me of the Thin Mint Girl Scout cookies that my mom used to buy. Although the look and shape is different, they have the same great mint chocolate taste. The green chips are kitschy and make them irresistible to kids, but if you are serving an adult crowd, use the chocolate mint chips instead. My husband and kids love these. The cookies freeze well.

makes 3 dozen

2¼ cups all-purpose flour
¼ cup unsweetened cocoa powder
1 teaspoon baking soda
½ teaspoon salt
1 cup unsalted margarine, at room temperature
¾ cup granulated sugar
¾ cup packed light brown sugar
2 eggs, at room temperature
1 teaspoon vanilla extract
1½ teaspoons peppermint extract
1 cup chocolate chips or chunks
1½ cups green mint chips, peppermint flavored candies, white chips, or dark chocolate mint chips

Preheat oven to 350°F. Line two baking sheets with parchment paper or Silpats.

Combine flour, cocoa powder, baking soda, and salt in a mixing bowl. Stir and set aside.

Using an electric mixer, beat margarine until creamy, about 3 minutes. Add sugar and brown sugar, beating until light, about 3 minutes more. Add eggs one at a time, beating between each addition. Then add vanilla and peppermint extracts. Add dry ingredients and beat slowly until fully incorporated. Stir in both chips.

Place about 1 rounded tablespoon of dough on baking sheets about 2 inches apart. Flatten cookies a bit. Bake for 12 minutes, until cookies are lightly crisped on the edges and soft in the center. Remove from oven and cool for 3 minutes. Move to wire rack to finish cooling completely. Store in airtight container.

Make Ahead

Can be prepared 2 days ahead of time. Store, covered, or freeze up to 3 months. Serve at room temperature.

Forgotten Meringues

Passover

Use Passover vanilla extract in place of pure vanilla extract.

Prep Ahead

For perfectly crispy meringues, they need to dry in the oven for a minimum of 7 hours and preferably overnight, so be sure to allow plenty of time.

Make Ahead

Can be made 2 days ahead of time. Store in airtight container until ready to serve or freeze up to 3 months.

I love these all year long, but especially on Passover. They come out cloud-like with a perfect crispiness and a nice soft center—and best yet, they cook while you sleep! Feel free to use any mix-in of your choice, such as other nuts, dried fruit, or even a swirl of gel food coloring. These are also delicious as a garnish or served with Lemon Curd (p. 338), Lemon Mousse (p. 272), or Hazelnut Mousse (p. 241).

makes 2½ dozen

2 egg whites
⅔ cup sugar
¼ teaspoon vanilla extract
Pinch of salt
1 cup chopped pecans
¾ cup mini chocolate chips or shaved chocolate
½ cup shredded sweetened coconut (optional)

Preheat oven to 350°F. Line a baking sheet with parchment paper or Silpat.

Beat egg whites until soft peaks form, about 4 minutes. Gradually add sugar and continue beating until they hold stiff peaks. Add vanilla and salt. Gently stir in pecans, chocolate chips, and coconut. Drop batter by the tablespoonful onto the baking sheet. Swirl top decoratively.

Place in oven, then turn oven off, leaving pan in overnight (or at least 7 hours) with door closed to help them dry out.

Tahini Thumbprint Cookies

My friend Galit, the owner of Geffen Gourmet, inspired this recipe. Her tahini cookies are the flakiest and tastiest tahini cookies I've ever tasted. No wonder the line is out the door on Thursdays! Her flavorful Sephardic dips are worth the wait! I wanted to create a recipe that had Shabbos presentation but included trendy tahini as an ingredient.

Make Ahead

Can be prepared 2 days ahead of time. Store, covered, or freeze up to 3 months. Serve at room temperature.

makes 2½ dozen

For the cookies:

1¼ cups all-purpose flour
½ teaspoon baking powder
½ teaspoon baking soda
1 teaspoon salt
¾ cup smooth natural tahini paste
½ cup (1 stick) margarine, softened
¼ cup packed light brown sugar
¼ cup granulated sugar
2 tablespoons vanilla sugar
1 egg
1 teaspoon vanilla extract
½ teaspoon fresh orange zest (optional)

For the filling:

4 ounces bittersweet or semisweet chocolate, finely chopped
1 teaspoon light corn syrup
2 tablespoons margarine
½ teaspoon coarse sea salt or kosher salt

Preheat oven to 350°F and line 2 cookie sheets with parchment paper or Silpat.

To make the cookies: Stir together flour, baking powder, baking soda and salt in a medium bowl. In a mixer, cream tahini and margarine until very smooth, about 2 minutes. Add brown sugar, granulated sugar, and vanilla sugar and mix until light and fluffy, about 3 minutes. Beat in egg, vanilla, and orange zest, if desired. Add dry ingredients in 2 batches, mixing until just blended after each addition. Refrigerate dough for 10 minutes or up to a few hours. Scoop 1 tablespoon of dough and roll into a ball. Repeat with remaining dough and set about 3 inches apart on the lined cookie sheets.

Bake for 10 minutes and remove from oven. (The cookies will still be soft.) With the bottom of a wooden spoon or the backside of a ¼ teaspoon measuring spoon, gently make an indentation in the center of the cookie that's deep and wide enough to hold the filling without going all the way through the dough. Return cookies to oven and bake for an additional 5 minutes, or until lightly browned. Remove from oven and let cool 5 minutes on baking sheet, and then transfer to a wire rack to cool completely.

To make the filling: Combine the chocolate, corn syrup, and margarine in a small saucepan over low heat. Stir until melted, smooth, and glossy. (Alternatively, place the ingredients in a glass bowl and microwave in 30-second intervals, stirring after each one, until the chocolate is almost melted. Continue stirring to melt the chocolate completely.)

To assemble: Let the chocolate filling cool slightly, and then fill the cookie indentations with the chocolate. Sprinkle the cookies with sea salt and allow the chocolate to set for at least an hour before serving.

Cinnamon-Swirl Shortbread Cookies

Make Ahead

Can be prepared 2 days ahead of time. Store, covered, in the refrigerator or freeze up to 3 months. Defrost in the refrigerator. Serve at room temperature. The rolled dough freezes well too. Defrost in the refrigerator, slice when dough is cold and firm but not frozen, then bake.

These are adorable and scrumptious. I make them often for bake sales or for Shalom Zachors because they have that fancy, you–fussed-over-them presentation. I like to stack them in a narrow, plastic box or cello wrap so that the gorgeous swirl can be seen at first glance. The finished cookies freeze well.

makes 4 dozen

Cookie:

1 cup (2 sticks) margarine, at room temperature

½ cup granulated sugar

¾ cup confectioners' sugar

½ teaspoon salt

1½ teaspoon orange zest

1 teaspoon vanilla extract

1 egg

2½ cups all-purpose flour

Filling:

5 tablespoons margarine, at room temperature

¼ cup packed light brown sugar

1½ teaspoons light corn syrup

1 tablespoon cinnamon

2 tablespoons all-purpose flour

Pinch of salt

½ teaspoon vanilla extract

For the dough: Using an electric mixer, cream margarine, granulated sugar, confectioners' sugar, salt, orange zest, and vanilla until light and fluffy, 4 to 5 minutes. Add egg and mix until incorporated. On low speed, add flour and mix until just combined.

For the filling: In a mixer, beat margarine, brown sugar, corn syrup, cinnamon, flour, salt, and vanilla until smooth, about 2 minutes. Set aside.

On a lightly floured surface, roll dough into a 12 x 12 inch square. Spread the cinnamon filling evenly over dough. Roll dough into a tight log. Wrap log in plastic wrap and freeze until firm, 15 to 20 minutes.

Preheat oven to 375°F. Line two baking sheets with parchment paper or Silpats.

Remove dough from freezer. With a sharp knife, cut into ¼-inch slices. Place slices on baking sheets about 1½ inches apart.

Bake until golden brown, about 12 minutes. Cool 3 minutes on pan and transfer to wire rack to cool completely. Store in airtight container.

Extreme Chocolate Drop Cookies

This is a combination brownie and cookie all in one. It's extra rich and moist, and yet has a little crunch like a cookie. This recipe made the cut for the book because, unlike other recipes for brownie type cookies, it's super simple. No chilling and re-chilling the dough, no extra steps, just make the batter and cook; plus, they freeze well.

makes 3 dozen

12 ounces good-quality dark chocolate (70% to 72% cacao), divided
¼ cup all-purpose flour
¼ teaspoon baking powder
¼ teaspoon kosher salt
3 tablespoons margarine
2 eggs
¾ cup sugar
1 teaspoon vanilla extract
2 cups coarsely chopped walnut or pecan pieces

Preheat oven to 350°F. Line two baking sheets with parchment paper or Silpats.

Chop half the chocolate finely for easy melting; chop the other half in larger chunks to stir into the cookie dough.

In a small bowl, mix together flour, baking powder, and salt.

In a heavy-bottom small pot, over very low heat, melt the 6 ounces of finely chopped chocolate with the margarine. Stir until melted. Remove from heat and cool slightly.

In a heavy-bottom, 3-quart pot, whisk eggs, sugar, and vanilla over very low heat. Stir until mixture is lukewarm to the touch. Remove from heat. Add the melted chocolate mixture, and then stir in flour mixture. Gently fold in nuts and the remaining 6 ounces chocolate chunks.

Scoop tablespoons of batter onto prepared pan, 1½ inches apart. Bake until surface of cookies looks dry and just set but center is gooey, about 12 to 14 minutes. Cool for 5 minutes on pan, transfer to wire rack to cool completely.

Passover

Use potato starch in place of flour. Use Passover vanilla extract in place of pure vanilla extract.

Make Ahead

Can be prepared 2 days ahead of time. Store, covered, or freeze up to 3 months. Defrost in the refrigerator. Serve at room temperature.

Tip

Scharffenberger, Callebaut, Guittard, and Vahlrona are all reputable vendors of high-quality chocolates. Scharffenberger and Callebaut offer pareve options.

קוסום

BARS & MINIS

One of my most special memories is baking with my grandmother. Her loving way of teaching me, her detailed instructions on melting chocolate, her patient demeanor as I tried to roll out the babka dough—these are images I can readily recall. My mother now bakes with my own children, and I love seeing her pass the tradition and love from one generation to another—especially such a delicious one as this.

Toffee-Caramel Blondies

Make Ahead

Can be prepared 2 days ahead of time. Store, covered, in the refrigerator or freeze up to 3 months. Serve at room temperature.

These are always a huge hit. The center is soft and cake-like and even tastes a bit like cookie dough. The glaze seeps into the bars, giving them extra sweetness. The toffee crunch topping gives the perfect contrast of crunch to make them sensational. The finished bars freeze well.

makes 20 or more bars

Blondies:

2⅔ cups all-purpose flour

1 teaspoon baking soda

¼ teaspoon salt

¾ cup (1½ sticks) margarine, at room temperature

1¼ cups packed light brown sugar

3 eggs

1 teaspoon vanilla extract

1½ cups chocolate chips

½ cup white chocolate chips

½ cup chopped toasted pecans (p. 335)

Topping:

1½ tablespoons margarine

¼ cup non-dairy creamer

⅓ cup confectioners' sugar

¼ cup packed light brown sugar

¾ cup coarsely chopped toffee candy (like Viennese crunch)

To prepare the blondies: Preheat oven to 350°F. Line a 13 x 9 x 2-inch baking pan with aluminum foil, allowing enough overhang to help remove bars from pan. Grease foil with nonstick cooking spray.

Whisk together flour, baking soda, and salt in a small bowl. Set aside.

With an electric mixer, beat margarine and sugar in a large bowl until light and fluffy, about 3 minutes. Add eggs and vanilla; beat until smooth. On low speed, add flour mixture; mix until just blended. Stir in chocolate chips, white chocolate chips, and nuts. Spread batter into prepared pan.

Bake about 25 minutes, or until golden brown. Cool for 15 minutes.

To prepare the topping: Heat margarine and non-dairy creamer in a small saucepan over medium heat until melted. Add confectioners' sugar and brown sugar and whisk until smooth. Bring mixture to a simmer; cook about 5 minutes, until thickened. Remove from heat.

Poke about 20 small holes into the blondies. Pour topping evenly over bars and sprinkle with toffee pieces. Gently press toffee pieces into the blondie. Cool on wire rack; store in refrigerator until ready to serve.

Cut into 20 or more bars.

Red Velvet and Cream Cheese Brownies

These rich and creamy brownies are as beautiful as they are delicious, and are a winner with everyone. Wrap leftovers and keep them in the freezer for another time.

makes 12 brownies

Brownies:

1 cup granulated sugar
½ cup (1 stick) margarine, melted
¼ cup unsweetened cocoa powder
1 tablespoon red food coloring
1 teaspoon vanilla extract
1 teaspoon distilled white vinegar
2 eggs
¾ cup all-purpose flour

Cream Cheese Layer:

1 egg
1 (8-ounce) package Tofutti cream cheese
¼ cup granulated sugar
3 tablespoons confectioners' sugar
½ teaspoon vanilla extract

Preheat oven to 350°F. Grease an 8 x 8-inch baking pan.

To prepare the brownies: Mix sugar, margarine, cocoa powder, food coloring, vanilla, and vinegar in a large bowl. Whisk in the eggs, one at a time, beating after each addition. Gently fold in flour until combined. Pour batter into prepared pan, reserving ¼ cup batter for the top. Set aside.

To prepare the cream cheese layer: Using an electric mixer, beat the egg, cream cheese, granulated sugar, confectioners' sugar, and vanilla together until smooth.

Gently spread cream cheese layer on top of the brownie batter in the pan. Dollop the reserved ¼ cup brownie batter over cream cheese layer. Use a chopstick or a knife to create swirl patterns in the cream cheese mixture with the red brownie batter.

Bake about 30 to 35 minutes, or until cream cheese layer is set. Cool completely before cutting into 12 bars. Store in the refrigerator.

Make Ahead

Can be prepared 2 days ahead of time. Store, covered, in the refrigerator or freeze up to 3 months. Defrost in the refrigerator. Serve at room temperature.

Creamy Cappuccino Layered Brownie Bar

Make Ahead

Can be prepared 2 days ahead of time. Store, covered, in the refrigerator or freeze up to 3 months. Defrost in the refrigerator. Serve chilled.

This brownie has layers of extra scrumptious flavor: rich chocolate base, cinnamon cream center, and a mocha chocolate ganache on top. I serve these as the main dessert, not as an extra on the table: they deserve to stand alone! Once the finished brownies are cut into bars, they can be wrapped and frozen.

makes 24 bars

Brownies:

8 ounces semisweet chocolate, chopped

¾ cup (1½ sticks) margarine, at room temperature

¼ cup water

2 tablespoons instant espresso powder

1½ cups granulated sugar

4 eggs

1 cup all-purpose flour

¼ teaspoon salt

Cream Cheese Layer:

2 (8-ounce) packages Tofutti cream cheese, at room temperature

6 tablespoons margarine, at room temperature

1½ cups confectioners' sugar

2 teaspoons ground cinnamon

1 teaspoon vanilla extract

Ganache:

12 ounces semisweet chocolate, chopped

½ cup pareve whipping cream

4 tablespoons margarine

2 tablespoons instant espresso powder

Preheat oven to 350°F. Grease a 13 x 9 x 2-inch baking pan.

To prepare the brownies: Stir together chocolate, margarine, water, and espresso powder in a large saucepan over medium-low heat until chocolate melts. Cool slightly; whisk in sugar. Add eggs, one at a time, mixing after each addition. Stir in flour and salt. Pour batter into prepared pan. Bake about 20 to 28 minutes, or until tester inserted into center comes out with moist crumbs (do not overbake). Cool and set aside.

To prepare the cream cheese layer: Using an electric mixer, beat cream cheese and margarine until light and fluffy. Add sugar, cinnamon, and vanilla; beat until blended, about 1 minute. Spread over cool brownies. Cover and refrigerate until chilled, about 2 hours.

To prepare the ganache: Melt chocolate, cream, margarine, and espresso in a medium saucepan over low heat. Stir until smooth. Cool. Pour over cream cheese layer and spread gently to cover.

Freeze brownies until set. Cut into 24 bars. Store in refrigerator until ready to serve.

White Chocolate, Pecan, and Berry Blondies

Make Ahead

Can be prepared 2 days ahead of time. Store, covered, in the refrigerator or freeze up to 3 months. Serve at room temperature.

Blondies are made even better with sweet fruit and delicious nut crunch. I sometimes use raspberries instead of strawberries. I love the way the berries swirl through the blondie bar so that every bite is divine. Wrap and freeze any leftovers.

makes 16 bars

2 cups all-purpose flour
1 teaspoon baking powder
½ teaspoon salt
¼ teaspoon baking soda
2 cups packed light brown sugar
¾ cup (1½ sticks) margarine, at room temperature
2 eggs
2 teaspoons vanilla extract
1 cup coarsely chopped toasted pecans (p. 335)
1 cup white chocolate chips
½ cup sliced fresh strawberries
½ cup fresh blueberries

Preheat oven to 350°F. Grease a 13 x 9 x 2-inch baking pan.

Stir together flour, baking powder, salt, and baking soda in a medium bowl; set aside.

In a mixer, cream sugar and margarine until light and fluffy. Add eggs, one at a time, beating after each addition. Stir in vanilla. Add flour mixture; mix until fully incorporated. Stir in pecans and chocolate chips. Gently fold in berries. Spread batter evenly in prepared pan.

Bake about 50 minutes, or until a tester inserted into the center comes out with moist crumbs. Cool completely. Cut into 16 bars and serve.

Pots de Crème

This is super simple and perfect for company. Be sure to make this a day ahead of time so that they have time to set. Serve them in cute demitasse or decorative cups. I love that they are lighter than some recipes because they are made with soy milk instead of non-dairy creamer. Trust me: you won't miss the creamer! Add chunks of chocolate, chopped nuts, coconut, or any topping you like just before pouring into the decorative cups for a crunchier pudding.

makes 16 (2-ounce) servings

2 eggs
2 cups semisweet chocolate chips
¼ cup sugar
⅛ teaspoon salt
1⅓ cups vanilla soy milk

Garnish:

Dollops of pareve whipped cream and raspberries or halved strawberries

Combine eggs, chocolate chips, sugar, and salt in a food processor or blender. Heat soy milk over medium heat in a small saucepan until warm but not boiling. Slowly pour into food processor. Blend 1 minute, or until smooth. Spoon into 2-ounce decorative cups and chill for at least 8 hours or best overnight.

Garnish each cup with a dollop of whipped cream and raspberries or half of a strawberry, and serve immediately.

Passover

Use non-dairy creamer in place of soy milk.

Prep Ahead

These lovely little custards need a minimum of 8 hours to chill before serving, so be sure to allow plenty of time.

Make Ahead

Can be prepared 2 days ahead of time. Store, covered, in the refrigerator. Serve cold or at room temperature.

Note

If you have any concerns with uncooked eggs, you can purchase pasteurized eggs at most groceries.

Macadamia, Pecan, and Coconut Tartlets

This is a great twist on traditional pecan tartlets. The filling is loaded with crunchy toasted nuts and coconut and then drizzled with chocolate for a professional presentation. To save time and effort, you can use store-bought shells for this recipe. We usually do! To make homemade tart shells, please see page 337.

makes 24 servings

Crust:

24 prepared individual tart shells (p. 337)

Filling:

2 eggs

⅔ cup light corn syrup

¼ cup packed light brown sugar

¼ cup (½ stick) margarine, melted

2 tablespoons cream of coconut (this is available in supermarkets in the mixed drink aisle)

1 teaspoon vanilla extract

1¼ cups toasted macadamia nuts, coarsely chopped (p. 335)

¾ cup toasted pecan pieces (p. 335)

½ cup shredded sweetened coconut

Glaze (optional):

½ cup semisweet chocolate chips

1 tablespoon margarine

To prepare the crust: Preheat oven to 350°F. Place tart shells on rimmed baking sheets. Bake 5 minutes. Remove from oven and cool.

To prepare the filling: Beat eggs, corn syrup, sugar, margarine, cream of coconut, and vanilla in a large mixing bowl until combined. Stir in nuts and coconut. Pour into tart shells. Bake 20 to 25 minutes, or until filling is puffy. Remove tarts from baking sheets to cool on wire racks.

To prepare the glaze: Melt chocolate chips and margarine in a small saucepan over low heat. Stir until smooth. Drizzle decoratively over each tart. Let cool before storing.

Make Ahead

Can be prepared 2 days ahead of time. Store, covered, in the refrigerator or freeze up to 3 months. To freeze, set finished tartlets on a rimmed baking sheet in the freezer until frozen solid, then wrap or pack inside an airtight container. Defrost in the refrigerator. Serve at room temperature.

Butterscotch Blondies

Make Ahead

Can be prepared 2 days ahead of time. Store, covered, in the refrigerator or freeze up to 3 months. Defrost in the refrigerator. Serve at room temperature.

I used to make these with dairy butterscotch chips, but had to forgo them on Shabbos. I was so excited a few years ago when butterscotch chips became available as a pareve ingredient. These became a regular sweet finish on Shabbos. Like fudgy brownies, you shouldn't overmix these, it will make them too dense. Start checking these after 20 minutes, but they may take up to 35 minutes to completely bake. They will freeze well once cooled.

makes 24 bars

1 cup butterscotch chips
½ cup (1 stick) margarine
1½ cups all-purpose flour
⅔ cup packed light brown sugar
2 teaspoons baking powder
2 eggs
2 teaspoons vanilla extract
1½ cups miniature marshmallows
1½ cups semisweet chocolate chips
1 cup salted peanuts or butterscotch chips (optional)

Preheat oven to 350°F. Grease a 13 x 9 x 2-inch baking pan.

Melt butterscotch chips and margarine in a small saucepan over low heat. Stir until smooth; cool slightly. Set aside.

With an electric mixer, combine flour, sugar, and baking powder. Beat in eggs, vanilla, and melted butterscotch mixture. Fold in marshmallows, chocolate chips, and peanuts or butterscotch chips, if using.

Spread batter into prepared pan. Bake 20 to 35 minutes, or until tester comes out with moist crumbs. Cool and cut into 24 bars.

Snap, Crackle, Pop Brownies

We run a lot of contests on Gourmetkoshercooking.com and this recipe for semi-homemade brownie submitted by Lauren was a big hit with readers. It can be made fully from scratch, with a brownie mix, or with store-bought brownies that you dress up with her peanut butter–Rice Krispies–marshmallow fluff topping. It is such a favorite that she won the Easy Best Brownie Contest by a huge margin. So when you're short on time and in need of a delicious and simple brownie option, try these chocolate brownies with a crunchy peanut butter and fluff topping. They definitely take me back to my childhood!

makes 12 individual cupcakes or 16 squares

Brownies:

8 ounces good-quality chocolate, chopped
6 tablespoons margarine
¼ teaspoon salt
¼ teaspoon vanilla extract
1 cup sugar
2 eggs
⅓ cup all-purpose flour

Topping:

1½ cups creamy peanut butter
1½ cups Rice Krispies cereal
2 cups marshmallow fluff
1½ cups semisweet chocolate chips
1½ tablespoons canola oil
Mini chocolate chips, for garnish (optional)

Preheat oven to 325°F. Grease a 12-cup muffin pan and line with paper cupcake liners.

To prepare the brownies: Heat a 2½-quart pot over very low heat. Add chocolate and margarine. Heat, stirring constantly, so that chocolate melts and does not burn. Mix until smooth and glossy.

Remove from heat and stir in salt, vanilla, and sugar. Add eggs one at a time, stirring after each addition, until incorporated. Add flour and mix batter vigorously until it is shiny and pulls away from the sides of the pot. Pour about 3 tablespoons of batter into each muffin cup and smooth the top.

Bake for 20 to 30 minutes or until tester inserted into the center comes out with moist crumbs. Cool completely.

To prepare the topping: Melt peanut butter in a saucepan over low heat. Add rice cereal and turn off the heat. Stir to coat cereal, and then spread mixture on top of each brownie cupcake. Place brownies in refrigerator for 30 minutes or in the freezer for 10 minutes.

Heat marshmallow fluff in the microwave or in a small saucepan and carefully spread on top of cereal layer. In another small pot, melt chocolate chips with the oil, stirring continuously until smooth. Pour melted chocolate on top of marshmallow layer, spreading to cover the top decoratively. Sprinkle with mini chocolate chips, if desired.

Place brownie cupcakes in the refrigerator to set completely. Remove paper liners and serve.

Make Ahead

Can be prepared 2 days ahead of time. Store, covered, in the refrigerator or freeze up to 3 months. Defrost in the refrigerator. Serve at room temperature.

Tip

These brownies can be made with 1 (20-ounce) box brownie mix, prepared according to package instructions, baked, and cooled. If using a 13 x 9 x 2-inch pan, use 2 cups peanut butter, 2 cups rice cereal, 3 cups marshmallow fluff, 2 cups chocolate chips and 1½ tablespoons canola oil for the topping. Prepare as instructed.

Chilled Chocolate Peanut Butter Balls

Make Ahead

Can be prepared 2 days ahead of time. Store, covered, in the refrigerator or freeze up to 3 months. Defrost in the refrigerator. Serve chilled.

These taste like the best peanut butter bonbons you've ever had, and they couldn't be simpler to make. They are excellent holiday or teacher gifts. I keep these in the freezer for up to 3 months and take them out about an hour before serving. On humid days, the dough can be very sticky. Dust your hands with confectioners' sugar before rolling the balls to help.

makes 20 balls

1 (18-ounce) jar creamy peanut butter
1½ cups confectioners' sugar
1 teaspoon vanilla extract
8 ounces chocolate, chopped

With an electric mixer or in a bowl with a whisk, beat peanut butter and confectioners' sugar until smooth. Mix in vanilla. With your hands, roll about 1 tablespoon of mixture at a time into balls and place on a waxed paper–lined tray. Place in the freezer for 1 hour.

Melt chocolate in a double boiler or small, heavy-bottomed pot over very low heat, stirring frequently. Remove from heat. (Alternatively, melt in the microwave in four 30-second intervals, stirring after each interval until melted.) Dip peanut butter balls halfway in chocolate, letting excess drip off, and set on the lined tray. With a fork, swirl some melted chocolate over the top of each ball. Refrigerate for at least 30 minutes before serving.

Chocolate Peanut Butter Cups

Make Ahead

Can be prepared 2 days ahead of time. Store, covered, in the refrigerator or freeze up to 3 months. Slightly defrost in the refrigerator and serve chilled.

This is my take on Reese's peanut butter cups, but a bit lighter. Everyone asks me for this recipe because they are so good. The finished cups freeze well, wrapped tightly.

makes 12 standard or 24 mini cups

½ cup margarine
¾ cup creamy peanut butter
¾ cup graham cracker crumbs (from 4 to 6 whole graham crackers)
¼ cup sugar
1 cup chocolate chips
¼ cup vanilla soy milk
¼ cup chopped roasted peanuts

Line 12 standard or 24 mini muffin pans with paper baking cups.

Melt margarine in a small saucepan over medium heat. Stir in peanut butter, graham cracker crumbs, and sugar. Mix well and remove from heat. Drop 2 tablespoons into each standard muffin cup or 1 tablespoon into each mini muffin cup. Chill for 15 minutes and up to overnight in the refrigerator.

Melt chocolate chips and soy milk in a separate small saucepan over medium heat. Stir until smooth. While still warm, spoon chocolate evenly over chilled peanut butter mixture. With an offset spatula or a knife, spread to cover peanut butter layer. Top with peanuts. Place in freezer to set for at least 2 hours before serving.

Apple Crumb Bars

I make these for Rosh Hashanah every year and my kids request them after an apple-picking outing too. The shortbread crust, sweet apple center, and crumbly topping make a wonderful fall dessert or an extra-special treat with a cup of coffee. For extra decadence, serve with pareve vanilla ice cream and drizzle with a little Red Wine Caramel Sauce (p. 338).

makes 16 to 24 bars

Crust:

1¾ cups all-purpose flour
¾ cup confectioners' sugar
¾ cup (1½ sticks) margarine, at room temperature
¾ teaspoon vanilla extract
¼ teaspoon salt

Apple Filling:

5 tart baking apples (like Granny Smith), peeled, cored, and thinly sliced
¼ cup granulated sugar
2 teaspoons fresh lemon juice
¾ teaspoon cinnamon

Crumb Topping:

1½ cups all-purpose flour
½ cup chopped walnuts (optional)
½ cup (1 stick) margarine, melted
½ cup packed light brown sugar
Pinch of salt
¾ teaspoon cinnamon
1 teaspoon vanilla extract

Garnish:

Pareve vanilla ice cream
Homemade caramel sauce (p. 338) or store-bought

Preheat oven to 375°F. Lightly grease a 13 x 9 x 2-inch baking pan and line with parchment paper or foil, letting the ends hang over the edges of pan.

For the crust: With an electric mixer, beat flour, sugar, margarine, vanilla, and salt until a dough forms, about 3 minutes. Press dough evenly on bottom of prepared pan. Bake for 20 minutes, or until lightly golden. Cool.

Lower oven temperature to 350°F.

For the apple filling: In a medium bowl, mix apples, sugar, lemon juice, and cinnamon. Pour over cooled crust and distribute evenly.

For the crumb topping: In a large bowl, stir flour, walnuts, margarine, brown sugar, salt, cinnamon, and vanilla together with a fork until moist crumbs start to come together. If necessary, use a bit more margarine. Topping should look slightly moist, crumbly, and coarse.

Top apples with crumb mixture, spreading evenly over apples.

Bake for 30 to 35 minutes, or until topping is lightly browned and toasted and apples are cooked through. Cool.

To serve: Cut in 16 or 24 squares. These bars can be served warm or cold, but they are best served warm with pareve vanilla ice cream and drizzled with warm caramel sauce.

Make Ahead

Can be prepared 2 days ahead of time. Store, covered, in the refrigerator or freeze up to 3 months. Defrost in the refrigerator. Serve at room temperature.

Tip

To keep caramel warm but not too thick, place caramel in a small glass bowl. Place that bowl into a large pot or bowl filled with a couple of inches of hot water. Be careful when placing caramel bowl in hot water: the water should not come up too high and spill into the caramel sauce. Stir sauce. This will keep sauce warm and creamy.

Pretty Little Honey Cakes

Make Ahead

Can be prepared 2 days ahead of time. Store, covered, or freeze up to 3 months.

Prettier and tastier than most honey cakes. These are a moist and wonderful addition to a Rosh Hashanah table. Wrap the cakes well, and they will keep in the freezer nicely.

makes 16 cakes

2 eggs
1 cup sugar
½ cup canola oil
¾ cup honey
1 cup strong brewed coffee
2½ cups all-purpose flour
1 teaspoon baking soda
1 teaspoon baking powder
1 teaspoon ground cinnamon

Preheat oven to 350°F. Grease and flour pretty muffin tins (ones shaped like flowers are nice) or standard 12-cup muffin tins. (There will be enough batter for 16 standard muffins.)

Stir together eggs, sugar, oil, honey, and coffee. In a separate bowl, stir flour, baking soda, baking powder, and cinnamon. Stir dry ingredients into wet. Put about ½ cup batter in each muffin compartment. Bake for 18 to 25 minutes. Let cool and then gently remove cakes from tin.

סעודה שלישית

SHALOSH SEUDOS

In the summertime, when days are longer, I like to invite guests for Shalosh Seudos and serve some of these dishes that feel uniquely perfect for the third meal—light, colorful, versatile, and all easy to make ahead of time.

Everything Bagel Romaine Salad with Smoked Salmon

Make Ahead

Dressing can be prepared 2 days ahead of time. Store, covered, in the refrigerator. Toss salad with dressing just before serving.

I get inspired to create recipes from the funniest things. The idea for this salad came to me when I looked at the bottom of the bag that had contained my fresh bagels. The crumbs and spices smelled so divine that I felt terrible wasting them. I quickly poured them into a container and turned them into a vinaigrette. The results were fantastic so I recreated it again and again, balancing the onions, garlic, and salt. Feel free to leave out the Tofutti sour cream if you prefer. I like it because it adds a bit of the same creaminess from the dairy cream cheese.

serves 8

Salad:

6 cups chopped romaine lettuce
1 cup sliced cucumbers
1 cup sliced cherry tomatoes
¼ cup thinly sliced red onion
5 ounces smoked salmon, diced into bite-size pieces
1½ cups seasoned bagel chips, bagel croutons, or pita chips (p. 337)

Dressing:

1¼ teaspoons onion powder
1 teaspoon garlic powder
1 teaspoon kosher salt
¼ teaspoon ground black pepper
1 teaspoon Dijon mustard
1 heaping teaspoon dried minced onion
1¼ heaping teaspoons dried minced garlic
1 tablespoon poppyseeds
1 tablespoon sesame seeds
¼ cup red wine vinegar
1 to 2 tablespoons Tofutti sour cream, or to taste
½ cup extra-virgin olive oil

To prepare the salad: Combine lettuce, cucumbers, tomatoes, onion, and salmon, in a large salad bowl. Mix and set aside.

For the dressing: Combine onion powder, garlic powder, salt, pepper, Dijon, minced onion, minced garlic, poppyseeds, sesame seeds, vinegar, and 1 tablespoon sour cream in a small bowl; whisk well. Slowly add oil, whisking vigorously until blended. Add another tablespoon of sour cream if you'd like it creamier.

To serve: Pour dressing over salad. Toss well, add bagel chips, and toss further. Serve immediately.

Hearts of Palm Salad with Sugar Snap Peas, Baby Corn, and Tomatoes, a.k.a. The Rabbi Salad

My friend Aviva shared this terrific salad with me. We used to joke that it was nicknamed the "Rabbi Salad" because none of the vegetables in this salad required careful washing and checking, and would therefore get Rabbi approval. Any salad that tastes this good and is so easy to make is a winner to me too!

makes 8 servings

Salad:

2 (15-ounce) cans baby corn, drained and sliced

2 (15-ounce) cans hearts of palm, drained and sliced

1½ pints grape tomatoes, halved

1½ cups sugar snap peas, halved

Dressing:

½ cup apple cider vinegar

½ cup canola oil

5 tablespoons packed light brown sugar

2 tablespoons soy sauce

¼ teaspoon garlic powder

¼ teaspoon ground ginger

To prepare the salad: Combine the corn, hearts of palm, tomatoes, and sugar snap peas in a large bowl; toss well.

To prepare the dressing: Whisk together the vinegar, oil, sugar, soy sauce, garlic powder, and ginger in a small bowl.

Pour dressing over salad; toss and serve.

Make Ahead

Dressing and salad can be made a 1 to 2 days ahead of time. Store, separately in the refrigerator. Toss dressing and salad just before serving.

Lighten Up

In the dressing, reduce the apple cider vinegar and the canola oil to ⅓ cup each. Reduce the brown sugar to 3 tablespoons and replace the soy sauce with 1½ tablespoons lite soy sauce.

Pizza Salad

How fun and cool-looking is this salad? I saw a version of this salad at Mario Batali's Eataly in NYC. His version had all sorts of ingredients that we do not eat, so I created my own version that pairs pizza crust with vinegary dressing and Italian salad ingredients. Voilà: delicious, gorgeous, and so kitschy, I love it!

serves 10

Dough:

2 tablespoons extra-virgin olive oil

1 ball store-bought pizza dough, at room temperature

½ teaspoon dried oregano

½ teaspoon minced dried garlic

½ teaspoon kosher salt

Dressing:

1 shallot, chopped

¼ cup red wine vinegar

1 teaspoon Dijon mustard

1 teaspoon dried oregano

½ teaspoon onion powder

½ teaspoon minced dried garlic

½ cup extra-virgin olive oil

½ teaspoon kosher salt

¼ teaspoon ground black pepper

Salad:

6 cups chopped romaine or mixed lettuces (I use mesclun, arugula, and romaine mixed together)

1 cup cherry tomatoes, halved

¼ cup sliced red onion

½ cup coarsely chopped marinated artichoke hearts

¼ cup sliced, roasted red peppers, from a jar or fresh

4 Persian cucumbers, sliced

½ cup sliced kalamata or green olives

For the dough: Preheat oven to 500°F with rack positioned in upper third of oven. Thoroughly grease a large rimmed sheet pan (13 x 18 inches) with oil. Place dough on the pan, pushing and stretching it with your hands to cover most of the pan. Do not worry if it does not cover the whole pan, just fill it as completely as possible. Brush dough with olive oil and sprinkle with oregano, minced dried garlic, and salt. Bake for 10 minutes, until golden brown, rotating pan midway through cooking. Cool completely before storing until ready to use. Wrap tightly with plastic wrap to store.

To make the dressing: Whisk shallot, vinegar, Dijon or lemon juice, oregano, onion powder, and minced dried garlic in a small bowl. While whisking, drizzle in olive oil. Season with salt and pepper.

To assemble the salad: Toss lettuce, tomatoes, red onion, artichoke hearts, red peppers, cucumbers, and olives in a large salad bowl. Pour dressing over salad and toss until thoroughly dressed. Chop salad into small bite size pieces, like a chopped salad.

Place pizza crust on a large platter or wood cutting board. Top with salad and dressing. Allow some of the dressing to soak into the pizza crust for about 10 minutes before serving. Serve with a large knife and salad tongs to cut pieces through crust and serve salad on top of crust.

Passover

Use toasted matzo in place of pizza dough. Place salad atop matzo just before serving. Use Passover mustard or lemon juice in place of Dijon mustard in dressing.

Make Ahead

Pizza dough and dressing can be made a day ahead of time. Store, covered, in the refrigerator. Serve pizza dough at room temperature.

Tip

This looks very pretty on a long narrow board or a wide rectangular wooden plate. Make the dough in whatever decorative shape you like. It's important to chop the salad into small shredded pieces so that it stays on top of every pizza slice.

Lighten Up

Reduce the oil to ⅓ cup in the dressing. Use whole wheat pizza dough.

Creamy Balsamic Tuna Fish

Passover

Use Passover mustard in place of Dijon mustard.

Make Ahead

Can be made up to 4 days ahead of time. Store, covered in the refrigerator.

My introduction to balsamic tuna came from Toddy's, a popular bagel store near my home that's a favorite of everyone around. They have excellent bagels, spreads, and caramel brownies, and they provided the inspiration for this recipe. I have fed my family with their delicious tuna and creamy balsamic dressing many a time. I hope you enjoy my version as much as I enjoy theirs.

serves 8

Dressing:

2 cloves garlic, grated
3 tablespoons mayonnaise
2 tablespoons fresh lemon juice
1 tablespoon Dijon mustard
3 tablespoons packed light brown sugar
¾ teaspoon garlic powder
2 teaspoons kosher salt
¾ teaspoon ground black pepper
½ cup balsamic vinegar
¾ cup extra-virgin olive oil

Tuna and Optional Mix-Ins:

3 (7-ounce) cans albacore tuna in water, drained, and flaked
¼ cup chopped scallions
¼ cup chopped green apple
¼ cup chopped celery
¼ cup chopped red pepper
¼ cup chopped red onion
¼ cup shredded carrot

For the dressing: Whisk together garlic, mayonnaise, lemon juice, Dijon, brown sugar, garlic powder, salt, and pepper until well combined. Add balsamic vinegar and whisk well. Using an immersion blender, slowly pour in olive oil to emulsify.

For the salad: Combine tuna with any mix-ins you'd like to use in a medium bowl. Add ½ cup creamy balsamic dressing and mix. Add more dressing if tuna is not moist enough for your taste.

Baked Salmon with Garlic and Sun-Dried Tomatoes

This recipe can be made with store-bought pesto (or basil compound butter made by blending 1 stick margarine with 1 cup basil leaves in a food processor), other tomato chutney or thick and spreadable sauce of your choice. For midweek cooking, I layer sliced tomatoes across the salmon. For Yom Tov or Shabbos, I use red and yellow grape tomatoes for a more elegant presentation. This can be made a day ahead of time and kept in the refrigerator until ready to serve. I serve it on Shabbos day, Yom Tov, or anytime.

serves 8

Whole side of salmon, 2 to 3 pounds, skin removed

8 to 12 cloves garlic

5 sun-dried tomatoes in oil, drained

3 tablespoons sliced fresh basil, or more to taste

½ cup chopped fresh parsley

1½ teaspoons kosher salt

½ cup extra-virgin olive oil

2 pints grape tomatoes, sliced in half, or 2 large tomatoes, thinly sliced

Place salmon on large jellyroll pan or other pan with low sides. Set aside.

Preheat oven to 350°F.

In a food processor or a blender, purée garlic, sun-dried tomatoes, basil, parsley, salt, and oil until a paste forms. Smear paste all over the top of the salmon. Decoratively place the tomatoes, cut-side down, on top of the garlic paste. Cover and bake 30 minutes, or until the salmon is almost cooked through.

Serve warm or at room temperature.

Passover

Perfect as-is!

Make Ahead

Can be prepared 2 days ahead of time. Store, covered, in the refrigerator until ready to serve. Serve chilled or at room temperature.

At the EMUNAH Ma'ayan Rivka Golden Age Restaurant in Petach Tikvah, I met an amazing women who is a long-time volunteer at this haven for lonely senior citizens in search of companionship.

Watermelon Tabbouleh

This is unlike any other tabbouleh you have tasted. The watermelon adds freshness, sweetness, and beautiful color to the traditional tabbouleh. This should be tossed together just before serving.

serves 8

- 1¼ cups water
- ¼ teaspoon kosher salt
- ¾ cup bulgur wheat
- 8 ounces watermelon (from about ½ small), peeled and coarsely chopped (about 1½ cups total)
- ⅔ cup coarsely chopped fresh parsley
- 2 tomatoes, coarsely chopped
- 4 scallions, thinly sliced
- 2 tablespoons fresh lemon juice
- 1 tablespoon plus 1 teaspoon extra-virgin olive oil
- 2 teaspoons finely grated lemon zest
- ½ teaspoon kosher salt

Bring water and salt to a boil in a medium saucepan over high heat. Add bulgur; stir and remove from heat. Let stand, covered, 15 minutes. Fluff with a fork, and let stand, uncovered, until cooled, 15 to 30 minutes.

Transfer bulgur to a large bowl; toss with watermelon, parsley, tomatoes, scallions, lemon juice, oil, lemon zest, and salt. Serve.

Passover

Use quinoa in place of bulgur. In a large pot, cook 1 cup quinoa in 2 cups water, bring to boil and simmer, covered, for 14 minutes or until water is fully absorbed.

Make Ahead

Salad without dressing or watermelon can be prepared a day ahead of time. Toss salad with dressing and watermelon just before serving.

Sensational Chunky Guacamole Plus Crazy Good Variations

Classic guacamole can be dressed up or dressed down as you like it. While some like a smooth, almost puréed guacamole, I like it with some texture—pieces of tomatoes, chunks of avocado, ample cilantro, and a hefty spritz of lime to cut through the fat of the avocado and brighten the whole dip. Make sure you try some of the crazy variations below. They will WOW and please your guests.

Passover

Perfect as-is!

Make Ahead

Guacamole needs to be prepared fresh. Or, more specifically, the avocados should be cut and mashed just before using. All the other ingredients that go into guacamole can be prepped up to a day in advance and refrigerated until ready to mix in the avocado.

If you must prepare the completed dip a few hours in advance, cover with plastic wrap, pressing the wrap directly into the surface of the dip to minimize oxidation. If the avocado still manages to turn a bit brown before serving, simply scrape off the thin layer of oxidized guacamole and discard. Give the remaining dip a stir and you're good to go.

serves 8

2 tablespoons grated onion
½ teaspoon kosher salt
2 (6- to 7-ounce) ripe Hass avocados
2 teaspoons fresh lime juice
1 tomato, chopped (optional)
¼ cup chopped cilantro (optional)

In a large bowl, mash the onion and salt to a paste.

Slice avocados in half, removing pit, and score the flesh with a knife, making a crosshatch pattern. Scoop the flesh gently into the bowl with the mashed paste. Add lime juice. Mix with a fork, mashing ingredients a bit, but leaving large chunks. Fold in tomato and cilantro, if using. Serve immediately

CRAZY GOOD VARIATIONS

Southwest Corn Guacamole

- 1 ear of corn, or ½ cup corn kernels from can, drained
- ½ teaspoon chili powder
- ¼ teaspoon ground coriander
- ½ teaspoon kosher salt
- 1 recipe Sensational Chunky Guacamole (p. 314)
- ¼ cup chopped fresh cilantro

Preheat broiler. Sprinkle the corn with chili powder, coriander, and salt and place in an ovensafe dish. Broil the corn for 2 minutes. Cool. Remove kernels from cob. Add corn to the Sensational Chunky Guacamole (p. 314). Gently mix in cilantro.

Indian Guacamole

- ½ teaspoon cumin
- ½ teaspoon ground coriander
- ½ teaspoon ground turmeric
- 1 recipe Sensational Chunky Guacamole (p. 314)

Stir spices into Sensational Chunky Guacamole (p. 314).

Papaya Guacamole

- ½ cup chopped papaya
- 1 recipe Sensational Chunky Guacamole (p. 314)

Combine the papaya with the Sensational Chunky Guacamole (p. 314) and serve immediately.

Roasted Jalapeño and Garlic Guacamole

- 2 jalapeños, quartered and seeded
- 3 scallions, chopped
- 2 cloves garlic, unpeeled
- 1 tablespoon extra-virgin olive oil
- 1 recipe Sensational Chunky Guacamole (p. 314)

Preheat oven to 400°F. Toss jalapeños, scallions, and unpeeled garlic cloves with oil. Place on roasting pan and roast for 20 minutes, or until charred.

Remove garlic from peel and mash in a medium bowl. Add charred scallions and jalapeños. Stir in the Sensational Chunky Guacamole (p. 314).

Crab Meat Guacamole

- ½ cup imitation crab meat, diced
- 1 tablespoon orange juice
- 1 tablespoon extra-virgin olive oil
- ½ teaspoon chipotle powder or chili powder
- 1 recipe Sensational Chunky Guacamole (p. 314)

In a medium bowl, mix together crab meat, orange juice, olive oil, and chipotle powder. Stir in the Sensational Chunky Guacamole (p. 314).

Seasonal Fruit and Heirloom Tomato Salad

I love home-grown or heirloom tomatoes in the summer. Their sweetness makes them almost fruit-like to me, which is what inspired me to create this recipe. I love the combination of sweet tomatoes with cantaloupe, papaya, or watermelon. If you prefer, omit the fruit and the salad is delicious too. In the summer, when Shabbos is late, I often add ½ cup crumbled feta cheese to the salad. It adds both creaminess and richness, and makes it a little more filling. I make this all year long with vine-ripe tomatoes, mangos, and cantaloupe.

serves 8

- 3 pounds ripe tomatoes (preferably heirloom tomatoes in mixed colors or vine-ripe tomatoes), cut in 1-inch chunks
- 4 cups cantaloupe, mango, papaya, watermelon, peaches, or other seasonal fruit, cut into 1-inch chunks
- 5 large fresh basil leaves, cut in a chiffonade (see note), or 3 tablespoons diced fresh basil
- 3 tablespoons chopped red onion or chives
- 1 teaspoon kosher salt
- ¼ cup extra-virgin olive oil
- 2 tablespoons balsamic vinegar

Combine tomatoes, fruit, basil, and onion in a large bowl. Toss gently (if using watermelon, assemble this just before serving. Other fruits can be prepared a few hours ahead of serving).

In a small bowl, whisk salt, olive oil, and balsamic vinegar. Pour over tomato mixture. Toss and serve immediately.

Passover

Perfect as-is!

Make Ahead

Dressing can be prepared a day ahead of time. Whisk before using and toss salad with dressing just before serving.

Note

To cut basil in a chiffonade, stack the basil leaves and roll them up like a cigar, starting from the thin long end, not the wide direction. Gently slice the bundle, forming long ribbons of basil. Slice the ribbons in half if you like or use as is.

The volunteers at the EMUNAH Ma'ayan Rivka Golden Age Restaurant are devoted to caring for the elderly patrons. Working with them was both inspiring and humbling.

Nut-Crusted Creamy Horseradish Salmon

My friend Naomi Nachman, the Aussie Gourmet and host of Table for Two *on the Nachum Segal Network, shared this amazing recipe with me. This is no ordinary nut-crusted salmon—it has a zesty layer of creamy horseradish that contrasts the sweet toasted nut topping. It can be made a day ahead of time, too, which makes it great as a Shalosh Seudos or Yom Tov option. It's simple and delicious, which Naomi always seems to master.*

serves 10

- ⅛ cup white or red horseradish
- ⅛ cup mayonnaise
- 2 to 3 pounds salmon fillet (one whole side of salmon or individual pieces)
- 1 cup shelled salted pistachios
- ⅓ cup packed light brown sugar
- 2 tablespoons fresh lemon juice

Preheat oven to 350°F.

Mix the horseradish and mayonnaise together in a small bowl. Place the salmon on a large baking sheet lined with parchment paper. Spread the mixture over the fish and set aside.

In a food processor, process the nuts until just coarsely chopped, but not too fine, lest they turn into pistachio butter. Add in the brown sugar and lemon juice, and mix until it looks like wet sand.

Pat nut mixture on top of salmon. Bake for 25 minutes, or until cooked through.

Can be served warm, room temperature, or chilled.

Passover

Perfect as-is!

Make Ahead

Can be prepared 1 day ahead of time. Store, covered, in the refrigerator. Serve at room temperature.

Pearl Barley Salad with Roasted Peppers, Sun-Dried Tomatoes, and Olives

Passover

Use quinoa in place of barley. In a medium pot, bring 1½ cups quinoa and 3 cups water to a boil over medium heat. Cover and simmer for 15 minutes or until water is absorbed. Use safflower or cottonseed oil in place of canola.

Make Ahead

This salad keeps well in the refrigerator for up to 2 days. I like to make it a day ahead of time to let the flavors blend.

I first saw this recipe in a 1993 edition of Gourmet magazine. I've adapted it over the years but go to it over and over again. I make it often for Shalosh Seudos. For a late Shabbos in the summer, I like to add about ½ cup of crumbled goat cheese or Boursin cheese to the salad for a creamy texture next to the chewy wheat berries, though you're welcome to substitute any grain you like.

serves 8

Barley Salad:

1½ cups pearl barley or wheat berries
5 cups water
1 teaspoon kosher salt
1 teaspoon canola oil
½ cup thinly sliced red onion
½ cup julienne strips of seedless cucumber
¼ cup julienne strips of drained bottled roasted red pepper
¼ cup julienne strips of drained bottled sun-dried tomatoes
¼ cup mixed minced fresh herbs such as parsley, mint, and dill
1 tablespoon chopped kalamata olives

Dressing:

2 tablespoons fresh lemon juice, or to taste
1 tablespoon red wine vinegar
1 tablespoon honey
1 teaspoon ground cumin
1 clove garlic, minced
¼ teaspoon crushed red pepper (optional)
½ teaspoon kosher salt
¼ teaspoon ground black pepper
5 tablespoons extra-virgin olive oil

To make the barley salad: Heat a 2½-quart pot over medium heat. Add barley, water, and generous pinch of salt and bring to a boil, reduce heat, cover, and simmer for about 25 minutes. Barley is cooked when water is mostly absorbed (drain if necessary) and it is fluffy and soft. Let cool.

If using wheat berries, heat a 2½-quart pot over medium heat. When pot is hot, add oil. Add wheat berries to pot and toast for about 3 minutes. The wheat berries should smell nutty and toasted. Add water and salt to pot and bring to a boil. Cover and turn heat down. Simmer for 30 to 40 minutes or until berries are cooked through. Drain any excess water. Cool. (Cooked wheat berries should be soft but still hold their shape. Some brands take up to an hour to cook, so taste before draining water).

In a large bowl, stir together cooked barley (or wheat berries), onion, cucumber, roasted pepper, sun-dried tomatoes, minced herbs, and olives.

To make the dressing: In a small dish, whisk lemon juice, vinegar, honey, cumin, garlic, red pepper flakes, salt, and pepper. While whisking, drizzle in olive oil until fully combined. Pour over salad and mix thoroughly. Serve or store in the refrigerator covered.

Peanut Soba Noodle Salad with Cucumbers and Carrots

Soba noodles are made from buckwheat and naturally gluten free, but look and taste like pasta. This Thai-inspired dish tastes great both warm and room temperature and can be made a day ahead of time.

serves 8

1 (10-ounce) package soba noodles
2 Persian cucumbers
6 tablespoons soy sauce
4½ tablespoons rice vinegar
3 tablespoons toasted sesame oil
3 tablespoons peanut butter
1 tablespoon packed dark brown sugar
1 cup roughly chopped cilantro or parsley
½ cup sliced fresh basil leaves
½ cup julienned carrots
¼ cup chopped roasted salted peanuts

Cook noodles according to package instructions until just tender. Drain, rinse well with cool water, and set aside. Cut cucumbers into ½-inch by 1½-inch pieces. Set aside.

Whisk together soy sauce, vinegar, oil, peanut butter, and brown sugar in a large bowl. Add drained noodles to peanut butter sauce, tossing to coat, and then add cilantro, basil, cucumbers, and carrots. Top with cucumbers and sprinkle with peanuts. Serve warm or at room temperature.

Make Ahead

Can be prepared 2 days ahead of time and stored, covered, in the refrigerator. Serve warm or at room temperature.

Salmon and Barbecued Corn Niçoise Salad

Niçoise salad is traditionally made with tuna. But I often make this with salmon because I think it's a bright change on the traditional Niçoise, plus salmon is much more affordable than fresh tuna and it's universally well liked. But feel free to use either in this recipe. This can be made a day ahead of time and assembled before serving.

serves 10

Vinaigrette:

4 hard-boiled eggs, whites and yolks separated (p. 49)

½ cup extra-virgin olive oil

⅓ cup red wine vinegar

2 tablespoons Dijon mustard

2 teaspoons sugar

1 teaspoon kosher salt

½ teaspoon dried basil

Salmon:

1 pound salmon or tuna fillets (about 4 fillets)

¼ cup prepared barbecue sauce

Salad:

2 ears fresh corn, kernels cut off the cob, or 1 (15-ounce) can corn, drained

20 small red potatoes

2 teaspoons kosher salt

10 spears asparagus, green or white, or fresh green beans

2 heads romaine lettuce

6 hard-boiled eggs, peeled and halved lengthwise (p. 49)

1 cup cherry tomatoes, halved

¾ cup pitted kalamata olives

To prepare the vinaigrette: Place cooked egg yolks (reserve whites for another use) in a small bowl; mash with a fork. Add oil, vinegar, Dijon, sugar, salt, and basil; whisk until fully incorporated. Refrigerate until ready to serve.

To prepare the salmon: Preheat broiler. Smother salmon with barbecue sauce and broil until cooked through, about 6 to 10 minutes. Remove from heat and cut into bite-size pieces; set aside.

For the salad: Place corn on low-sided baking sheet. Broil 3 to 5 minutes, or until lightly browned and beginning to caramelize. (Watch carefully to prevent burning. Note that canned corn will take 2 to 3 minutes longer). Remove from heat; set aside to cool.

Alternatively, grill salmon and corn: Heat a grill to 375°F and grease the grates. Grill salmon over indirect heat for about 9 to 13 minutes. Grill corn over indirect heat for about 3 minutes each side.

Combine potatoes and salt in a large stockpot. Add enough water to cover potatoes by 1 inch. Bring to a boil over high heat; reduce to a simmer and cook 10 to 15 minutes, until potatoes are just cooked through but still intact. Drain and cool. When potatoes are cool enough to handle, cut into thick slices; set aside.

Passover

Use kosher for Passover mustard in place of Dijon mustard. Omit corn. Substitute jícama or chopped apples or pears, if desired.

Make Ahead

Salmon, eggs, corn, potatoes, asparagus, and dressing can be prepared a day ahead of time. Store, covered, in the refrigerator until ready to use.

Place asparagus in a microwave-safe dish. Microwave 3 to 4 minutes for green asparagus and 5 to 7 minutes for white, until just soft-crisp (alternatively, steam or roast the asparagus). Set aside.

To assemble: Arrange lettuce on a large platter. Decoratively arrange salmon, corn, potatoes, asparagus, hard-boiled eggs, tomatoes, and olives on top of lettuce. Drizzle vinaigrette over salad and serve.

Southwestern Pasta Salad

This salad can be made with orzo, white or brown rice, quinoa, or any grain of your choice. If using pasta, I often opt for the fun shapes of bowties or wagon wheels. For a lighter, healthier dish, I use quinoa.

serves 8

1½ teaspoons kosher salt, divided
1 teaspoon cumin
1¼ teaspoons coriander
½ teaspoon cinnamon
4 tablespoons extra-virgin olive oil, divided
1 (1-pound) box bowtie or wagon wheel pasta
1 (15.5-ounce) can black beans, drained and rinsed
2 Persian cucumbers, diced
1 cup halved grape tomatoes
1 cup fresh or canned corn kernels
1 red pepper, diced
⅓ cup sliced scallions
¼ cup chopped fresh parsley or cilantro
¼ cup fresh orange juice
1 tablespoon plus 2 teaspoons fresh lime juice
2 teaspoons minced fresh garlic
2 teaspoons honey
½ cup pine nuts or slivered almonds, toasted (p. 335)

In a small dish, combine ½ teaspoon kosher salt with the cumin, coriander, cinnamon, and 1 tablespoon olive oil. Set aside.

Bring a large pot of water to a boil and add remaining teaspoon salt. Add pasta and stir. Cook until just al dente, about 7 to 9 minutes, and then drain. Pour warm pasta into a large bowl and immediately stir in oil and spice mixture. Let cool.

In a large mixing bowl, combine black beans, cucumbers, tomatoes, corn, pepper, scallions, cilantro, orange juice, remaining 3 tablespoons olive oil, lime juice, garlic, honey, and ½ teaspoon salt. Stir. Add cooled pasta mixture and mix well. The flavors will blend as it sits. Garnish with pine nuts just before serving.

Make Ahead

Can be prepared 2 days ahead of time. Store, covered, in the refrigerator. Serve at room temperature.

מזווה

PANTRY

Here's a secret to enhancing the flavors of all of your regular dishes without enrolling in cooking school: Fill your pantry and fridge with some of my bold-flavored, homemade staples. I obsessively buy new condiments— different kinds of mayonnaise, ketchup, chutneys, and vinaigrettes—and recreate them in simplified versions for my own kitchen. I've only included the best of the best of all my experiments here. These must-have recipes will help you season your dishes, transform the ordinary to the extraordinary, and impress your guests. Combine these with a few basic techniques, and you've got the foundation you need for successful Shabbos cooking.

Honey Mustard Sauce

Passover

Replace the ¼ cup Dijon mustard and the ¼ cup whole grain mustard with ⅓ cup Passover mustard in total.

Make Ahead

Can be prepared 2 weeks ahead of time. Store, covered, in the refrigerator or freeze up to 3 months. Defrost in the refrigerator.

The mayonnaise adds a creaminess to this staple. Serve it with It's So Easy Anyone Can Make It Corned Beef (p. 174), Fork-Tender Sliced Pastrami (p. 175), Pesto Flounder Pinwheels (p. 62), or Everything Bagel Marinated and Grilled Chicken (p. 138).

makes 1¼ cups

½ cup honey
¼ cup Dijon mustard
¼ cup whole grain mustard
2 tablespoons mayonnaise
1 tablespoon fresh lemon juice
¼ teaspoon kosher salt
⅛ teaspoon ground black pepper

Combine all ingredients in a small bowl; whisk until smooth.

Grainy Mustard Dipping Sauce

Make Ahead

Can be prepared 2 weeks ahead of time. Store, covered, in the refrigerator or freeze up to 3 months. Defrost in the refrigerator.

Tip

If you have any concerns with uncooked eggs, you can purchase pasteurized eggs at most groceries.

For a slightly more grown-up flavor than the Honey Mustard Sauce above, give this grainy mustard sauce a try. Serve it with Everything Bagel Marinated and Grilled Chicken (p. 138), Chicken and Pistachio Terrine (p. 75), or Cornbread-Crusted Turkey London Broil (p. 143).

makes ½ cup

1 tablespoon plus 1 teaspoon Dijon mustard
1 egg yolk or 1 tablespoon mayonnaise
2 teaspoons fresh lemon juice
¼ teaspoon kosher salt
⅛ teaspoon ground black pepper
½ cup extra-virgin olive oil
2 tablespoons whole grain mustard
1 tablespoon water
2 teaspoons white horseradish

Whisk together Dijon, egg yolk, lemon juice, salt, and pepper in a medium bowl. Add oil in a slow stream, whisking constantly until emulsified and thickened. Whisk in whole grain mustard, water, and horseradish. Thin with more water if necessary.

Use as a dip for steaks, grilled chicken, or pastrami.

Zesty Ketchup

In this easy recipe, I jazz up regular ketchup, cooking it up with wine and spices to create a fantastic dipping sauce. I use it on everything from veggies to chicken to grilled meats.

serves 8

¾ cup ketchup
¼ cup red wine vinegar
¼ cup packed light brown sugar
2 teaspoons curry powder
¼ cup red wine
1 teaspoon kosher salt
¼ teaspoon ground black pepper
Pinch of ground cloves

Combine all ingredients in a small saucepan and set over high heat. Bring to a boil, stirring to dissolve the sugar. Continue cooking until the mixture has slightly thickened, about 10 minutes. Let cool, and then store in the refrigerator until ready to use.

Passover

Substitute 1 teaspoon cumin for curry powder.

Make Ahead

Can be prepared 2 weeks ahead of time. Store, covered, in the refrigerator for up to 2 weeks or freeze up to 3 months. Defrost in the refrigerator.

Citrus Aïoli

This garlicky dip tastes fabulous with Citrus Marinated Chicken Cutlets (p. 138) or as a dip for freshly steamed asparagus or artichokes.

makes 1 cup

¾ cup mayonnaise
1½ tablespoons fresh lemon juice
1 tablespoon orange juice
2 teaspoons Dijon mustard
2 teaspoons lemon zest
1 teaspoon orange zest
½ teaspoon kosher salt
2 cloves garlic, minced

Whisk together all ingredients in a small bowl until well combined. Serve immediately or refrigerate, covered, until ready to use. Serve with Citrus Marinated Chicken Cutlets (p. 138).

Passover

Substitute Passover mustard for Dijon.

Make Ahead

Can be prepared 5 days ahead of time. Store, covered, in the refrigerator.

Peanut Dipping Sauce

Make Ahead

Can be prepared 7 days ahead of time. Store, covered, in the refrigerator or freeze up to 3 months. Defrost in the refrigerator and stir before using.

This versatile East Asian dipping sauce goes will with everything from grilled chicken to a crudités platter. Serve with the Minute Steak with Peanut sauce (p. 174) or the Sesame Chicken Hand Rolls (p. 58).

makes ¾ cup

¼ cup creamy peanut butter
2 tablespoons soy sauce
2 tablespoons water
2 tablespoons packed light brown sugar
¼ teaspoon cayenne pepper

Combine all ingredients in a small bowl; whisk until smooth. Serve at room temperature.

Passover Version:

1 cup almond butter
2 tablespoons hot water
2 teaspoons freshly grated ginger
2 cloves garlic, minced
1 teaspoon apple cider vinegar
2 scallions, chopped
1½ teaspoons Passover soy sauce (optional)
2 tablespoons chopped fresh cilantro or parsley (optional)
¼ teaspoon black pepper
Salt, if needed

For the sauce: In a small bowl, whisk almond butter, hot water, ginger, garlic, vinegar, scallions, soy sauce, cilantro, and black pepper until creamy. Add salt if needed, or if the almond butter has no salt in it; start with about ¼ teaspoon kosher salt.

Spicy Peanut Sauce

Make Ahead

Can be prepared 7 days ahead of time. Store, covered, in the refrigerator or freeze up to 3 months. Defrost in the refrigerator.

Like the regular peanut sauce, this sauce goes well with the Minute Steak (p. 174) and Sesame Chicken Hand Rolls (p. 58), as well as any variety of grilled chicken, beef, raw veggies, or noodles.

makes 1 cup

½ cup creamy peanut butter
½ cup coconut water
1 tablespoon Sriracha sauce
1 tablespoon soy sauce
2 tablespoons fresh lime juice
1 teaspoon finely grated peeled fresh ginger
1 clove garlic

In a food processor or blender, combine all of the ingredients and purée until smooth.

Sri-Rancha Sauce

Remember the first time you had spicy chicken wings dipped in ranch sauce, with the buffalo sauce adding a fiery zip to every bite and cool ranch calming your burning tongue? Well, it's the same here, only it's elevated an extra notch by replacing the buffalo sauce with today's new favorite condiment, Sriracha. You'll be the hit of the party with this dip. Besides wings, this dip works well with the Chicken and Pistachio Terrine (p. 75), It's So Easy Anyone Can Make It Corned Beef (p. 174), and Spicy Grilled Brisket (p. 179).

Make Ahead

Can be prepared 2 weeks ahead of time. Store, covered, in the refrigerator.

makes 1¼ cups

1 cup store-bought ranch or Pareve Caesar Salad Dressing (p. 333)
1 tablespoon fresh lemon juice
2 tablespoons Sriracha sauce, or to taste

Combine ingredients in a small bowl and whisk until smooth. Store in an airtight container in the refrigerator until ready to use.

Spicy Mayonnaise

Use this as a dipping sauce for the Salmon Croquettes (p. 57) or some homemade French fries.

Make Ahead

Can be prepared 7 days ahead of time. Store, covered, in the refrigerator for up to 3 weeks.

makes 1¼ cups

1 cup mayonnaise
3 tablespoons fresh lime juice
4 teaspoons chili powder
1 teaspoon kosher salt
2 cloves garlic, crushed

Combine all ingredients in a small bowl; whisk until smooth. Refrigerate, covered, until ready to serve.

My Favorite Vinaigrette

Thank you Susie Fishbein!

makes 1 cup

1 shallot, minced
2 tablespoons white wine vinegar
2 tablespoons balsamic vinegar
2 teaspoons Dijon mustard
½ teaspoon kosher salt
¼ teaspoon ground black pepper
⅔ cup extra-virgin olive oil

Whisk together shallot, both vinegars, Dijon, salt, and pepper in a small bowl. Gradually add olive oil, whisking continuously until emulsified and smooth.

Passover

Substitute Passover mustard for Dijon mustard.

Make Ahead

Can be prepared 7 days ahead of time. Store, covered, in the refrigerator. Bring to room temperature before using and shake well.

Sweet Poppyseed Dressing

Serve this dressing with spinach, lettuce, strawberries, and toasted nuts for a fresh, summery salad. Or try with arugula, sliced mushrooms, hearts of palm, and cooked quinoa as a side to grilled meats. It also makes a great sweet dip for vegetable crudités.

makes 3 cups, enough for 3 large salads

1 egg
⅔ cup red wine vinegar
¼ cup sugar
3 tablespoons grated yellow onion, plus juice from the grating
1 tablespoon Dijon mustard
½ teaspoon kosher salt
2 cups canola oil
3 tablespoons poppyseeds

Combine egg, vinegar, sugar, grated onion and juice, Dijon, and salt in the bowl of a food processor fitted with a steel blade. Process 1 minute.

With motor running, add oil in a slow, steady stream. Transfer mixture to a bowl with a lid, and stir in poppyseeds. Refrigerate, covered, until ready to use.

Make Ahead

Can be prepared 2 weeks ahead of time and stored, covered, in the refrigerator. Bring to room temperature and shake well before using.

Pareve Caesar Salad Dressing

Double this recipe and use it all week for freshly dressed salad greens to go with dinner.

makes ¾ cup

½ cup extra-virgin olive oil
1½ tablespoons red wine vinegar
2 teaspoons fresh lemon juice
¼ teaspoon ground dry mustard
1 teaspoon Worcestershire sauce, non-fish variety
2 cloves garlic, minced
1 teaspoon ground black pepper
5 drops Tabasco sauce, or to taste
1 egg yolk

In a food processor or with an immersion blender, blend all ingredients together until fully combined and mixture is slightly thickened. Store in the refrigerator until ready to use.

Make Ahead

Can be prepared 5 days ahead of time. Store, covered, in the refrigerator. Shake well before using.

Tip

If you have any concerns with uncooked eggs, you can purchase pasteurized eggs at most groceries.

Homemade Breadcrumbs

Homemade breadcrumbs, also called gremolata, can elevate the quality of a dish from good to great. They're a quick make and store well. You can use any bread or combination of breads like whole wheat, challah, and spelt. Leave the crusts on if you don't mind a little extra crunch. Feel free to change the flavor profile with different herbs and spices. For an Italian twist, for instance, add some fresh or dried oregano, and a pinch of crushed red pepper. The possibilities are endless.

serves 8

6 pieces stale bread, crusts removed (optional)
2 teaspoons extra-virgin olive oil
2 cloves garlic, minced
Zest of 1 lemon
1 teaspoon fresh lemon juice
½ to 1 teaspoon kosher salt
½ teaspoon ground black pepper
3 tablespoons chopped fresh parsley

Place the bread in a food processor and pulse into crumbs.

In a sauté pan, heat oil over medium-high heat. Reduce the heat and add breadcrumbs and garlic. Cook until garlic is soft and bread is toasty. Add lemon zest, juice, salt, pepper, and parsley and cook an additional minute so that all the juice is absorbed and the flavors are incorporated.

Make Ahead

Can be prepared 7 days ahead of time. Store, covered, in an airtight container or freeze up to 3 months.

Homemade Croutons

Make Ahead

Can be prepared 7 days ahead of time. Store, covered, in an airtight container.

Serve these with any salad in the book, such as the Wild Mushroom and Arugula Panzanella Salad (p. 113), Kale Caesar Salad (p. 122), or the Everything Bagel Romaine Salad with Smoked Salmon (p. 304). Or float them in a creamy soup for a contrasting crunch. Add just before serving, of course!

makes 3 cups

3 cups leftover bread, cut into ½-inch cubes
3 tablespoons margarine
2 cloves garlic, minced
½ teaspoon kosher salt

Preheat oven to 400°F. Line a baking sheet with parchment paper or aluminum foil. Arrange bread cubes on the prepared sheet.

Melt margarine in a small skillet over medium heat; add garlic and cook 2 minutes, stirring until fragrant but not browned. Pour over bread cubes, sprinkle with salt, and toss to coat evenly. Bake the croutons 10 to 15 minutes, or until browned.

Roasted Garlic

Passover

Perfect as-is!

Make Ahead

Can be prepared up to 1 week in advance. Store, covered, in the refrigerator or freeze for up to 3 months. Defrost in the refrigerator.

Roasting garlic mellows its normally sharp flavors and brings out a natural sweetness. I use it in the Savory London Broil with Sweet Onions and Mushrooms (p. 160), Roasted Garlic Potatoes (p. 190), Roasted Garlic Hummus (p. 40), and Succulent and Crispy Five-Hour Roast Chicken (p. 148). Honestly, though, it's just as good smeared on a nice piece of toasty bread and drizzled with some fresh olive oil and a sprinkling of salt.

makes 3 tablespoons

1 head garlic
1 to 2 tablespoons extra-virgin olive oil, as needed

Preheat oven to 400°F.

Slice the top off the head of the garlic. Set the garlic on a large piece of aluminum foil. Drizzle oil over the garlic, allowing the oil to cover the garlic completely. Wrap tightly with the foil and place directly on wire rack. Roast for 45 minutes, or until the garlic is softened. Remove from oven to cool, and then squeeze the roasted garlic from the skins.

Toasting Nuts

Toasting nuts adds a real depth of flavor to them, but you must watch them carefully. They can go from toasty to burned in a split second! Follow these directions below for any type of nut. For best results, toast each type of nut separately, as they can cook at different rates.

Set a medium saucepan over medium-low heat. Add nuts and cook until lightly browned and fragrant, shaking pan every 30 seconds or so to prevent burning. Alternatively, preheat oven to 350°F. Place nuts on a small baking sheet and bake for about 10 minutes, until slightly brown and fragrant.

Passover

Perfect as-is!

Make Ahead

Store toasted nuts in an airtight container for 2 weeks or in the freezer for up to 3 months.

Pesto

Pesto encompasses the fresh taste of summer. Use it as dip, on pasta, or as a marinade for chicken, meat, or fish. In this book alone, it's used with Garlicky Pesto-Stuffed Mushrooms (p. 211), Pesto Flounder Pinwheels (p. 62), Seared Cod with Corn Vinaigrette (p. 68), and Rich Red Pepper Soup with Basil Drizzle (p. 99). Double the recipe and keep half in your freezer for a quick pasta dinner. I like to freeze mine in ice cube trays, and then pop them out as needed.

makes about 4 cups

4 cups fresh basil leaves
1 tablespoon minced garlic
½ teaspoon kosher salt
¼ teaspoon ground black pepper
1 cup extra-virgin olive oil
3 tablespoons pine nuts, toasted (see above)

Combine basil, garlic, salt, and pepper in a food processor. With the motor running, add oil in a slow, steady stream. Add pine nuts and blend until smooth.

Passover

Perfect as-is!

Make Ahead

Can be prepared 7 days ahead of time. Store, covered, in the refrigerator or freeze up to 3 months. Defrost in the refrigerator.

Fresh, Active Dry and Instant Yeast, What's the Difference?

Fresh yeast, also called cake or compressed yeast, has a bold, fresh flavor and it's my favorite choice when baking challah. It's perishable, and the water to activate the yeast must be 80 to 90 degrees. You do not need to add sugar during the proofing process. Remember to buy it only a few days ahead of time and keep it refrigerated until ready to use. To proof, dissolve yeast in warm water. Stir, and place in a warm, dry place for approximately 15 minutes, or until yeast is foamy and slightly puffed up.

Active dry yeast is a bit more forgiving. It's made by putting yeast on a dryer to remove 90 percent of its moisture. This harsh process kills many of the yeast cells, which then form a hard coating around each granule of active yeast. The granules must be proofed or soaked in water at a temperature of 100 to 115 degrees before they are used, which is hot enough to dissolve the hard coating and awaken the active yeast within. To proof, place in warm water with a teaspoon of sugar. Leave in a warm dry place for approximately 15 minutes, or until foamy.

Instant yeast, also known as rapid rise, requires no proofing. The drying process is gentler than the process for active dry yeast, so fewer cells are killed. The yeast is faster acting and can be added directly to dry ingredients. The liquid you add to make the dough should be warm—110 to 130 degrees—to activate the yeast. It is more potent so you should use 3/4 teaspoon of instant yeast to 1 teaspoon of active yeast.

Both types of dry yeast keep up to a year at room temperature. and all types will be killed with water above 132 degrees. For faster challah, use the rapid rise yeast. Simply combine all the ingredients together—no proofing necessary. For an extremely "fresh bread" taste, try the fresh yeast.

Yeast Conversion Rates

.6 ounce cube fresh yeast = 2 ¼ teaspoons (1 package) active dry yeast = 2 teaspoons rapid rise yeast

Homemade Tart Shells

Use in Macadamia Pecan Tartlets (p. 291), fill with creamy Lemon Curd (p. 338) or with Hazelnut Mocha Chocolate Mousse (p. 241).

makes 16 shells

2½ cups all-purpose flour
½ cup sugar
⅛ teaspoon kosher salt
1 cup (2 sticks) unsalted margarine, chilled and cut into ¼-inch slices
1 egg
1¼ teaspoons vanilla butter nut extract or vanilla extract

Place flour, sugar, and salt in a food processor and pulse to combine. Add margarine slices; pulse several times, until mixture has the consistency of cornmeal.

Whisk together egg and butter/vanilla extract in a small bowl. With the food processor motor running, pour egg mixture into food processor bowl. Process until the ingredients form a ball. Remove the dough to a work surface. With the heel of your hand, press the dough together until it is smooth and cohesive.

Divide the dough into 16 equal pieces, just over ¼ cup each. Roll out each piece and press into tartlet shells or miniature pie pans. Prick bottom and sides of dough with a fork so that the crust doesn't bubble when baked. Prebake tart shells 8 to 11 minutes, or until lightly browned, or fill and bake as directed by recipe.

Make Ahead

Can be prepared 5 days ahead of time. Store, covered, in the refrigerator or freeze up to 3 months. Defrost in the refrigerator.

Homemade Pita Chips

These crunchy chips make every dip better. Try them with Roasted Garlic Hummus (p. 40) or Triple Onion and Spinach Dip (p. 43). But don't limit yourself—they go equally well with Chicken Livers with Brandy, Mushrooms, and Cherries (p. 37), Dressed-Up Salmon Ceviche (p. 35), and Everything Bagel Romaine Salad with Smoked Salmon (p. 304), too.

serves 8 to 10

4 tablespoons extra-virgin olive oil
1 clove garlic, smashed
½ teaspoon kosher salt
¼ teaspoon ground black pepper
5 whole pita rounds, cut into 8 wedges

Preheat heat oven to 375°F.

Pour olive oil into a bowl and add garlic, salt, and pepper. Brush pita wedges with olive oil mixture. Arrange wedges on baking sheet in a single layer and bake for 12 to 15 minutes, until golden brown and crispy.

Make Ahead

Can be prepared 7 days ahead of time. Store, covered, in an airtight container.

Lemon Curd

Passover

Perfect as-is!

Make Ahead

Can be prepared 5 days ahead of time. Store, covered with plastic wrap directly on the top of the lemon curd, in the refrigerator or freeze up to 3 months. Defrost in the refrigerator.

Note

Lemon curd is delicious eaten by the spoonful or dolloped into Homemade Tart Shells (p. 337). It also works well with the Easy Creamy Lemon Tart (p. 220), Berry Custard Tart (p. 247), and Forgotten Meringues (p. 272).

This recipe is best if made with fresh lemon juice. The fragrant and strong flavors of fresh lemons yield a much better tasting lemon curd. Of course, store-bought lemon juice can be used and lemon pie filling can be substituted for lemon curd in a pinch. Fair warning: Once your family has tasted this homemade version, they may refuse to go back to store-bought.

makes 2 cups

3 large eggs
½ cup sugar
½ cup fresh lemon juice
2 teaspoons finely grated fresh lemon zest
¾ stick (6 tablespoons) margarine, diced
Pinch of salt

Combine eggs, sugar, lemon juice, and zest in a 2-quart saucepan; whisk well. Add margarine and set over medium-low heat, whisking frequently, until lemon curd is thick enough to coat the spoon and just begins to bubble, about 6 minutes. Add salt and stir.

Transfer mixture to a small bowl. Cover with plastic wrap placed directly on lemon curd to prevent any skin from forming. Chill at least 1 hour before using and store in the refrigerator until ready to use.

Red Wine Caramel Sauce

Passover

Perfect as-is!

Make Ahead

Can be made 5 days ahead and stored, covered, in the refrigerator. To serve, rewarm over a low heat, whisking frequently.

Note

This caramel sauce adds extra decadence to the Chocolate Caramel Pecan Pie (p. 229), Apple Galette (p. 230), and Apple Crumb Bars (p. 299).

serves 8

1 cup red wine
1½ cups packed dark brown sugar
1½ cups pareve whipping cream
6 tablespoons (¾ stick) unsalted margarine
¼ teaspoon coarse salt or kosher salt

In a small saucepan, heat red wine over medium heat. Bring to a gentle simmer and cook until reduced to ½ cup, about 10 minutes. Set aside.

Combine sugar and pareve cream in a heavy saucepan over medium-high heat, and bring to a boil, whisking constantly until sugar dissolves. Boil until caramel thickens enough to coat spoon, whisking often, about 10 minutes. Add margarine and red wine and cook until margarine is melted and caramel is thick, about 4 minutes. Remove from heat. Sprinkle with coarse salt. Serve warm or cover and chill. If rewarming, whisk over low heat until ingredients are fully mixed and caramel is warm.

Mastering Meringue

Beating egg whites is one of the most important steps in so many dishes. Follow this step-by-step guide for perfect meringue every time.

- Don't attempt to make meringue on a humid day. It'll never dry properly and always remain chewy. If you must, then place your meringues in a closed oven. The heat from the pilot light will help them dry.
- Use old eggs. They whip better.
- Use cold eggs. They separate better.
- Separate the eggs perfectly. If there's even a trace of yolk, the whites will not whip. And since that's hard to guarantee with each egg, separate them one at a time into 2 cups, and then pour each egg white into the mixing bowl as you go. That way, if a yolk breaks with a single egg, it won't mess up the whole batch. If you do break a yolk into a white, use a piece of eggshell or paper towel to extract it. If you are not fully confident that every trace of yolk has been removed, then discard or use that egg for something else.
- Use room temperature eggs for beating. They will increase in volume more than cold ones.
- Use a copper or stainless steel bowl and a wire whisk. A glass bowl will work, but not quite as well. Avoid plastic bowls and whisks. Make sure everything is completely clean, dry, and grease free.
- Stabilize the peaks with an acid, such as vinegar, lemon, or cream of tartar. If using a stainless steel or glass bowl, rub a cut lemon or a paper towel moistened with white vinegar on the inside of the mixing bowl. (Copper bowls do not need this step.)
- Cream of tartar further stabilizes whipped egg whites and helps hold the peaks stiff. It also helps add the shine to the egg whites. A recipe with 3 egg whites just needs ¼ teaspoon cream of tartar. Omit if not available.
- Do not add the sugar until the egg whites are whipped to soft peaks. And then, do it slowly, tablespoon by tablespoon. Superfine sugar dissolves faster. Continue beating until stiff peaks form, and then fold in any remaining ingredients called for in the recipe.
- When cooking meringues, do so at a low temperature so that the moisture gradually evaporates. A high temperature will make the outside crunchy and the inside chewy and sticky. Let the meringue continue drying in the oven after baking to further remove any chewiness.

MY FLAVOR BOOSTING PANTRY STAPLES

Having a well-stocked pantry means ensures that almost any recipe can be prepared with great success. I call most of these items, flavor boosters and rely on them when a touch of heat, sweetness, brightness, acidity, tang, richness, or crunch is needed. Stock up!

- A variety of oils, including olive, canola, peanut, sesame, and chili oils
- A variety of vinegars including balsamic, white, white wine, red wine, raspberry, apple cider, and rice wine vinegars
- Grains including pasta, quinoa, couscous, rice, brown rice, barley, and wheat berries
- Canned tuna
- Canned tomatoes including, stewed, crushed, fire-roasted, tomato paste, and tomato sauce
- Chicken stock, vegetable stock, and beef stock
- Mustards including Dijon, whole-grain, and any variety you like
- Dried herbs and spices—all of them, but in small quantities to ensure freshness
- Panko or breadcrumbs
- Coconut milk
- Soy sauce
- Kosher salt
- Pepper grinder or ground black pepper
- Maple syrup
- Sugars, including white, light brown, dark brown, and confectioners' sugar
- Honey
- A variety of flours, including white, wheat, white whole wheat, and high-gluten
- Baking powder
- Baking soda
- Vanilla and almond extracts
- Ramen noodles
- Sriracha sauce
- Worcestshire sauce
- Canned beans, including garbanzo, black beans, white beans, and kidney beans

FRESH STAPLES

- Lemons and limes
- Garlic—both fresh and frozen cubes
- Ginger—both fresh and frozen cubes
- Onions, including yellow, red, shallots, scallions, and chives
- A variety of toasted nuts, stored in the freezer

FRESH STAPLES SUBSITUTIONS

If you've run out of an ingredient, see if there's a substitute in your kitchen that you can use:

fresh tomato = grape or cherry tomatoes = whole peeled canned tomato

turkey = chicken

lamb = beef

brisket = French Roast= square roast = Delmonico roast

minute steak = London broil

skirt steak = hanger steak

spinach = kale

broccoli = cauliflower

white potato = sweet potato

white rice = brown rice = Israeli couscous = quinoa

root vegetable = any other root vegetable

shallot = yellow onion=white onion

chives = scallions=leeks

any fresh herb = flat leaf parsley

lime = lemon

sour cream = Tofutti sour cream

cream cheese = Tofutti cream cheese plus 2 tablespoon powdered sugar

pine nuts = almonds = walnuts

white wine vinegar = distilled white vinegar = lemon juice

balsamic vinegar = red wine vinegar

maple syrup = honey = brown sugar

panko = breadcrumbs

METRIC CONVERSIONS

These standard conversion tables can be used to adjust a recipe to metric standard measurements, although every recipe has not been tested with metric conversions.

TABLESPOONS > OUNCES > GRAMS

1 teaspoon (liquid) = 5.0 grams
3 teaspoons = 1 tablespoon = ½ ounce = 14.3 grams
2 tablespoons = 1 ounce = 8.35 grams
4 tablespoons = 2 ounces = ¼ cup = 56.7 grams
8 tablespoons = 4 ounces = ½ cup = 113.4 grams
16 tablespoons = 8 ounces = 1 cup = ½ pound = 226.8 grams
32 tablespoons = 16 ounces = 2 cups = 1 pound = 453.6 grams

TEMPERATURES: FAHRENHEIT TO CELSIUS

-10°F = -23.3°C *(freezer storage)*
0°F = -17.7°C
32°F = 0°C *(water freezes)*
68°F = 20°C *(room temperature)*
212°F = 100°C *(water boils)*
325°F = 162.8°C
350°F = 177°C *(standard baking)*
375°F = 190.5°C
400°F = 204.4°C
425°F = 218.3°C
450°F = 232°C
500°F = 260°C *(broiling)*

KEEPING A HEALTHY, KOSHER KITCHEN

I have asked **Kimberly Rothstein, MS, RD**, a highly respected dietitian who focuses on healthful kosher cooking, to give us some helpful tips to use with our own families. Here's what she has to say:

I'm so delighted to be a part of this wonderful cookbook. Shabbos cooking comes up frequently with my clients, and I love to help make their meals delicious but also nutritious. They frequently ask how they can prepare large meals with multiple courses for Shabbos and holidays, while still being a nutritious and conscious cook. Or, how do we prepare and serve exquisite and delicious meals without feelings of guilt that we've overindulged or served our guests and families far more than any one person can eat?

Can you make Shabbos more nutritious and still be delicious? Of course you can!

So many delicious foods and recipes (like the ones in this book!) can fit into a healthy diet and lifestyle. The key when planning your menus, both Shabbos and weekday, is to make good choices. Opt for whole grains, more fruits and vegetables from a variety of colors, eat less red meats, and use natural ingredients. I add more herbs and spices to enhance the flavors in dishes. Make homemade sauces to reduce the need for store bought sauces and marinades, which are usually filled with unnecessary amounts of salt, sugars, and fat.

One of my favorite tips on how to eat more nutritiously isn't about the food, but how you enjoy it: Eat slowly! Savor every bite! If it's a good recipe, it's worth it! Be mindful of the foods you're choosing and how much of them you put on your plate. When I eat too quickly, I tend to overindulge, having not given my body a chance to realize I've eaten my fill.

Throughout *Celebrate* I've offered suggestions on how to "lighten up" certain recipes and give you a healthier alternative to the original. But first, I'm sharing some of my experience on how to improve the nutrition of your everyday and Shabbos cooking.

Here's my secret: The 4 R's of Healthy Cooking—Replace, Reduce, Relish, and Relax. Keep these in mind and you'll be in great shape (pun intended!).

Replace: Replace full fat items with lower fat alternatives. For instance, Egg Salad with a Twist (page 36) and Persian Spiced Meat Roll (page 189) will still taste equally good and satisfying. Replace high sodium products with no salt added or low sodium options so that you can control the amount of salt in a recipe. Replace solid fats (such as margarine) with heart-healthy liquid varieties (such as canola oil). Replace enriched white flour, white rice, or couscous with whole wheat flour, brown rice, quinoa, bulgur, or other whole grain choices, as we did in the Whole Wheat Challah (page 16) and the Spelt Challah (page 26).

Reduce: Reduce salt, fats, and added sugars. Reduce fatty red meats, sweet side dishes, and sugary desserts. In most cases, one can reduce the sugar in a recipe by ¼ cup without affecting the integrity of the finished dish. The same rule applies when reducing the salt—you can reduce it by half in most recipes without affecting the finished dish. Reduce the oil in dressings and marinades to trim some calorie-dense fats from a dish, as we did with the Roasted Beet and Asparagus Salad on page 115. Reduce nuts and other garnishes if you need to trim some added calories.

Relish: Relish the flavors of the foods you eat. Take the time to enjoy your meals. When you choose a special dessert, enjoy each bite. Or choose a dessert you won't feel guilty about enjoying, like fresh fruit or the Pots de Crème on page 289 . Be conscious of what you choose, but then enjoy it without guilt. Life is too short.

Relax: Balance and moderation are the keys to an attainable, maintainable healthy lifestyle. Don't make it stressful—make small changes to your menu and your techniques. Relax…Shabbos is coming!

More adorable, happy faces of the children from Bet Elazraki Children's Home and of the smiling and compassionate volunteers from Ma'ayan Rivka Golden Age Restaurant, including Ada Krell, the founder of the Ma'ayan Rivka Golden Age Restaurant.

PASSOVER RECIPE LIST

Each of these recipes can be prepared for Passover, either as-is or with the substitutions listed on their original recipe page. Check with your local rabbi regarding the use of quinoa on Passover.

GLUTEN-FREE RECIPE LIST

These recipes are gluten-free. Make sure to buy brands that are gluten-free for ingredients such as soy sauce, chicken broth, Worcestershire sauce. Additionally, many other recipes can be gluten-free with simple substitutions for graham crackers, flour, pretzels, couscous and breadcrumbs, with the readily available gluten-free equivalent products. I often use the gluten-fee graham cracker crumbs, flour and panko with great success. These recipes are not on this list.

INDEX

Page numbers in italics refer to other recipes that use the entry, that are used as part of the entry, or that accompany the entry.